The Master's Carpet

Or Masonry and Baal-Worship Identical

by

Edmond Ronayne

ISBN: 978-1-63923-153-9

The Master's Carpet

Or Masonry and Baal-Worship Identical

Printed: November 2021

Cover Art By: Paul Amid

Published and Distributed By:

Lushena Books
607 Country Club Drive, Unit E
Bensenville, IL 60106
www.lushenabks.com

ISBN: 978-1-63923-153-9

Printed in the United States of America

CONTENTS.

ILLUSTRATIONS.

PREFACE.

In all the most popular Manuals of Freemasonry and in its standard works of the highest authority and merit, there are four well authenticated claims set up on behalf of that institution, as follows:

1st.—That it is a religious philosophy, or a system of religious science.

2nd.—That it was REVIVED in its "present outward form" in 1717.

3rd.—That all its ceremonies, symbols, and the celebrated legend of Hiram in the Master Mason's degree, were directly borrowed from the "Ancient Mysteries," or the secret worship of Baal, Osiris or Tammuz, and

4th.—That a strict obedience to its precepts and obligations is all that is necessary to free man from sin, and to secure for him a happy immortality.

The design of this work, then, is to discuss these claims in a clear, simple and intelligible manner, and to demonstrate beyond the possibility of dispute or doubt, on the part of any Freemason, that the Masonic system, as it exists to-day, is precisely the same religious philosophy, and the same form of *secret* worship, that used to be taught and practiced in honor of the "god of nature" in the old temples of paganism. All the proofs adduced to establish these facts are designedly drawn from the testimony of Masonry itself, and are so arranged as to be recognized at a glance, and must be found of great value for immediate reference in all possible discussions on this important subject. The work is also profusely illustrated—the interior of the lodge, the position of its various officers, the ceremonies through which the candidate is made to pass, and the emblems and symbols of its different degrees, being accurately represented by wood-engravings, specially prepared for this exposition, and passed upon by some of the former members ot the Order, while the legend of Osiris in the Egyptian Mysteries, and the celebrated legend of Hiram in the Masonic Mysteries, are compared with such minute ness of detail that none can fail to note their absolute identity.

This constitutes the *real secrets* of a Master Mason, and was never before alluded to by any seceder nor in any exposition of its pretended mysteries.

The unmistakable coincidence between Masonry and Romanism is also set forth, and it is demonstrated with positive certainty that both systems have sprung from the same pagan source—the one being the old pagan BEAST of Revelation and the other the *Image of the Beast.* Although I have been a member of the fraternity for a number of years, though I have been exalted to the highest office among my brethren in the lodge, and have received the unanimous plaudits of the Grand Lodge of Illinois, in 1872, yet accepting God's Word as the rule of my faith and practice, I insist upon it that I have just as much right to secede from the institution of Freemasonry, and to cast off all allegiance to its extra-judicial and iron-clad oaths, its inhuman death penalties, and its anti-Christian and idolatrous worship as I had to secede from the idolatrous worship of Rome just thirty years ago. Acting upon this principle then, I claim that a father, although a Freemason, is in duty bound to warn his son against affiliation with the Masonic institution, and in doing so, to give him a full exposition of its principles and philosophy. And hence the conversation between Mr. Barton and Henry.

That in this manner I may be the humble means of liberating some of my former brothers from the despotism of the lodge, as well as saving others from its wicked entanglements, that through the instrumentality of this book the pure, spiritual, heartfelt worship of God through Christ may be better appreciated, and the Redeemer's name be glorified and exalted, is the sincere and earnest prayer of the author.

EDMOND RONAYNE,

Past Master Keystone., No. 639, Chicago.

Chicago, March, 1879.

THE MASTER'S CARPET
EXPLAINED AND EXPOSED.

CHAPTER I.

INTRODUCTION.—Masonic Laws opposed to parental duty.—The "Good Man" argument.—Masonic Charity.—Pure Selfishness.—Chicago Fire.—Masonic Board of Relief.—Masonic Benevolence rewarded.

"And so, Henry, you tell me that some of your Masonic friends have been trying to persuade you to become a Mason? Well, I can hardly say that this astonishes me, as I am well aware that considerable recruiting is almost everywhere practised, though indirectly, to induce men to join that order. But it is rather singular, however, that, knowing my sentiments in regard to the Masonic institution, as many of our Masonic friends do, any effort should be made on their part toward inveigling you into an organization which they have every reason to believe is highly distasteful to me, and to which they ought to know very well I should never give my consent to your connecting yourself. But what is your own opinion on this subject? Have you had any very serious notions about joining the lodge? Or have you given the matter any more than a mere passing thought?"

"Well, the truth is, that I have been thinking somewhat on the subject of Masonry, and I confess that I have been very strongly tempted to send in my petition. Before doing so, however, it was my full intention to submit the whole case to your judgment and ask your advice, and it is partly with this object in view that I have broached the subject this morning. But you rather astonish me when you say that you should never consent to my joining the lodge. I understand that, as a general thing, Freemasons do not solicit men to become members, and hence I was fully prepared to believe that you would not depart from the usual practice; but when you tell me that so far from requesting me to join the Masonic institution, you would actually withhold your consent to my doing so, then, indeed, you not only surprise me very much, but I confess that you greatly excite my curiosity as well."

"At first sight this may astonish you, it is true, but upon calm reflection I think you will ap-

prove of my action in the premises. If Freemasonry were a good honorable institution, of course you know very well, I would be only too glad that you should become a member of it, and not only that, but I would of course be the first man to take in your application myself; but knowing, as I do, that the Masonic institution is nothing but a hollow sham, a consummate swindle, a gigantic falsehood, the most corrupt and the most corrupting system on the face of the globe, I cannot and will not consent that my son should have any connection whatever with it.

"Freemasonry is far too serious a matter for any man to assume its villainous obligations without due reflection; for, once you have crossed the threshold of the lodge room, divested of your own clothing, and wearing the habiliments of the order, and when once you become, as it were, bound by the *cable tow* of Satan to the altar of Baal, 'there is no place for after repentance,' though, like Esau of old, you may 'seek it carefully with tears.' Living or dead, Freemasonry will never give you up. The law of Romanism is, 'once a priest, always a priest,' and so it is in Masonry; 'once a Mason, always a Mason.' If I were back again where I was before joining the Masonic institution, I would much rather have my right arm cut off than to have taken such a terrible leap in the dark. No, my son, I shall certainly never consent to your becoming a Freemason, and I strongly advise you to banish the subject entirely from your mind and to have nothing whatever to do with it."

"Why, father, I never before heard you say so much as that about Masonry. I always had a sort of a vague impression that it was a tolerably good institution, and in fact that its members to a certain extent were a sort of privileged characters; but will you not please explain your reasons for thus advising me to avoid Freemasonry? Of course, if you insist upon it, I shall think no more about it, but when you tell me it is bad and wicked, thus demolishing, as it were, al lmy preconceived good opinions of the institution, you surely cannot refuse to explain your meaning and to show me in what its wickedness consists, so that I may judge for myself, and, if I am convinced at all, that I may be convinced upon reasonable grounds, and upon the evidence of testimony which cannot be either denied or controverted?"

"My dear son, you don't know what you are asking. Why, to comply even in the very smallest degree with your reasonable request, is considered an unpardonable crime in Freemasonry. Every Mason is sworn in every degree that '***he will always hail, ever conceal and never reveal,***' and 'Silence and Secrecy' are two of the 'most precious jewels' of the order, and, consequently, if I give you the explanation you desire, and which you undoubtedly ought to have, I shall be violating my obligation and committing the one unpardonable crime, as I have just said, which a Mason can commit."

"But surely, Freemasonry does not bind a man against performing a secret duty toward his child? It does not—it cannot forbid a father to teach, to advise or to admonish his son, even on the subject of Freemasonry itself?"

"Yes it does. Freemasonry forbids everything and denies everything that comes in contact with its despotic sway. A father cannot explain anything concerning Freemasonry to his son any more than he can to the greatest stranger in the land; and so when I warn you against the terrible snare of the Masonic system, and when I admonish you to 'have no fellowship wlth the unfruitful works of darkness,' as they are exemplified in the lodge room, and at the same time explain to you my reasons,—derived from long experience and study—for so doing, then I am cutting right into the very foundation of the institution, and aiming a deadly blow at its most vital part, and hence Freemasonry forbids what it would term such a 'sacriligious act."'

"Why, my dear father, this is a very singular

state of things! You caution—you warn me to avoid Freemasonry as I would the bite of the most venemous serpent, and when I ask you for an explanation, you answer me that the laws of Masonry and its obligatoins and penalties forbid you to explain! Is this reasonable? Is this honorable? Or even is it honest for any institution, no matter by what name it may be called, to thus lay the ax at once even to the root of free inquiry, and to interpose its man-made edicts in the way of parental duty? Why, this caps the climax of any absurdity and wickedness that I have ever heard of."

"Masonry is nothing but absurdity and wickedness throughout, as you shall clearly understand by and by. Its obligations would fain bind my whole being, my heart, my affections, my conscience, my religious convictions, my faith, my parental duty, and it would, if it could, prevent me from offering you any explanation whatever why I advise you not to join the Masonic fraternity. But my duty to God, my duty to my family and my duty to myself have a higher claim to my allegiance and consequently a prior right to demand and receive all my obedience; and hence, holding Freemasonry to its own part of the contract entered into between us when I was made a Mason—that there was nothing in the obligations, and consequently nothing in Masonry, that could conflict with anv of those exalted duties *which I may owe* to GOD, my country, my neighbor, MY FAMILY OF MYSELF, —it shall be both my pride and my pleasure, as I consider it my bounden duty, to satisfy you in every respect that my advice regarding Masonry has not been prompted by any mere capricious whim, but that it is based upon the Word of God, upon reason, upon common sense, upon history, and upon the very *best books* and other standard works of the institution itself. However, as I perceive that I am now likely to be busy pretty soon, I shall defer my promised explanation of the entire Masonic system to some other time in the near future; but before you leave me, my dear Henry, may I request that you'll take no further steps toward being initiated until such time as we have fully examined the system and have learned in reality what Freemasonry is."

"You need have no fears, my dear father, on that score. I shall do nothing toward taking part in your monster procession on the 24th, without fully advising you of my intent; and now, of course, as you have already given me somewhat of an insight into the arbitrary character of Masonry, I could scarcely bring myself to join it—even were I ever so much inclined—without having a fuller knowledge of what I was going to do. So I shall try and keep you to your promise at an early day;

and now, as I may possibly interfere with other important business, I shall at once say good-bye, and leave for down-town."

"Good-bye, my son, and don't forget to look out for all Masonic friends."

This conversation took place in the city of Chicago on a beautiful morning in the early part of June, 1874, between Mr. George Barton, a prominent Freemason, belonging to Keystone Lodge, No. 639, and his son Henry. The latter, as the reader has already learned, had been frequently importuned, in various indirect ways, to allow his name to be taken into one of the Masonic lodges in that city. Before doing so, however, he felt it his duty to consult his father in the matter and to seek his advice in regard to such an important step, and Mr. Barton, as we have seen, promptly and cheerfully accedes to his son's earnest desire. Now the question arises, was Mr. Barton wrong in doing this? Is it wrong or wicked in a father to advise his son as to whether or not he ought to join the Masonic or any other institution of which he may have knowledge? And in giving this advice, ought a father to say simply "yes" or "no," without offering any further explanation on the subject? Is it not a parent's duty to warn and advise his child against any and every wrong doing, and hence, why may he not warn him against becoming a

Freemason, if he has cause to know that Freemasonry is bad and wicked? And in offering this warning, is there any valid reason why he should not fully explain his reasons for so doing? And, lastly, is there anything in the institution of Freemasonry itself that will operate against a father giving such counsel and advice and offering such explanation to his son? That such a bar actually exists will scarcely be admitted by any member of the Masonic fraternity, as the ritual of every degree most emphatically affirms that in Freemasonry "there is nothing which can conflict with any of those exalted duties which a man may owe to his family." And what duty more "exalted" than that which requires a parent to bring up his children "in the nurture and admonition of the Lord?" Every man is first of all morally bound to do right, and every law, rule, edict or decree, no matter where any such may be found, that intervenes between a father and the performance of his bounden duty, is radically and intrinsically wrong and wicked, and ought at once to be set aside. Every one, therefore, must honestly concede that Mr. Barton is simply performing his duty, and nothing more, when he explains the full nature of the Masonic institution to his son Henry.

The law of God requires this, conscience dictates it, and parental love, breaking through all artificial bounds, impels him to it; and if the laws of Freemasonry come in direct conflict with the laws of God, the honest requirements of conscience and the natural promptings of a father's love, then, indeed, it must be confessed that Freemasonry, with all its sinful, selfish brood of other smaller secret associations, is one of the most vicious, the most wicked and the greatest enemy to the well-being of the family, that has ever existed in any age or in any nation.

But we had better hear what Mr. Barton himself has to say on this subject, as we find him conversing with Henry a few evenings subsequent to the day already mentioned.

Mr. Barton: Well, Henry, is there any more news this evening from our Masonic friends? Have they made any further advances in their efforts to induce you to become a Mason? Or have you yourself given the matter any further thought since our last brief conversation on the subject?

Henry: Yes, Freemasonry is now more or less the subject of conversation every day, especially that grand turnout which all seem so anxiously to look forward to, on the occasion of laying that corner-stone of the Custom House. This theme, just now, seems to absorb all others, and if the brethren are to be believed, Freemasonry is one of the noblest, if not *the* noblest, tinstitution in the world. "Its members," they say, "assist each other in distress. It is purely benevolent. It is petted and patronized by the government, encouraged and upheld by ministers of the gospel. It can count within its membership some of the very best and greatest men in the community," and they argue, and, I must confess, not without some show of reason, that "if Freemasonry were as bad as its enemies would make it out to be, all those great and good men would not continue to be members of it."

Mr. Barton: The laying of that corner-stone by the Masonic fraternity, on the 24th inst., is, in my opinion, one among the many of those things that ought to condemn this institution in the estimation of every honest mind. What right has Freemasonry to arrogate to itself privileges and prerogatives which cannot be fully enjoyed by all the rest of the community? Why should the Freemasons more than any other class of men be called upon to lay the corner-stone of a building for the erection and subsequent maintenance of which the public at large pay heavy taxes? But if Masonry does this, then Masonry must submit to be publicly examined and discussed. So long as Masonry steps in and claims the exclusive right of performing certain acts of public service in matters where the entire community is interested, then every man, woman and child *in* that community has a perfect right to inquire by what authority Freemasonry does this; and, furthermore, they have a full right to examine what Freemasonry is, and, if possible, to learn all about it.

And as for ministers of the gospel and good men being members of this organization, I do not see how that can be any better proof that Masonry is good, any more than it is that hundreds and thousands of bad men within our lodges prove that the system is wicked and vicious.

Take Freemasonry, for instance, in this city and tell me how many really good men can we find connected with all our Chicago lodges? How many good men in Blaney, in Blair, in Covenant, or in Kilwinning lodges? How many really good men in Thos. J. Turner, Dearborn or Wm. B. Warren? How many could we count in Cleveland, Chicago or National lodges? How many good men compose even the Grand Officers of the Grand Lodge of Illinois? Strickly speaking, not one. You can fairly challenge the entire Masonic fraternity of the city of Chicago, to-day, to produce half a dozen truly good men from among the whole fraternity. Take every one of our public officers, for instance, in this town, from the notorious ex-sheriff Fischer down to ex-postmaster McArthur, and tell me to which one of them all would you apply the epithet "*good?*"

There are a few honest and respectable men, to be sure, in all our lodges, here as well as elsewhere, but to the one honest and respectable man standing inside the lodge room door, there are a hundred men, better acquainted with its principles, just as honest at least, and quite as respectable, who oppose Freemasonry and stand upon the outside. Will the very few respectable men within the lodge prove the extreme goodness of the Masonic institution, any more than the hundreds of respectable men outside of it prove its extreme badness?

Ask any of those "good men" whom the base ones of the craft and the Jack Masons are so constantly boasting about, the simplest question on the subject of Masonry, and will he return a truthful and straightforward answer? Ask any one of these supposed 'good men" if Boaz, Jachin, Shibboleth, Tubal-cain and Mah-hah-bone are Masonic passwords, and he will immediately answer, they are not. Ask any one of them if "Ronayne's Hand Book" or "Duncan's Ritual" are correct revelations of Masonic so-called secrets, and he will unhesitatingly deny it. Let even the wife or child of any of those wonderfully "good men" put these questions, and a negative answer will in every case be returned, and in every one of these denials those supremely "good men" say what they know to be absolutely and positively false. Now, for the very life of me, I cannot see how this is a token of any extraordinary degree ot goodness in these men. It seems to me that a truly good man will always speak the truth, while prevarication, quibbling and falsehood are the sure characteristics of an opposite quality.

And, again, if it be any proof of the goodness of the Masonic system that some of the ministers belonging to the Methodist, Congregational and Baptist Churches fraternize with the Universalist, the Unitarian, and the infidel on the floor of the Masonic lodge room, and assume the very same obligations administered to the rum-seller, the profane swearer and the libertine—I say if this be any proof that the system of Masonry is good—ought not the fact that hundreds of the very best men and ministers of the most exemplary piety who secede from the institution every year, and who positively affirm that they could not consistently lead a Christian and a Masonic life at the same time, be proof equally strong, at least, and equally convincing that the system is false, wicked and Antichristian.

But, are there any better men in Masonry, or any more of them, than are to be found in the Romish Church? Can Freemasonry reckon any more *good* ministers among its membership than the

Church of Rome can count good ministers and bishops and cardinals among *its* membership? And if Freemasonry be a good institution on the simple ground that a few good men, ministers and others may be claimed as its members, then, upon the same ground and for precisely the same reason, we can prove Romanism, Buddhism, Mohammedanism, Mormonism, or even Molly Maguireism, to be all good institutions, and equally worthy of our esteem and respect.

And again, if we account Freemasonry to be a good institution because a few ministers, comparatively speaking, among Methodist, Baptist and Congregational Churches are wicked enough to be enrolled among its membership, so by a parity of reasoning the traffic in human slaves was a much better institution, because not only the whole Protestant Church south of Mason and Dixon's line, but also a large proportion of their brethren in the North, upheld that peculiar institution of slavery, not very many years ago, in this country.

I know it is a very common thing for Masons to point to ministers of the gospel who are members of the Order as a proof that the institution *must* be a good one; "otherwise," they say, "these good men would not remain connected with it;" and it is notorious that it is the most worthless characters in the lodge who generally use this argument. But is it a fact that ministers of the gospel, as such, are regarded as really *good*, *reliable*, *pious*, *God-fearing* men by the rulers of Masonry and by those men, even, with whom these misguided ministers seek association and fellowship? If a minister is a really good, reliable, pious, God-fearing man, why do Masons insist upon it that he shall take an oath just the same as a rum-seller, a profane swearer or a libertine does, when being made a Mason? If the minister is considered such a *good* man, why not take his simple promise or even affirmation? But no; he must "solemnly swear" by the Holy Bible, Square and Compass, as all others do. If Masonry considers the minister a good, reliable, honest man, why cause him to swear "not to cheat, wrong or defraud a lodge of Master Masons, or a brother of that degree?" If he is a pure-minded, pious, God-fearing man, why require him to swear "not to violate the chastity of a Master Mason's wife, mother, sister or daughter?" If he be such a good man, why not accept his simple promise? But no, his word cannot be taken; he must "solemnly swear." This proves conclusively that, as far as his moral worth is coneerned, the minister of the gospel is considered by Masonic law as no better and no worse than the vilest and the most miserable rum-seller or rum-drinker in the lodge-room, and that his word or promise is of no more value than theirs.

And how a man whom the Masonic institution itself thus degrades and mistrusts can be pointed to as a proof of the extreme goodness of Masonry, is one of those unfathomable mysteries so frequently met with in discussing the merits of a system which has not the least shadow of support, either from history, from scripture, from reason, or from common sense, but, in fact, is diametrically opposed to them all. Degrade a minister to the level of a common *rough*, in order to make him a Mason, and then afterwards point to that same minister as a proof that Masonry *must* be a good thing! If this is not an insult to the ministerial character, then I am at a loss to understand how a minister could be insulted.

"Freemasonry is good," exclaim the Masonic rabble and their cousins, the "Jacks;" "because some good men and ministers of religion are members of it."

"Jesus Christ is a bad and a wicked man," exclaimed the Jewish priests and Pharisees; "because none of the rulers or of the Pharisees believed on him."

"And some of them would have taken him, but no man laid hands on him. Then came the officers to the chief priests and Pharisees, and they said unto him 'why have ye not brought him?' The officers answered: 'Never man spake like this man.'

"Then answered them the Pharisees: 'Are ye also deceived? Have any of the rulers or of the Pharisees believed on him? But this people who know not the law are cursed.' "—John vii. 44–49.

This is precisely the argument used to-day in support of Freemasonry, and it is as valid in the one case as it was in the other.

But you have stated that "Freemasons help one another when in difficulty," and, like a good many other young men, you very foolishly conclude that that must be a good point in its favor. Now if this be an argument to show that Freemasonry is a good institution, that it ought to be respected and upheld, and that men ought to blindly swear to support all its laws and requirements, whether "right or wrong," then, on the same ground, and for similar reasons, burglary is good, horse-stealing is good, gambling or Molly Maguireism is good, and ought, therefore, to be supported, because in all these institutions their members help one another as much as Masons do when in difficulty, according to the tenor and letter of their several obligations.

This is no proof that a man should join the Masons any more than it is that he should become a gypsy, and indeed there is but very little difference between the oath taken by a man in being adopted into a tribe of gypsies and that taken by a man in being made a Master Mason. And if Masons help one another when in difficulty, they do nothing more than their sworn duty, or even what the gypsies do.

What thanks ought a man to receive for doing a thing which he positively swears to do? If a Mason swears to help a brother Mason in difficulty, does it argue a single whit in favor of the goodness of Freemasonry because he simply does what he absolutely swears he would do? I think not. It merely proves he very reverse. If Masonry required its members to help all men and women in distress, then it would have some show of reason for proclaiming its goodness and parading its noble character before the world, but as it is, all that can be said of it is, that it is purely and positively selfish in every single act and movement of its whole being. (*See Appendix.*) (Note A.)

And, lastly, you are laboring under the erroneous opinion that Freemasonry is charitable or benevolent even to its own members. But this, my dear Henry, is as great a delusion as any of those to which I have already alluded. Freemasonry a charitable or benevolent institution! In the name of goodness and common honesty, where are the tokens of its charitableness or benevolence? We know that Masonry has existed in one form or another from the year 1717 to the present time, and we also know that here in the United States its lodges have been in operation since the year 1733, but during all this long period of nearly a century and a half, what has it done to exemplify its benevolent character? Has it built even one really charitable institution or performed one single act of public charity in all that time? Not one. There is not to-day, in America, a single hospital, a single house of refuge, or a single institution of any kind whatever, where the old and decrepit Mason can be received, and where he may end his days in peace, and not one for the Mason's widow, except that miserable excuse in Louisville, Ky. Masonry has never done anything to mark it out as a benevolent institution, but on the contrary, it has left numerous foot-prints on the sands of one hundred and fifty years, like the Wandering Jew, which distinctly point to it as a hollow mockery, a gigantic swindle, and a selfish, vicious, wicked falsehood. The purely selfish character of the Masonic system is very strikingly presented (though of course unwittingly) by Past Grand Master Morris, in his edition of "Webb's Monitor of Freemasonry," p. 296, under the word "TRAVEL." He says:—

"A Master Mason on his travels has a right to visit every regular lodge in his way. Every well-regulated lodge will have a seat and a welcome for him, every intelligent brother a hand and word of greeting."

This is doubtless very pleasant and very comforting to the traveling brother; but let us now see the conditions upon which these little social amenities are to be extended to him. Dr. Morris goes on to explain:—

"To *secure* this greeting and this welcome, the

traveling brother must have 'the pass of King Solomon.' He must be at least in outward semblance mentally, morally and physically perfect."

What a good, noble, charitable institution truly Masonry must be, when those to whom its "intelligent" members are to extend a "welcome" and a "word of greeting" must all be stout, hale, healthy fellows,—"mentally, morally and physically perfect." Now it could lay some claim to benevolence if it extended even its "welcome" and its "word of greeting," if nothing more, to the poor and the needy, or to the halt, the maimed, the lame, and the blind; but no! its seat and its welcome, as well as its word of greeting, are only to be extended to members of its own order, and then only to those who are "mentally, morally, and physically perfect, at least in outward semblance."

But again Dr. Morris informs us:—

"If his limbs are mutilated or his senses deficient *so that he cannot give and receive all the Masonic means of recognition in the ancient Masonic manner*, he is physically imperfect and cannot visit the lodge."

"If he is unable from original ignorance or forgetfulness to explain to the satisfaction of his examiners all the ceremonials of Blue Lodge Masonry, together with the rational intention of the same, and do it all *in the peculiar phraseology of York Masonry*, he is mentally imperfect and cannot visit the lodge."

In both these cases he has not got "the pass of King Solomon," and although he may have been a Mason for eight, ten or a dozen years and, of course, paid regularly all just dues and demands against him, yet under the peculiar circumstances mentioned he is not only excluded from any possible chance of being financially relieved, but he is even debarred from temporarily occupying a seat in the lodge. And yet this thing will call itself a charitable institution! When the great fire came and burned down the fairest and best portion of our city, destroying nineteen lodges, and reducing hundreds of Masonic families to absolute want, every one thought that then at least Freemasonry would exemplify its benevolence and show to the world that it makes no empty boast when it claims "to soothe the unhappy, to sympathize with their misfortunes, to compassionate their miseries, and to restore peace to their troubled minds." But how was it at that terrible time in Chicago? Every intelligent Mason among us is well aware that the farce known by the name of a "Masonic Board of Relief," organized by the Grand Master to disburse the fruits of Masonic selfishness miscalled "Blessed Charity," was one of the biggest humbugs and the grandest and most gigantic swindle that was ever witnessed by the Masonic fraternity within the memory of the present generation. After numerous solicitations Grand Master Cregier, who was at that time, by virtue of his office, President of that so-called "Board of Relief," was enabled to gather together the handsome sum of $90,634.50, as we learn from page 42 of his "Final Report."

On page 11 of the same "Final Report" Mr. Cregier acknowledges that "in nearly all letters accompanying the donations, the instructions as to the disposition thereof were explicit, and it may be worthy of note," he says, "that these letters, coming as they did from so many different parts of the continent, should contain language almost identical, viz: that the donations were intended '*for the relief of worthy Master Masons, their widows and orphans who were sufferers by the fire of the eighth and ninth of October.*'" According to Bro. Cregier's own showing, then, the money he received at that time was for the relief of suffering Masons and the widows and orphans of deceased brethren, and not for lodges or to be given away as presents or donated to personal friends. His instructions he says, "were explicit as to the proper distribution of those funds," but how did he act in the very face of those "explicit instructions?" Assisted by his little factotum, Harry Duval, he simply misappropriated $60,000 out of the $90,634 which he received.

He gave $20,267 to "Burned-out Lodges"—he gave $5,301 to "Lodges *not burned out*"—he gave $200 of a donation to his little henchman,

Harry, besides allowing him $100 a month salary as Secretary of the Board. He gave $100 donation to James Morrison, besides allowing him also $100 a month salary as Superintendent. He gave $52 a month to old John P. Ferns, the Grand Tyler of the Grand Lodge. He gave $6,000 to form a sham arrangement, yclept "Board of Relief," to care for the needs of those *only* who come from abroad; he returned $20,000 to the Grand Lodges from whose jurisdictions donations had been received; he spent $1,304.57 in printing and publishing his ,'Blessed Charity," and in the largeness of his heart, and in the extreme greatness of his benevolence, he felt himself at liberty, after the foregoing generous *donations* tc his numerous cronies, to distribute the munificent sum of $30,631.37 "among three thousand one hundred and forty-five *needy* brethren, widows and children," or an average of about $9.47 a-piece. Of the $30,631.37 which Cregier and Duval could find it in their generous hearts to distribute among their poor suffering brother Masons, there was $1,387 paid to R. H. Mason for stoves, not one of which was worth $2 except to break it up and sell it to some rag-merchant for old iron, as you remember I did with the one they gave me. This man Mason—ex-Mayor Mason's son—hunted up all the worthless old refuse of stoyes spoiled in the manufacture that he could possibly find—opened a bogus store on North Dearborn street, and to him Harry Duval sent all his poor, distressed brother Masons for stoves, and charged for the smallest of them (No. 7,) nineteen dollars a-piece. And some very good Masons even to this day are wicked enough to believe that Duval and Mason divided the profits. Of course when these worthless old stoves were all disposed of, the concern very suddenly collapsed and our worthy brother betook himself elsewhere to practice charity and benevolence according to the peculiar requirements of his tender conscience quickened by the noble teachings of the "Ancient Craft."

This, my son, is a general exemplification of Masonic benevolence and the peculiar manner in which Masons assisted one another during that terrible winter subsequent to our Great Fire in October, 1871.

Even the paltry sum that Cregier and Duval could afford to spend for the relief of their suffering brothers and the widows and orphans of deceased Masons was wilfully and grossly mismanaged and misapplied. Instead of giving each needy applicant a few dollars with which to help himself, a shiftless English greenhorn, who knew as much of what a family ought to have as he did of the Conic Sections, was appointed to purchase supplies of all kinds, and then when a poor, destitute, burned-out Master Mason wanted some little assistance for his suffering family, either himself or his wife had to trudge wearily along through snow and ice to the corner of Halsted and Randolph streets, and present himself, basket in hand, before the large-hearted Duval, to beg for any little miserable pittance which that capricious individual may see fit to dole out to him. Insults and not necessary relief was what poor suffering Masons were most largely treated to during that cold fearful winter. Freemasonry charitable! Why the notorious sham—Freemasons themselves even do not really believe in any such hollow mockery. They have a by-word among them; and when they desire to reflect very severely upon anything, they say "it is as *cold* as Masonic charity." But suppose a destitute Mason or even a suffering widow should receive a few paltry dollars from a Masonic lodge, what is that but giving back a very small part of their own? Does Masonry ever assist any one from whom it has received no previous equivalent? Never. Does Masonry ever assist even its own suffering deserving poor? It does not, as many here in Chicago can testify. What difference is there between the benevolence of Freemasonry and that of a well-conducted Life Insurance Company? The latter is a thousand per cent. better and without the terrible oaths and blood-curdling penalties of the Masonic lodge. Freemasonry a benevolent institution! Humbug! Why, during that fearful time that tried men's souls, if the Masonic institution could not even manifest common respect towards its own suffering members, how could we expect either goodness or benevolence from it on ordinary occasions? But "like people, like priest." At the time of the Chicago fire, Harmon G. Reynolds late of Springfield, Illinois, was the immediate Past Grand Master, and also publisher of a Masonic magazine. Through the medium of that periodical he solicited aid for the Masonic sufferers, and received in all $641.41. This money he kept and applied to his own use, never once pretending that he had ever received a single penny of it. And the Worshipful Master, of Keystone Lodge, No. 639—he who is now publicly working the Masonic degrees—at the Grand Lodge meeting held in October, 1873, preferred "charges" of gross, immoral and unmasonic conduct against this same man Reynolds for committing larceny as bailey—for theft—for perjury, for wilfully and wickedly violating his obligations, and for a great many other crimes too numerous to mention. After a long debate and repeated solicitations on the part of old Harrison Dills and others, the charges were withdrawn on the expressed condition that he (Reynolds) should receive no further assistance from the Grand Lodge, but notwithstanding the fact that every member of the Grand Lodge knew well that he was guilty, yet he is to-day a member of the Masonic fraternity in good standing, and what is more, they made him a present of $500 at that very meeting.

The following is the expression of the special report of the Finance Committee in relation to the peculiar method adopted by Most Worshipful Past Grand Master Reynolds, in relieving *a brother in distress.*

"Grand Lodge Report of Illinois" for 1873, page 85:—

"Your committee to whom was referred the special report of the Grand Secretary in regard to certain moneys paid him by P. G. M. Reynolds, have had the same under careful consideration and would respectfully report that this case presents so much that is praiseworthy and noble on the part of the lodges contributing the money and *so much of an apparently opposite character in the brother who received it from them, but who withheld it from those for whom the generous doners designed it, that we find it difficult to properly express our admiration for the acts of the one, and our pain at having to refer to the conduct of the other.*"

A certain "lone widow" by the name of Mrs. T——, who claimed to have tidings from the West, was pounced upon by little Harry and the great Cregier, and brought up before a Chicago Police Court for obtaining a few worthless straw matresses under false pretences, but Past Grand Master Reynolds, who absolutely stole $641.41 from his suffering brother Master Masons when they sorely needed it, was not only not punished for his crime but was actually rewarded for his ***charitable intent*** by a handsome donation from the Grand Lodge of $500. But then you must remember Mrs. T—— was a woman, and never had the cable-tow round her neck while Reynolds was Past Grand Master, and whatever happens, the fame of Masonry must be preserved—and the Right Worshipful Grand Chaplain—a minister of the gospel—at that very meeting which voted Reynolds the money had the temerity to thank God for the Masonic institution, and for the existence of the Illinois Grand Lodge.

Every thing connected with that miserable abortion—the "Executive Board" of the Masonic Relief Committee was so disgracefully mismanaged and so glaringly insulting to the moral sense of every member of the Masonic fraternity at that unfortunate period that even the German Masons here in Chicago called several indignation meetings condemning in no unmeasured terms the notorious conduct of both the President and Secretary of the Board, and frequently manifested other very serious symptoms of a general revolt.

In 1872, the Grand Lodge of Illinois, expended in salaries, lodge parapharnalia, music, printing, &c.,

the enormous sum of $25,015.59, and but only $10c in charity, according to the "Grand Lodge Report" for that year, pages 45 and 46.

In 1873, there were expended for similar purposes the still larger sum of $28,822.19, and not a penny in charity, while in 1874, the Grand Lodge saw fit to expend upon a few of its own most favored members alone, the unprecedented amount of $11,363.60, but not a nickle piece in charity, according to the "Grand Lodge Report" of these years, pp. 62 and 25 respectively.

All my experience in and out of the Masonic lodges, has gone to establish the fact in my mind that Freemasonry in all its departments is the most corrupt and wicked, and contains the greatest amount of falsehood of any other institution on the face of the globe.

It is positively and absolutely selfish in every single element of its pagan composition, and can truthfully lay no more claim to charity, benevolence or goodness of any other name or description than could any of the heathen organizations which Christian civilization has long since banished from the world. (Note B.)

It excludes from even its pretended benefits all old men, all young men under twenty-one, all women, all blind men, all deaf and dumb men, all cripples, all men with the left or right knee stiff-jointed, all one-armed men, all men even with the right thumb or first finger of the right hand off, all negroes or colored men, and ALL POOR MEN. In a word it rejects seventy-five per cent. of the entire human family from any participation whatever in any of its boastful privileges and wonderful benevolence, and how an organization doing all this can lay claim to charity or goodness is something more than I have ever been able to understand.

CHAPTFR II.

MASONRY A RELIGIOUS INSTITUTION.— Teaches piety. — Lodge meetings strictly religious.— Opened and closed with prayer. — Masonry of divine origin.— Teaches divine truth. — Lodges consecrated to holy purposes. — Not Christian.

Henry:—Well, my dear father, I cannot say that you have impressed me very favorably in regard to Masonry, so far as its mutual aid and its claims to a wonderful benevolence are concerned, but now suppose you tell me something of its internal workings. Outside of any particular virtue which it may pretend to possess, what on the whole does Freemasonry claim to be? And what are its general objects?

Mr. Barton:—Freemasonry claims to be a *religious institution* or a system of *religious philosophy*; nothing more and nothing less. The very construction of the organization itself clearly establishes this fact, and in this respect its claim (not as in the case of its benevolence) is something more than mere pretense. Masonry *is* undoubtedly a religious system. All its prayers, its mystic rites, its numerous ceremonials, its hymns of praise, its altars, its burial and baptismal services, its consecration and dedication ceremonies, its priests and high-priests, and all its other various religious formulas demonstrate the fact beyond any question even in the absence of documentary evidence, if necessary, that Freemasonry is a religious institution, that and nothing more. But above and beyond all this, every one of its manuals, monitors, text-books, lexicons and law-books, in fact all Masonic literature, positively assert this in language that cannot be doubted, and the religious character of the institution is so thoroughly understood by the members of the fraternity generally, that we hear the sentiment daily echoed from every lodge-room in the land, that "Masonry is a good enough religion for me." This is the universal belief among Masons. "If Masonry don't save a man," they say, "then he cannot be saved." But in order to have a perfect understanding of this peculiar feature of the Masonic system, and to place it beyond the possibility of a doubt, that this is indeed the true character and design of Freemasonry, I must at once refer you to the different text-books or manuals in general use among the craft, and also to those various standard Masonic works which are intended to teach Masonry to Masons. It is only from Masonic literature that we can obtain any accurate and authentic knowledge of Masonic teaching, and hence, in all our future investigations we must confine ourselves exclusively to the authorized and standard monitors, manuals, lexicons and law-books of the lodge and chapter, and in this way, my son, you will be able to obtain that true, proper, legitimate and correct information concerning the entire Masonic system and its symbolic teaching, to which it is my earnest desire, as it shall be my greatest pleasure to direct your attention.

In "Webb's Monitor of Freemasonry" by Dr. Robt. Morris, Past Grand Master of Kentucky, we read on p 7:—

"Masonry is a system, teaching symbolically PIETY, morality, science, charity and self-discipline."

Now you will observe, if Masonry teaches piety, if it claims to make a man pious, it must undoubtedly be a religious institution, for nothing but religion of some sort can possibly do that. A purely secular or scientific institution cannot do it, even a benevolent society will not do it. Nothing but religion can make a man pious, and therefore Masonry, according to this definition, must, of necessity be a religious institution.—PIETY and religion are synonymous terms. See Webster's Dictionary.

But whoever saw or even heard of a man, whom Freemasonry had made pious? If it be really a fact, as stated by Dr. Morris, that Masonry teaches *piety*, then, without doubt, some one of its members—some Grand Master, Grand Chaplain, Grand High Priest, some Sublime Prince or Worshipful Master, or some one of its members, high or low, grand or otherwise, must have been made pious through his connection with the lodge, and ought assuredly to manifest this piety in his walk and conversation in life.

But if it be the object of Freemasonry to teach piety, why not extend its privileges to all? If Masonry teaches PIETY why deny the benefits of its pious teachings to the Mason's wife, any more than to the Mason himself? And if Freemasonry teaches MORALITY why is it a standing rule that a man must already be strictly *moral* before applying for admission? An institution having for its sole object the inculcation of piety and moral principles, ought to have no dread of public discussion, but yet it is a notorious fact that every Mason is absolutely forbidden to enter into any controversy whatever on the subject of Masonry. Freemasonry professes to make men pious, and yet as we have already seen, it utterly closes its doors against seventy-five per cent. of the whole human race, and positively refuses to discuss its principles. Romanism, also, professes to make men pious and send them to heaven, but like the Masonic institution it absolutely refuses to do so except upon the payment of certain sums of money, and it too declines to be publicly discussed. Perhaps some Masonic Protestant minister will be able to discern the difference between Freemasonry and Romanism in these respects.

But again in "Webb's Monitor" p.13, I read:—

"No lodge *can be* regularly opened or closed without *religious services* of some sort."

"Religious services of some sort" must be engaged in before a lodge of Masons can proceed with work or business of any kind, and also before closing its labors, and this alone is enough to establish the religious character of the institution.

Again in "Webb's Monitor," p. 231 under the word "CHAPLAIN," we read:—

"The Master of the Lodge is its *priest*, and the director of its religious ceremonies. His duty is to select the scriptures, prayers, &c., and he should be present at the burial of the dead. A meeting of a Masonic Lodge *is a religious ceremony*." "Masonry in many features *is* a religious as well as moral institution."

This, I think, places the question of the religious character of Freemasonry beyond the possibility of dispute. The Worshipful Master is the priest of the lodge, and his duties there are precisely the same as those of a Methodist, Baptist, Congregationalist or any other minister of religion in the Christian Church. But lest any doubt should remain on the subject, it is distinctly stated in plain easy language, that "the meeting of a Masonic lodge is a religious ceremony, and that "Freemasonry is a religious institution." This is the testimony of the "father of American Masonry," and surely a father ought to know the real character of his own off-spring.

But we have stronger testimony still on this point, or rather the same principle expressed in more forcible language.

In "Webb's Monitor," p. 284, under the word "RELIGION," we read again:—

"The meeting of a Masonic lodge is *strictly a religious ceremony*." * * * The *religious* tenets of Masonry are few and simple, but fundamental." * * * "No lodge or Masonic assembly can be regularly opened or closed without prayer." * * * So broad is the *religion* of Masonry," &c.

Here it is positively affirmed that in the strictest sense of the word the meeting of a Masonic lodge is a religious ceremony, that its religious tenets are few but fundamental, and lastly, that the *religion* of Masonry is a *broad religion*. All establishing beyond controversy that Freemasonry is a system of religious philosophy or religious institution. So much from Webb.

Now we may turn to another text-book where, in fact, we shall find even stronger testimony, if any stronger than this can exist.

In the "Manual of the Lodge" by A. G. Mackey, p. 40, it is stated that :—

"As Masons we are taught never to commence any great or important undertaking without first invoking the blessing and protection of deity, and this is because *Masonry is a religious institution*."

Here you will observe Dr. Mackey assigns as the reason why prayer is always offered in Masonic lodges, that "Masonry is a religious institution," and you and I must be very well aware that Past Grand Master Albert G. Mackey would be very far from publishing anything in his "Lodge Manual," or making use of any remark which he thought would not be endorsed by the general craft, or be denied as the correct teaching of the Order.

But that Freemasonry is a *religious* philosophy, Dr. Mackey further proves in his "Manual of the Lodge," p. 57. He says :—

"Speculative Masonry, now known as Freemasonry is, therefore, the scientific application and the religious consecration of the rules and principles, the technical language, and the implements and materials of operative Masonry to the worship of God as the Grand Architect of the Universe, and to the purification of the heart, and the inculcation of the dogmas of a religious philosophy."

Reducing this to plain, common, every-day language, we learn that Freemasonry pretends to worship God, to purify the heart, and to inculcate the *dogmas of a religious philosophy* through its religious consecration of the rules, principles, technical language, implements, and materials of operative Masonry ; all of which manifestly proves that Freemasonry is a religious system.

And now we shall turn to another text-book.

In the "Lexicon of Freemasonry" by Mackey, p. 371, under the word "PRAYER," we read :—

"All the ceremonies of our Order are prefaced and terminated with prayer, because *Masonry* is a religious institution."

And again, under the word "ORDER," on p. 336 :—

"An order is defined by Johnson to be among other things 'a regular government, a society of dignified persons, distinguished by marks of honor, and a *religious fraternity.*' In all of these senses Masonry may be styled an Order."

That is to say, Freemasonry may be styled an Order, for three reasons: First, because it is a *regular governmeut.* Second, because it is a society of dignified persons; and Third, because it is a *religious fraternity.*

Again in the "Traditions of Freemasonry" by A. T. C. Pierson, p. 13:—

"The Order known as Freemasonry appears to have been instituted as a vehicle to preserve and transmit an account of the miraculous dealings of the Most High with his people in the infancy of the world, for at that early period Freemasonry may be identified with religion."

The writer of this, Mr. A. T. C. Pierson, the present Grand Secretary of the Grand Lodge of Minnesota, is a "Sovereign Grand Inspector General" of the "Holy Empire" of Freemasonry, and it is rather curious to notice his claim for that organization, that it was "instituted as a vehicle to preserve and transmit an account of the dealings of the Most High with his people in the infancy of the world."

Now, I think, we may lawfully inquire here, by whom was the Masonic philosophy instituted? If its sole object, as Pierson claims, was to "transmit an account of the dealings of the Most High with his people, in the infancy of the world," then of course the inference is undeniable that this thing now called Freemasonry must have been instituted by God himself. But we learn from the Word of God *all* that is necessary for us to know of the dealings of the Most High with his people in the infancy of the world; we learn that he promised them a Redeemer: that all their daily sacrifices and religious worship typified his coming, his sufferings and his death, and that all his dealings with his people at that early period were specially intended to keep before the minds of men the sublime truth, that reconciliation with God and a restoration to their lost condition could only be effected through the atonement of the promised Messiah. And if Mr. Pierson claims that Freemasonry must have been instituted by the Most High, then he simply affirms that the Most High instituted one system of religion as revealed in the Old Testament, embodying all the types and shadows of a future Saviour, and another system of religion as revealed in Freemasonry, which absolutely denies, rejects, disowns, and dishonors that Saviour. That is to say, God is the author of two distinct and different systems of religion, the one pagan, the other Christian; the one false as the serpent, the other true as God himself. In the very next sentence to the one already quoted, it is distinctly affirmed, that "the identity of the Masonic institution with the Ancient Mysteries" *i. e.* with pagan secret worship "is obvious," and strange to say it is boldly asserted of Masonry, that it was instituted by the Most High. That is to say, Masonry and the secret worship of paganism are one and the same, and as "it is claimed for Masonry that it has been instituted as a vehicle to preserve and transmit the dealings of the Most High with his people in the infancy of the world," therefore, it follows that the debasing, licentious worship of Baal and Osiris in Samaria and Egypt, was the true religion of God, and consequently that the Bible is worse than an old wife's fable. This is the natural deduction, if I accept Pierson's theory, and in this way the word of God is made of none effect by "Masonic tradition."

But again we read on p. 14:—

"But the Order of Freemasonry goes further than did the Ancient Mysteries, it becomes a conservator as well as a depository of *religion*, science and art."

And again on p. 15:—

"Thus, without any reference to forms and modes of faith, it furnishes a series of indirect evidences, which silently operate to *establish the great and general principles of religion*." And

In the "General Ahiman Rezon" by Sickles, p. 57, we read:—

"That our rites embraee *all* the possible circumstances of man—moral, social and spiritual—and have a meaning high as the heavens, broad as the universe, and profound as eternity."

If this does not mean that Freemasonry is a religious philosophy, then I must confess myself unable to comprehend the plain import of words. No stronger language than this can be used in reference to Christianity.

Again, in the "Symbolism of Freemasonry," p. 11, Dr. Mackey says:—

"Now, I contend that the philosophy of Freemasonry is engaged in the contemplation of the divine and human character."

What more can be said of the Christian religion than this—that it is engaged in the contemplation of the divine and human character?—and if we do not believe from this testimony that Freemasonry is a system of religion, then why should we believe from testimony not a whit stronger that Christianity is a system of religion?

But Dr. Mackey sets this whole matter of the religious character of Freemasonry at rest in his "Text-book of Masonic Jurisprudence," p. 95, where he says:—

"The truth is, that Masonry is *undoubtedly a religious institution*, its religion being of that universal kind in which all men agree."

And in his celebrated "Masonic Lexicon" he not only asserts in the plainest possible terms the religious character of the Masonic institution, but he also affirms in language which cannot be mistaken or misunderstood, the sort of a religion it is, and the universal law which all must observe in relation to it.

In the "Lexicon of Freemasonry," p. 404, he says:—

"The religion then of Masonry is *pure theism*, on which its different members engraft their own peculiar opinions; but *they are not* permitted to introduce them into the lodge, or to connect their truth or falsehood with the truth of Masonry."

From all this vast array of Masonic testimony, then, furnished as it is by its accredited text-books and by the very highest and most honored rulers of the order. you will at once understand that Freemasonry is claimed to be a religious institution and nothing more; not a mere benevolent or social organization, but simply a religious system established, as we have already seen, for the "purification of the heart and the worship of God," through the spiritual consecration of the implements and materials of a handicraft Mason.

But we have still further evidence, and one equally convincing, that Freemasonry is a religious institution, namely: The "chief design which constitutes all its teachings," and which is asserted to be the "elucidation and enforcement of divine truth." I shall now give but a very few extracts from the text-books upon this point, as I intend to refer to it more at length at another time.

In the "Manual of the Lodge," p. 26, Dr. Mackey says that:—

"Search of truth is the great object of all Masonic labor."

And again, on p. 29:—

"Spiritual light, which is but another name for Divine truth—the truth of God and the soul—the nature and essence of both, which constitute the chief design of all Masonic teaching."

And again, on p. 93:—

"Now, what are the wages of a speculative Mason? Not corn, nor wine, nor oil. All these are but symbols. His wages are *truth*."

And again, from the "Symbolism of Freemasonry," by Mackey, p. 149:—

"He (the candidate) craves an intellectual illumination, which will bring to his view as an eyewitness *the sublime truths of religious philosophy* and science, which it is the great design of Freemasonry to teach."

And, last of all, Freemasonry is proved to be a religious institution, from the fact that its halls and temples are said to be consecrated or set apart for sacred and holy purposes, as distinguished from profane edifices.

In the "Text-book of Masonic Jurisprudence," by Mackey, p. 288, we read as follows:—

"CONSECRATION.—The ceremony of consecrating *religious* edifices to the *sacred* purposes for which they are intended by mystic rites, has been transmitted to us from the remotest antiquity. 'History,' says Dudley, 'both ancient and modern, tells us that extraordinary rites, called rites of consecration or dedication, have been performed by people of all ages and nations on the occasion of the first application of altars, or temples, or places to *religious* uses.' "

And, after citing the examples of Moses, Solomon, and the "returned exiles" from the Babylonish captivity, he goes on to say:—

"Among the pagans, ceremonies of the most magnificent nature were often used in setting apart their gorgeous temples to the purposes of worship. A Masonic lodge is, in imitation of these ancient examples, consecrated with mystic ceremonies to the *sacred* purposes for which it had been constructed. By this act it is set apart for a holy object, the cultivation of the great tenets of a Mason's profession, and becomes, or should become, in the mind of the conscientious Mason, invested with a peculiar reverence as a place where, as he passes over its threshold, he should feel the application of the command given to Moses: 'Put off thy shoes from off thy feet, for the place whereon thou standest is holy ground.' "

Such language as this can only be used in reference to a religious institution, and the examples adduced by the Masonic law-giver, namely: that of anciently consecrating "altars, temples or places" to religious uses, such as the Tabernacle, the first and second Temples, and likewise the gorgeous temples of the pagans, in imitation of all of which Masonic lodges, halls and temples are set apart for holy purposes, clearly demonstrate the fact that Freemasonry is a religious institution, and even that it is of so sacred a character that in fact the very floor of its lodges is "holy ground."

And again, on p. 293:—

"The consecration and dedication may be considered as the religious formularies, which give a sacred character to the lodge, and by which it is to be distinguished from a *profane* association, intended only for the cultivation of good fellowship."

Comment on this is entirely unnecessary, for it is scarcely possible to utter language in any plainer words. The lodge must be "distinguished from a *profane* association," or even from a society of men "where only good fellowship is cultivated." It must ever be regarded in its true *sacred* character, and the mystic rites of "consecration and dedication" are the "religious formularies," which "give this sacred character to the Masonic lodge."

Thus it has been clearly established, that Freemasonry claims to be a religious institution, and (what is more) that it attempts to prove and sustain that claim beyond the possibility of a dispute, or the shadow of a doubt. It claims to be a religious institution. First, because of the principles it inculcates. Second, because of its prayers and benedictions. Third, because of the character of its lodge work. Fourth, because of its professed object. Fifth, because of its consecration ceremonies, which alone are sufficient to distinguish it from a profane association, and, lastly, because of its divine origin.

Henry:—Yes, I'm thoroughly satisfied on that point. I am fully convinced that Masonry is, without any doubt, a religious institution, else of course, all its various text-books, manuals, monitors, and lexicons, would never dare to assert in such very strong and positive language that it is so; but, after all, may not Freemasonry be a Christian institution, just as the Methodist, Baptist, or Congregational Churches are? And indeed, I suppose, I am justified in thus judging of its religious character, from the fact that very many of the ministers of these different churches are members of the order.

Mr. Barton:—No, my son, Freemasonry is not a Christian institution, nor does it even pretend in the very remotest degree to be any such thing. But it is, nevertheless, a religious system, just as Mahommedanism, Buddhism, Judaism, and Romanism, are religious systems. On this point ignorant Masons generally make a very great mistake. They confound the word "*religion*" with Christianity, and hence they deny that Masonry is a religious institution at all, while they simply mean only to deny that it is the Christian religion. Christianity is the *true* religion established by the Father, through the Lord Jesus Christ, for man's redemption and for his restoration to holiness and fellowship with Himself, while Masonry is but a base counterfeit, and was only established, or rather revived, in the early part of the last century, in a London grog-shop. But this I shall more fully explain to you at another time. For the present, however, let us remember that as regards the religious character of Freemasonry, there can be no controversy.

In "Webster's Unabridged," the word "religion" is defined as being:

1st. "The recognition of God as an object of worship, love and obedience."

2d. "Any system of faith and worship."

3d. "The rites or services of religion."

Now, Masonry claims to recognize God as "an object of worship and obedience," and hence, on this ground, it is a religious institution. Again, Masonry is a "system of faith and worship," and therefore in this sense, also, it is a religion, while its various "rites and services" most unquestionably establish its religious character. But, as already stated, it is nothing more than a base counterfeit, and yet (with shame be it stated,) every minister and professing Christian who is initiated into its pretended mysteries must bind himself under oaths, which are enforced by the most terrible death penalties, that he will "conform to and abide by, and ever maintain and support, every edict, rule, law, decree and regulation" of this false religious philosophy, no matter what its nature or requirements may be.

CHAPTER III.

THE MASONIC RELIGION EXAMINED.—Moral law of nature.—Purely antichristian.—True God entirely ignored.—Grand Orient of France.---Masonic despotism.---Obedience right or wrong. Masonry and Romanism.---Pure theism.---Masonic religion not founded on the Bible.—Masonic traditions.—Romanism and Masonry compared.—Condemned by the word of God.

Henry:—I begin to feel a deeper interest in the study of the Masonic philosophy than I ever thought I shonld. I always had an idea that it was simply an association established merely for benevolent purposes only, with a little conviviality or sociability thrown in to render its meetings more interesting, and to encourage its members to attend lodge more regularly, but I never thought of it as being a system of religion. I am now, however, thoroughly convinced on that point. Indeed, I cannot see, in the face of the evidence adduced, how any one can deny it. But what sort of a religion does Freemasonry inculcate? And what "rights and benefits,"

if any, does it pretend to confer on its adhering members?

Mr. Barton:—The subject to which your questions allude, my dear Henry, is exceedingly important and ought to be thoroughly investigated, and fully and clearly understood.

The silly so-called secrets of the Masonic system have been exposed and explained time and again during the last fifty years at least. Its passwords, signs, grips, and the clownish buffoonery of its initiatory ceremonies, have all been published to the world over half a century ago, and hence, to direct attention in an especial manner to the Masonic ritual, or to explain to you merely how Masons are made, would be only to demonstrate how very foolish and stupid men are sometimes capable of acting. All this is fully set forth in the "Hand-book of Freemasonry," and to that work I would therefore refer you for the genuine secrets of the craft. But that we may fully understand and thoroughly appreciate the absolute wickedness and the infidelity of the whole Masonic philosophy, we must carefully examine and expose its true religious character, and the source from which it is derived. To begin with, then:

It is claimed for the religion of Freemasonry, by its authorized exponents and teachers, that it is a UNIVERSAL RELIGION.

In reference to this point, I shall direct your attention first of all to the oldest Masonic document now in existence, namely: The "Charges of a Freemason," originally published in London by one James Anderson, in 1723, and the basis of the written law of Masonry. This document we find in the "Manual of the Lodge," by Mackey, p. 215:

CHARGE I.—"CONCERNING GOD AND RELIGION."

"Though in ancient times Masons were charged in every country to be of the religion of that country or nation, whatever it was, it is *now* thought more expedient only to *oblige them to that religion in which all men agree.*"

Here then we have it positively asserted that the *religion* of Masonry is "that religion in which all men agree," and further, that Freemasons, as such, are now everywhere "obliged" to profess that religion. Now this "religion," whatever else it is, cannot possibly be Christian, for in *that* all men do not agree—never have, and during the present dispensation never will. Neither is it Romanism, Judaism, Mohammedanism, or Mormonism, for in none of these systems do "all men agree." The religion of Masonry, therefore, must be a religion entirely peculiar to itself, from the very nature of which it borrows its vaunted universality, and by means of which it boastingly pretends to associate upon one common religious platform men of every country, and kindred, and tongue, and people, and nation. But how is this pretended universality sought to be established? And what is that peculiar feature of the Masonic system which, it claims, renders it thus acceptable to all classes of religionists, but in reality to men of no religion at all?

The answer to this is found, and can only be found, in the fact that it virtually ignores the law of God as revealed in the Bible, and that it positively repudiates and rejects the divinity and the mediatorship of the Lord Jesus Christ. On this subject we have the most ample testimony that can possibly be furnished by Masonic works of the highest standard.

In the "Text-book of Masonic Jurisprudence," by Mackey, on p. 502, it is stated that:—

"Every Mason is obliged by his tenure to obey the moral law." (Old Charges of 1722.) "Now this moral law is not to be considered as confined to the decalogue of Moses, within which narrow limits the ecclesiastical writers technically retain it, but rather as alluding to what is called the *lex naturæ*, or the *law of nature*."

Or, in other words, when the Almighty delivered his law for man's government he gave it so very imperfect, so incomplete, and so utterly inadequate to the purpose for which he intended it, that it is found to be entirely "too narrow," and too "limited" to be accepted as the standard of right in Masonic lodges, and hence Freemasonry very judiciously manufactures a much superior law for its own especial use, which it calls the "*lex naturæ*, or law of nature," which it proclaims as its only religious standard, and which every one of its members "by his tenure is bound to obey." If this is not turning the truth of God into a lie, will some Masonic divine have the goodness to say how otherwise it could be done, and to better effect?

But Dr. Mackey continues:—

"This is the 'moral law' to which the old charge already cited refers, and which it declares to be the law of Masonry. And this was wisely done, for it is evident that no law less universal could have been appropriately selected for the government of an institution whose prominent characteristic is its universality."

Of course it was "wisely done!" Why should such a noble institution as Freemasonry—so broad in its philosophy—so universal in its membership, and so extensive in its wonderful benevolence, be governed by so "narrow," and so "limited" a code as the law of God? Freemasonry, which is so exceedingly generous and expansive in the immensity of its charity as to exclude, by stern decree, at least seventy-five per cent, of the whole human family from the very least of its boasted benefits, must have something better! Why should such a noble institution as this be governed by so "limited" a set of precepts as are to be found in the moral law of Jehovah? No, no, that would never do. Freemasonry must have a code of laws far superior to that, and entirely more suitable to its own peculiar morality, and so it has set up for itself a something called the "*lex naturæ*," or "law of nature." But let us hear the great Masonic Dr. Mackey out. He says, in continuation:—

"The precepts of Jesus could not have been made obligatory on a Jew; a Christian would have denied the sanctions of the Koran; a Mohammedan must have rejected the law of Moses, and a disciple of Zoroaster would have turned from all to the teachings of his Zend Avesta. The universal law of nature, which the authors of the old charges have properly called the moral law, is, therefore, the *only* law suited in every respect to be adopted as the Masonic code."

Here lies the secret of the whole matter. "The precepts of Jesus" must be rigidly excluded, the law of nature must be substituted for the law of God, and a religious philosophy, founded upon this law, must be substituted for the religion of the Bible; and upon this broad infidel platform it is boasted that men of every clime and every religion, or of no religion at all, may and do harmoniously associate together. But how can a professing Christian, and more especially a Christian minister, solemnly swear to "maintain and support" such a wicked combination as this? Or if he is unwittingly led into such an infidel conspiracy how can he consistently remain a member of it, and thus by the very example he sets encourage others to do the same?

Taking the very best possible view of Freemasonry, is there any one single doctrine, or any one duty inculcated and enforced by the Masonic philosophy, which is not found to be inculcated by God's law and within the pale of the Christian church? "The church of the living God is the pillar and the ground of the truth," (1 Tim. iii. 15) which the Lord Jesus Christ has "sanctified and cleansed with the washing of water by the word, that he might present it to himself a glorious church, not having spot or wrinkle or any such thing, but that it should be holy and without blemish." (Eph. v. 26 27.) Can this be said of the Masonic institution? Is that miserable system of sin and folly "without spot or wrinkle?" And are the laws and precepts of Freemasonry, its obligations, death penalties, and its foul philosophy of selfishness, deceit, and cunning, "holy and without blemish?" Why, to compare the church of Christ to Masonry would be about the same as comparing the brightness of the sun to the darkness of midnight, or the glory of the Mount of Transfiguration to the blackness of despair in the regions of eternal woe. Upon what hypothesis then can a professing Christian, and more especially a Christian minister, justify his conduct in connecting himself with the Masonic institution, and in swearing to support its laws, rules and edicts, whether "right or wrong?"

Secondly, *the religion of Masonry places the gods of paganism on a level with the God of the Bible, and its laws and edicts are especially antagonistic to Christianity.*

Of course, when it accepts the "*lex naturæ*, or law of nature," as of equal authority with the Decalogue of Exodus, it necessarily follows that it honors the "god of nature" as much as it does the true God. As regards this point, we read in

"Webb's Monitor of Freemasonry," by Rob. Morris, p. 280, as follows:—

"So BROAD is the religion of Masonry, and so CAREFULLY ARE ALL SECTARIAN TENETS EXCLUDED FROM THE SYSTEM, that the Christian, the Jew, and the Mohammedan, in all their numberless sects and divisions, may, and do harmoniously combine in its moral and intellectual work with the Buddhist, the Parsee, the Confucian, and the worshiper of Deity under every form."

Here, in plain, simple language, we have the true nature of the Masonic religion very accurately defined, and its one great leading characteristic of the positive rejection of every feature of Christianity authoritatively declared and set forth:—

First, it is a "*broad*" religion. Secondly, it is *so broad* that "all sectarian *tenets are carefully excluded from the system.*" Thirdly, this religion of Masonry is so "*broad*," that the Christian, the, Jew, the Parsee, the Mahomedan, the Confucian, and the worshipper of Deity under every form including the wild Arab and the American savage, "may, and do harmoniously combine in its moral and intellectual work." And in order to become a living, working member of this truly accommodating institution, the minister and the professing Christian must bind himself by the most solemn obligations to "conform to, and abide by all its laws and teachings."

Again in "Webb's Monitor," by Morris, p. 284, it is asserted that:—

"The religious tenets of Freemasonry are few, simple, but fundamental. The candidate must profess a belief in Deity before initiation."

This is the Mason's creed, and the one sole article of faith of the Masonic religion, as practised in the United States. It professes to demand "belief" in a God. But in what God does Freemasonry require its candidates to profess a belief? The claim is made that "the Budhist, the Parsee, and the Confucian," according to Masonic law and usage "may, and do harmoniously combine with the Máhomedan, the Jew, and the Christian in the moral and intellectual work" of the Masonic institution, but surely all these do not believe in the same God. The Confucian believes in the God

Josh ; the Mahomedan believes in the God of the Koran ; while the Budhist and the Parsee are idolatrous pagans of the most pronounced and positive type. And hence, of course, the God of Masonry must be anything and everything that the capricious fancy of any or of all these people may choose to make him. The words "God" and "Lord," it is true, are very frequently used in the Masonic ritual, but these names, Masonically expressed, can have no more reference to the true God and to his worship than the square of the Worshipful Master has to the cross of Calvary. If the God of the Bible is the true God, and if in that book He has given us a revelation of Himself, then most assuredly the Masonic philosophy is a libelous falsehood, and the God of Masonry a senseless myth.

But the Christian believes and worships the one only living and true God, everlasting—Father, Son and Holy Ghost, "who at sundry times, and in divers manners, spake in time past unto the fathers by the prophets," and who, in the person of the Lord Jesus Christ, "appeared once in the end of the world to put away sin by the sacrifice of himself." How can it be truthfully asserted then by the rulers of Masonry, that a professing Christian, or a Christian minister can harmoniously combine with Chinese, Turks, and pagan Budhists, in the various religious exercises of the lodge, especially when the law is expressly laid down that, from the peculiar construction of the Masonic philosophy, the name of Christ must be "carefully excluded." (?)

No man can serve two masters; and no Christian can worship God, through Christ, in the church, while he pretends to worship the pagan's God, without Christ, in the lodge. No, the Masonic claim in this respect is a mere shallow pretense, and hence, while American Freemasonry requires all candidates to profess a "belief in deity," it nowhere inculcates, nor can it consistently inculcate faith and trust in the God of heaven.

The Grand Orient of France, however, the highest Masonic authority in that country, and in fact the foster parent of the Freemasonry of America, is more honest in its expression in regard to its religious tenets, and more true to the real principles of the Masonic philosophy, than the Grand Lodges of the United States; for while the latter hypocritically pretend to inculcate faith in God, while they reject Christ, the latter, by a decree passed at its last Grand Annual Conclave, has ordered the name of God to be entirely stricken out from every part of its work and ritual. To require a belief in God, while the Lord Jesus Christ is disowned and rejected, is a piece of the most consummate hypocrisy, and hence the French

Freemasons recognizing this fact, and believing tn... no God at all is quite as good, if not better and more preferable, than God without Christ, have come out in their true Masonic colors, and have rejected God altogether, and when their brethren in this and other countries will follow their example, is only a mere question of time.

But again in "Webb's Monitor," by Morris, p. 285 we read:—

"The Ten Commandments *or their equivalent* embrace the gist of the *Masonic religion.*"

In this simple assertion of the Masonic lawgiver we have three things very distinctly affirmed. First: that there is a Masonic religion. Second: that the gist of the Masonic relgion is embraced in the Ten Commandments, and Third: that the Masonic authorities allow that the Ten Commandments may have an equivalent.

The first of these propositions has been already fully established by numerous quotations, both from the ritual and from the standard works of the institution ; the second is an additional proof of the antichristian character of its religious philosophy, while the third savors very strongly of the rankest blasphemy. If Freemasonry admits that God's law may have an "equivalent," and that that "equivalent" can be found in the writings of Mahomed, Confucius, or Joe Smith, then it simply affirms that the God of heaven is no better and no wiser than a mere sensual adventurer, a tyranical usurper, or an ambitious pretender.

Thirdly, *The religion of Masonry is a system of absolute despotism, and like that of Rome, demands a blind unquestioning obedience to all its laws, rules, and edicts, whether "right or wrong."*

While Freemasonry is a religious philosophy, pretending to teach piety and morality though its laws and landmarks are so framed and interpreted as to exclude from its system every particle of the Christian faith, and while it admits that any pagan philosopher may frame a code of laws equal in every respect to the moral law of God, yet lest any of its members, lay or clerical, should repent of his wicked folly in entering such a notorious combination of fraud, deception, and infidelity, and so secede from its ranks, it requires every candidate by a most terrible obligation to enter into a life-long covenant with it, and to bind himself forever to obey, without questioning, every law, rule and decree of the system under any and all circumstances.

This purely despotic principal is very clearly asserted in the following extracts from the Masonic obligations:—

In the Fellow Craft's Obligation, section 2:—

"I furthermore solemnly promise and swear that I will *stand to* and *abide by all* the laws, rules and regulations of the Fellow Craft degree, so far as the same shall come to my knowledge."

And again, in the Master Mason's Oblig ation, section 2:

"I furthermore solemnly promise and swear that I will *conform to* and *abide by all* the laws, rules and regulations of the Master Mason's degree *and of the lodge of which I may herefater become a member*, and that I will *ever maintain* and *support* the constitution, laws and edicts of the Grand Lodge under which the same shall be holden, so far as the same shall come to my knowledge."

"To all of this I most solemnly and sincerely promise and swear, with a firm and steadfast resolution to keep and perform the same without any equivocation, mental reservation, or secret evasion of mind whatever, *binding myself under* no less a penalty than that of having my body seyered in twain, my bowels taken from thence and burned to ashes, and the ashes scattered to the four winds of heaven, so that no more trace or remembrance might be had of so vile and perjured a wretch as I, should I ever, knowingly or willingly, violate or transgress this, my solemn obligation as a Master Mason; so help me God, and keep me steadfast in the due performance of the same." See "Hand Book," pp. 66 and 99.

If such an oath as this were published in any of the daily papers, with a statement that it was administered in the dead of night, and at a secret meeting, guarded by an armed sentinel, by the Molly Maguire or Ku-Klux societies to a joining member, the whole country would be horrified, and these wicked institutions justly ranked as among the very worst of their kind in the world. And yet, every minister in being made a Master Mason must take this oath.

Now compare this with the following from the oath administered by the Romish church to every one of her converts and mark the difference.

In the Creed of Pope Pius IV. Art. xii we read:—

"I, N. N. do at this present freely profess and truly hold this *true Catholic faith without which no one* CAN BE SAVED, and I promise most constantly to retain and confess the same entire and inviolate with God's assistence *to the end of my life.*"

And then every priest, bishop and ecclesiastic must further swear:—

"And I will take care as far as in me lies, that it shall be held, taught and preached by my subjects, or by those, the care of whom shall appertain to me in my office; this I promise, vow and swear—so help me God and the holy gospels of God."

Is the Romish system then any more exacting or any more despotic then the system of Masonry?

Again in the Masonic ritual the following questions and answers occur, and while they serve to indicate the true source of all Masonic piety and morality, they also point out the only bond which could otherwise cement this wicked conspiracy together:

"What makes you a Mason?" "My obligation."

"What makes you a Fellow Craft?" "My obligation."

"What makes you a Master Mason?" "My obligation." (See "Hand Book," pp. 36, 182, 259.)

Thus we see that the Masonic obligations are the very foundation of the whole system, and without which this miserable, wicked sham would fall to pieces in a year; and the only condition upon which obedience to the requirements of these obligations is demanded and enforced is explained by Dr. Rob. Morris, Past Grand Master of Kentucky, in language so plain and easy that no Mason can fail to understand his duty.

In "Webb's Monitor," p. 196, he says:—

"The *first duty* of the reader of this synopsis is to *obey* the edicts of his Grand Lodge. *Right or wrong, his very existence as a Mason hangs upon obedience to the powers immediately set above him.* The *one unpardonable* crime in a Mason is *contumacy or disobedience.*"

From this, I think we can have a pretty clear conception of the deep-rooted conspiracy and the crafty design of the Masonic institution. First, the candidate is made to swear eternal obedience to all Masonic laws and edicts, and without having the slightest knowledge of any one of them; then the law peremptorily excluding the name of Christ is submitted for his acceptance, and, lastly, in perfect harmony with the requirements of his Masonic obligation, a blind, implicit, unwavering obedience to this law is demanded of him whether "*right or wrong.*"

In direct opposition to this terrible system of mental and moral enslavement and as if in utter condemnation of this very principle of the Masonic institution, the word of God distinctly affirms in Lev. v., 4 5., that:—

"If a soul swear, pronouncing with his lips to do evil or to do good *whatsoever it be that a man shall pronounce with an oath and it be hid from him* when he knoweth of it then he shall be guilty in one of these, and it shall be when he shall be guilty in one of these things that he shall confess that he had sinned in that thing."

Freemasonry says to every candidate; "swear, although what you are called upon to swear to is hidden from you." The word of God on the other hand says "if you do this you sin against God and you shall be guilty."

Fourthly, *The religion of Freemasonry is* PURE THEISM, *acknowledging* A GOD *but denying revelation.*"

This is very clearly asserted under the word "Religion" in the

"Lexicon of Freemasonry," by A. G. Mackey, p. 404:—

"THE RELIGION THEN OF MASONRY IS PURE THEISM on which its different members engraft their own peculiar opinions, *but they are not permitted to introduce them into the lodge* or to connect their truth or falsehood with the truth of Masonry."

In the extract before us, my dear Henry, we have as clear and emphatic a statement as can possibly be found anywhere, of the real character of the Masonic religious philosophy. It is PURE THEISM. Nothing more and nothing less; and upon the broad platform of this *pure theism* it pretends to unite all classes and conditions of men. Now the Jew, the Turk, the Confucian and the Brahmin in joining the Masonic fraternity, binds himself to support and maintain this *pure theism.* But when the professing Christian or minister of the gospel becomes a Mason, what does *he* swear to support and maintain? Why this very same system of *pure theism.* And when the Jew, the Mahomedan and the Unitarian are initiated, or when they visit a lodge, what does Masonic law require them to "*exclude*" from the system? Nothing; absolutely nothing. Their religion, if they have any, is *pure theism* already, and consequently they compromise nothing whatever religiously by being made Masons. But when a Christian minister is made a Mason and lives up to his obligations, what is he called upon to *exclude* and what does he maintain and support? He must "carefully exclude all sectarian tenets." That is he cannot use the name of Jesus Christ in the lodge room in connection with any Masonic prayer or religious ceremony. He cannot introduce any of, what Masonry calls, his peculiar Christian opinions into the lodge, nor "connect their truth or falsehood with the truth of Masonry," and hence he willfully compromises his Christian character. And should a professing Christian or minister so far forget his duty as a good Mason as to use the name of Christ when called upon to pray in any Masonic Assembly he simply violates his obligation as a Master Mason and thus in reality becomes as much a "perjured villain" as if he had proclaimed its silly, senseless secrets upon the housetops. Having solemnly sworn that "he will conform to and abide by ALL THE LAWS, rules and regulations of the Master Mason's degree," and it being one of the most fundamental laws, rules and regulations of that degree that "all sectarian tenets must be carefully excluded," he is bound to submit to this inexorable mandate or else willfully violate his obligation, and thus incur the penalty of expulsion if not death itself.

But what is "*pure theism?*" Polytheism we know is a belief in *many* gods, Atheism is a belief in *no* God at all, and *theism* is the belief in *a* God, and hence Dr. Mackey uses the term *pure theism* in this place, evidently to assert that the religious philosophy of Freemasonry merely recognizes the existence of *a something* which it calls god, but which is not to be understood as embodying a plurality of persons in that god; or, in other words, it is a positive denial of the Trinity.

Freemasonry, as we shall find hereafter, is the "secret worship" of paganism *revived*, and this doctrine of pure theism enunciated here by the Masonic lexicon is simply the same principle which in all pagan countries distinguished their secret from their public worship. This sáme idea of the Masonic religion is elsewhere referred to by Mackey and others, as "the unity of God," and, together with the doctrine of immortality, is claimed to constitute the sole religious belief of the Masonic philosophy.

Referring to these doctrines, and the manner in which they were communicated and preserved in early times, the "Symbolism of Freemasonry," by Dr. Mackey, p. 15, states as follows:—

> "But those among the masses—and there were some—who were made acquainted with the truth, received their knowledge by means of an *initiation into certain sacred mysteries* in the bosom of which it was concealed from the public gaze."

Hence, then, the *pure theism* which constitutes the sum and substance of the Masonic philosophy is precisely the same doctrine and mode of faith which is claimed to haye existed in the pagan mysteries, after the dispersion of mankind in the plains of Shinar; and to this pagan philosophy of the lodge every candidate, be he minister or layman, "must, with reverence, most humbly bow," according to the tenor of his obligation.

In direct opposition to this pagan idea of lodge theism, the word of God very distinctly affirms a plurality of persons in the God-head.

In Genesis i. 26, we read:—

"And God said, let us make man."

Again in John i. 1 14:—

"In the beginning was the WORD, and the WORD was *with* God, and the WORD was God."

"And the WORD *was made flesh, and dwelt among us.*"

See, also, in Matt. xxviii. 19:—

"Teach all nations, baptising them in the name of the Father, and of the Son, and of the Holy Ghost."

And again in John v. 7:—

"There are three that bear record in heaven, the Father, the Word, and the Holy Ghost, and these three are one." And

Lastly, *The religion of Masonry is both unscriptural and antiscriptural, and like Romanism, wholly based on corrupt traditions.*

In the "Digest of Masonic Law" by Geo. Wingate Chase, pp. 207, 208, I read:—

"The Jews, the Chinese, the Turks, each reject, either the New Testament or the Old, or both, and yet we see no good reason why they should not be made Masons. In fact *Blue Lodge Masonry has nothing whatever to do with the Bible; it is not founded upon the Bible.* If it was, it would not be Masonry, it would be something else."

This is the unchangeable law in the case, absolute and beyond controversy. Chinese, Turks and Jews may become Freemasons, although they reject either a part or the whole of God's word, and the reason given for the existence of this universal principle is that "Masonry has nothing whatever to do with the Bible. It is not founded on the Bible; if it was it would not be Masonry it would be something else."

You will observe that here four things are explicitly affirmed. First, that a man who rejects the Bible altogether may become a Mason. Second, that Freemasonry is not founded on the Bible. Third, that if Masonry were founded on the Bible it would not be Masonry, and Fourth, that the religious system of Masonry is "something else" than what the Bible teaches.

Now with regard to the first point —that men who reject the Bible may become Masons.—How is it that the candidate is obligated on the Bible in all American lodges? And why is he required to salute it with his lips, after taking his obligation? Kiss a Bible which he may despise and reject! Take an obligation on a Bible, one word of which he may not believe? Why, this is solemn mockery—an insult to common sense, to reason, to the religion of the Bible and to God. And yet as Masons we ask God to help us to keep steadfast in and carry out this wicked hypocrisy to the end of life. (See "Hand Book," p. 185, last clause of obligation.)

But again, suppose one of these men who disbelieve the Bible, (and there are thousands of them in Masonry) should be the Master of the lodge, when a minister or a deacon of a Christian church is being initiated, how can such a man truthfully and consistently assure the candidate, then standing before him, that there is nothing in the obligation which he is about to take that can "conflict with any of those exalted duties he may owe to God?" Or how can a Christian minister, with any show of consistency or truthfulness, submit his own judgment to the judgment of such a man? We condemn Romanists, and pityingly refer to their ignorance and blind superstition in yielding their private judgment to the will and judgment of a priest; but in the Masonic lodge we find that the minister of a purely Protestant and evangelical church at his initiation may be, and very often is, called upon, to yield his private judgment to the will and judgment of a rum-seller, a profane swearer, a gambler, or even an infidel. (See "Hand Book" p. 181. Master's address to candidate before taking the obligation.)

With regard to the second point—that Masonry is not founded on the Bible—then on what is it founded? Of course, "pure theism" is not and cannot be founded on God's Word. What then is the foundation of speculative Freemasonry?

In the "Lexicon of Freemasonry" by Dr. A. G. Mackey, pp. 491, 492, we read:—

"TRADITIONS".—"The legends or traditions of Freemasonry constitute a very considerable and important part of its ritual. In many instances these *traditions* have been corrupted by anachronisms and other errors which have crept into them."

"All that can be claimed for them is that in some there is a great deal of truthful narrative more or less overlaid with fiction."

The Masonic philosophy then recognizing only what it calls "the moral law of nature," has nothing to sustain it but a system of lying traditions and legends, borrowed from the old pagan religions, and which its best and most intelligent authors candidly confess, have been falsified and corrupted almost beyond recognition.

Now it is very singular that the religion of Romanism is also claimed to be based on the same fabulous and unreliable foundation.

In the creed of Pope Pius IV, article 1, we read as follows:—

"I most steadfastly admit and embrace *Apostolical* and *ecclesiastical traditions*, and all other observances and constitutions of the same church."

And again, in the Abridgement of Christian Doctrine, p. 10:—

"Is it not enough to believe all that is written in the Bible?"

"*No it is not*, for we must *also* believe *all Apostolical traditions*."

Now, what difference, may I ask, is there between the senseless and corrupt traditions and legends of Freemasonry and the numerous "ecclesiastical" and so-called "apostolical traditions" and lying legends of Romanism? Not a particle. One is just as good authority as the other, and just as worthy the same degree of credit, while, at the same time, both are false and unscriptural. And in what particular respect does the blind credulity demanded of the Mason differ from the ignorant, superstitious belief of the Roman Catholic? A poor, ignorant, Irish Catholic, who never knew, and who perhaps, never had an opportunity of learning any better, bows submissively and yields his judgment to the will of his priest, accepting as literal truth all the stupid legends and traditionary fables of superstitious monks and hermits; but a Protestant minister, holding, perhaps, his diploma of D. D. from some famous university, and claiming to be, himself, a teacher of truth and a guide to the ignorant, bows with equal submissiveness to the will of his Masonic superior, and accepts, with the same degree of blind credulity, all the disgustingly stupid fables concerning Hiram, Solomon, Zerubbabel, the Saints John, and other Bible worthies, with which the ritual and manuals of Masonry abound. If a Protestant minister *protests* against the error of "*Romish tradition*," how can he consistently accept "*Masonic tradition*," which is not a bit more reliable if, indeed, it is as good? But what is still more singular, how can he solemnly swear to "abide by and support" all those fables and teach them to others as truth?

How exceedingly consistent a man must act when once he becomes a Mason!

Fabulous tradition is the only foundation of both Masonry and Romanism, and, as we shall find further on, the superstructure in either case is the same in principle, and is condemned with equal severity in God's Word.

In Matt. xv. 3, 6 and 9, we read:—

"Why do ye also transgress the commandment of God by your tradition?"

"Thus have ye made the commandment of God of no effect by your tradition."

"But in vain they do worship me, teaching for doctrines the commandments of men."

See also Col. ii. 8:—

"Beware lest any man spoil you through philosophy and vain deceit after the tradition of men, after the rudiments of the world and not after Christ."

CHAPTER IV.

What Masonry Claims to Do.—The new birth.—Temple building.—Mental illumination. Romanism and Masonry compared.—Both opposed to God's Word.—Freedom from sin.—"Justification by works"—Masonic precepts.—Masons in search of divine truth.—Never find it.—Masonry above the true religion.—Masonry a wicked counterfeit.

Mr. Barton:—Having thus examined the *character* of the Masonic religion and the basis upon which it rests, the next point of interest to which I desire to call your attention is the extraordinary goodness which it claims to possess, or, as the ritual expresses it, its "rights, lights and benefits."

Every religion, no matter by what name it is known, professes, of course, to contain within itself some wonderful advantages. What are the great results then to be derived from Masonic affiliation? And what are the pretended privileges which Masonry professes to confer upon those who become initiated into its antichristian mysteries and pagan ceremonials?

First:—*The Masonic religion claims to renew man's nature and to accomplish in every candidate the "new birth."*

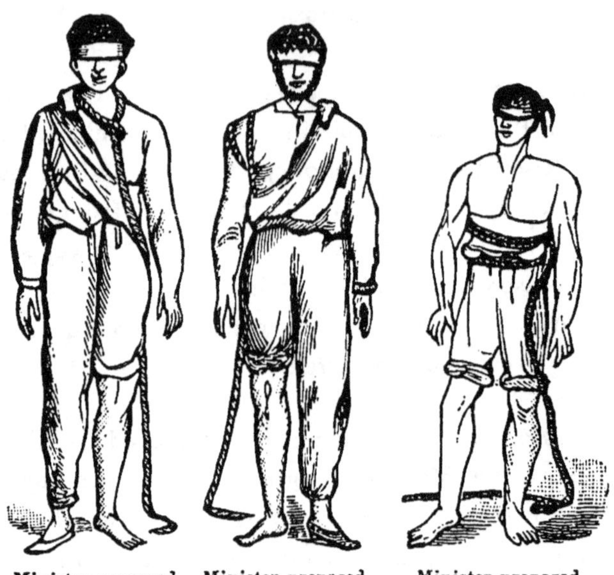

Minister prepared in E. A. Degree. Minister prepared in F. C. Degree. Minister prepared in M. M. Degree.

The above figures represent the candidate as he stands outside the door of the lodge prepared for initiation. He is divested of all his clothing—shirt excepted—dressed in an old pair of drawers; the left leg, arm and breast are bare, in the first degree; his right leg, arm and breast, in the second; and both legs, both arms and both breasts are bare in the third degree. A rope is put once round his neck, in the first; twice round his right arm in the second, and three times round his body in the third degree; and in each degree a hoodwink is carefully fastened over his eyes.

Speaking of him thus, the "Manual of the Lodge," by Mackey, p. 20, says—

"There he stands, without our portals, on the thereshold of his new Masonic life, in darkness, helplessness and ignorance. Having been wandering amid the errors, and covered over with the pollutions of the outer and profane world, he comes inquiringly to our doors, SEEKING THE NEW BIRTH, and asking a withdrawal of the vail which conceals *divine truth* from his uninitiated sight." (See "Hand Book," pp. 30, 31.)

And again, on page 21:

"Masonry stands before the neophyte in all the glory of its form and beauty, to be fully revealed to him, however, only WHEN THE NEW BIRTH *has been completely accomplished.*"

Here you will observe that, according to Masonic teaching, the *new birth* is to be accomplished in every candidate, without any exception whatever by the influence of the Masonic religion and through means of the initiatory ceremonies of the Masonic degrees. And it is also represented that every candidate—rum-seller, infidel or doctor of divinity—up to that time, has been "covered over with the pollutions of the outer and profane world," that he has been "in darkness, helplessness and ignorance," and that during all his life previous he had been "wandering in error," and that now, at last, he comes to the only place where "divine truth" can alone be found; where his "darkness" is to be changed into marvelous brightness, where his "help lessness and ignorance" are to be removed, where the clouds of "error" by which he had been heretofore enveloped are to be dispelled, and where he is to be accepted into the joyful companionship of the "Sons of Light" and receive the glorious privilege of "the new birth." What an honorable position this for a Christian minister to occupy, and what an exalted opinion Freemasonry entertains of his Bible, his church, his knowledge, his Christianity and his God, when it thus degrades him to the level of the rough, the rumseller and the dancing master; and yet this same minister takes fifty-four solemn obligations never to tell anybody anything whatever about this, and to be ever strictly obedient to all the "laws, rules and regulations" of the system, whether "right or wrong."

The Apostle John tells us, "Behold what manner of love the Father hath bestowed upon us that we should be called the sons of God. Beloved, now are we the sons of God, and it doth not yet appear what we shall be, but we know that when he shall appear we shall be like him, for we shall see him as he is." (1 John iii. 1, 2.)

Does a child of God require to go to a Masonic lodge for divine truth—to have his mental darkness dispelled, and his helplessness and ignorance removed? Or does he need to pass through the sham jugglery of Masonic initiation in order to receive the "new birth?" The word of God declares that the Lord Jesus

Christ is "the true light, which lighteth every man that cometh into the world," (John i, 9,); that he is "the root and the offspring of David, and the bright and morning star," (Rev. xxii. 16,); and he himself says; "I am the light of the world; he that followeth me shall not walk in darkness, but shall have the light of life." (John viii. 12.) But Freemasonry "carefully excludes" the Lord Jesus Christ from the lodge and chapter, repudiates his mediatorship, rejects his atonement, denies and disowns his gospel, frowns upon his religion and his church, ignores the Holy Spirit, and sets up for itself a spiritual empire, a religious theocracy, at the head of which it places the G. A. O. T. U.—the god of nature—and from which the one only living and true God is expelled by resolution; and by virtue of the silly ceremonies of this religious system, it professes to renew man's nature and secure for him in the hereafter a happy immortality in "the Grand Lodge above."

If Freemasonry, then, according to its own showing, be not the ANTICHRIST, it is impossible to understand what antichrist means, and every man, minister, or layman, deacon, or drunkard, class-leader, or gambler, initiated into Masonry swears to maintain and support this terrible antichrist for ever.

Freemasonry represents the "new birth" as being accomplished in the lodge, and through pagan initiations. The Holy Scriptures teach that the "new birth" is to be accomplished through the word of God, and by the operations of the Holy Ghost. Which ought to be believed, Freemasonry or God? Which is to be obeyed, the law of Masonry or the law of Christ?

The Lord Jesus Christ says:—

"Except a man be born again, he cannot see the kingdom of God."

"Except a man be born of water and of the Spirit, he cannot enter into the kingdom of God." John iii. 3, 5.

And again, 1 Peter i. 23:—

"Being born again, not of corruptible seed, but of incorruptible, by the word of God, which liveth and abideth forever."

How different this from the vain jugglery and foolish buffoonery of Freemasonry!

Secondly:—*Operative Masonry being the art of building temporal edifices, free or speculative Masonry professes to erect a spiritual temple in the heart.*

In the "Manual of the Lodge," p. 35, we read:—

"The speculative Mason is engaged in the construction of a spiritual temple in his heart, pure and spotless, fit for the dwelling place of Him who is the author of purity; where God is to be worshiped in spirit and in truth, and whence every evil thought and unruly passion are to be banished, as the sinner and the Gentile were excluded from the sanctuary of the Jewish temple."

And again, in the "Symbolism of Freemasonry," by Mackey, p. 162:—

"The speculative Mason, then, if he rightly comprehends the scope and design of his profession, is occupied from his very first admission into the order until the close of his labors and his life in the construction, the adornment, and the completion of this spiritual temple of his body."

And again, in "The General Ahiman Rezon, or Freemason's Guide," by D. Sickles, 33°, Secretary General of the Supreme Council Northern Jurisdiction, p. 71:—

"Masons are called moral builders. In their rituals they declare emphatically that a more noble and glorious purpose than squaring stones and hewing timbers is theirs—fitting immortal nature for that spiritual building not made with hands eternal in the heavens. The pyramids were mausoleums, in which the bones of the mighty dead might repose in imperial magnificence. Masons are erecting a structure in which the God of Israel shall dwell forever."

This, then, is the one grand pretended object of Freemasonry. "The Mason is supposed to be engaged in the construction of a spiritual temple in his heart pure and spotless." And this spiritual temple is to be constructed, adorned and completed by himself alone, without any reference whatever to the full and free salvation of Christ, the divine influence of the Holy Spirit, or without the remotest allusion to God's plan of salvation, as revealed in the Scriptures.

St. Paul, writing to the Corinthian Christians, speaks of them as follows:—

1 Cor. 3, 10:—

"Ye are God's husbandry, ye are God's building," and the reason they were so is further explained in Chapter i, 2, where he calls them "the Church of God, which is at Corinth, them that are sanctified in Christ Jesus;" and in Chapter iii. 11, he distinctly asserts that "other foundation can no man lay than that is laid, which is Jesus Christ," and all believers in the Lord Jesus Christ are living stones, built up by God's Holy Spirit—not by Masonry—into a "spiritual house, a holy priesthood," and they worship God in spirit and in truth by offering "spiritual sacrifices, acceptable to God by Jesus Christ." See 1 Peter ii. 5.

This, and this only, is God's appointed means; but Freemasonry, as we have seen, has a different plan. The Jew, the Mohammedan, the Chinese, the Buddhist, the Parsee, the wild Arab, the American savage, and the worshiper of deity under any and every form, may and do harmoniously combine in the Masonic work, according to Past Grand Master Morris, of Kentucky, and each one of these pagans and unbelievers is "engaged in the construction of a spiritual temple in his heart, pure and spotless, where God is to be worshiped in spirit and in truth;" and each one of them, before the close of life, is supposed to have succeeded in constructing, adorning and completing this temple. This is surely more blasphemous and wicked, because couched in language more calculated to deceive, than the very worst and most abusive tirades against Christianity of either Voltaire, Volney, Rousseau or Tom Paine.

Third:—*Freemasonry claims to enlighten the understanding of every candidate, to purify his evil nature, and to rescue him from the world.*

Concerning the extraordinary efficacy of the Masonic religion in these respects, we read in the "Manual of the Lodge," by Dr. Mackey, p. 39, alluding to the darkness produced by the hoodwink worn at initiation:—

"Applied to Masonic symbolism, it (the darkness) is intended to remind the candidate of his ignorance, which Masonry is to enlighten; of his evil nature, which Masonry is to purify; of the world in whose obscurity he has been wandering and from which Masonry is to rescue him."

And in the "Book of the Ancient and Accepted Scottish Rite of Freemasonry," by Charles T. McClenachan, 33 °, and "Past Grand Master of Ceremonies, of the Supreme Council of the Northern Jurisdiction of the United States," is contained a very extensive ritual or rubric for the administration of "Masonic Baptism." This rubric ordains that this extraordinary ceremony shall be performed only in the first or Entered Apprentice degree; that it is intended chiefly for infants; and it prescribes, further, that the elements to be used in administering this *rite* are water, oil, salt, lighted candles, and god-fathers and god-mothers, precisely as we find all these things in the baptismal service of the Romish Church. From this Masonic ritual I quote, on p. 576, as follows:—

"Worshipful Master:—In the name, and under the auspices of the Supreme Council of Sovereign Grand Inspectors General of the thirty-third and last degree, I proclaim these children to be *purified by* Masonic baptism, and anointed with the oil of consecration to Masonic duty. Proclaim it along your columns, brethren, Senior and Junior Wardens, and charge all Free and Accepted Masons over the surface of the two hemispheres to know and acknowledge them as such."

The Senior and Junior Wardens make the necessary proclamation as ordered, and the ceremony of baptising infants according to the formula prescribed by the Masonic lodge is over. And now in view of the strange doctrine thus strongly promulgated by Masonic law, I would like to ask some Masonic minister of the Protestant Evangelical Christian church, what does he understand by Masonry purifying a man's evil nature and by children being purified by Masonic baptism? Purified in what way? Purified from what? Will some Baptist Masonic minister have the goodness to say whether, or no, he believes this doctrine? And if he does not believe it, then why did he swear to "conform to, and abide by it," and "ever maintain and support it?" and, what is worse, why does he still adhere to it? Or, if he does believe it, then will he kindly inform us why should not Christian baptism be as efficacious in purifying a little sinless infant as Masonic baptism is? And, lastly, I would like to know how a bishop or minister of the Reformed Episcopal Church can consistently reject the doctrine of "infant regeneration" as held and taught by the Church of England, while at the same time he believes and swears to uphold and maintain the doctrine of "justification by works" as held by Maonry, and of infant regeneration by Masonic baptism? What reply can Bishop Fallows and his co-laborers in church reform make to this inquiry? And what a strange inconsistency that men who are very loud in their protestations against the errors of Romanism, as practiced in the chapel, should swear solemnly to "maintain and support" the very selfsame errors when practiced in a Masonic lodge; for on this subject of the purification of man's nature, Freemasonry and Romanism again are similar.

In the Roman Catholic catechism, entitled "Abridgement of Christian Doctrine," p. 112, we read:—

Q:—What is Original Sin?

A:—It is a privation of original justice, which we inherit from our first parent Adam, being all by course of nature conceived and born in that privation, or in original sin.

Q.—What are the effects of original sin?

A.—Concupiscence, ignorance, evil inclination, proneness to sin, sickness and death.

And again, in the "General Catechism," p. 25:

Q.—What other particular effects followed from the sin of our first parents?

A.—Our whole nature was corrupted by it; it darkened our understanding, weakened our will, and left in us a strong inclination for evil.

This is precisely the natural condition of man, as set forth by the Masonic philosophy. And now mark the infallible remedy prescribed by the Church of Rome.

"Abridgment of Christian Doctrine," p. 112:

Q.—How is original sin removed?

A.—By holy baptism.

Again, in the "Catechism of the Council of Trent," p. 257:—

"Baptism is a sacrament, because it *washes away all*, particularly original sin; penance also washes away *all* sins of thought and deed committed after baptism; on the same principle, therefore, penance is a sacrament."

And again, in the "Council of Trent," Sess. 7, Can. viii, we read:—

"Whoever shall affirm that grace is not conferred by these sacraments of the new law, *by virtue of the act performed*, but that faith in the divine promise is all that is necessary to obtain grace, LET HIM ACCURSED."

From all this testimony, then, we learn two things: 1st, that, according to Romish teaching, sin, both original and actual, is forgiven, the nature purified, the understanding illuminated, the man rescued from the captivity of the world, the flesh and the devil, by means of baptism and other sacramental ceremonials: and, 2nd, that this purification, enlightenment and liberty are secured simply by the mere *performance* of those ceremonies. According to the Romish system, a man is purified and made holy by the ceremonies of the chapel; according to the Masonic system, he is made pure and holy and spiritually intelligent by the ceremonials of the lodge and by the pagan jugglery of the Hiram Abiff tragedy. And yet ministers and other professing Christians who claim to be Protestants absolutely swear to conform to the end of life to one of the foulest doctrines of the idolatries of Rome.

In direct opposition to this wicked system of demon or man worship, both of the Romish and Masonic religions, the Holy Scriptures everywhere declare that faith alone in the divine promises of God *through the Lord Jesus Christ* is all that is necessary to obtain all needed grace and secure man's salvation.

First:—Grace in the pardon of sin, as in Rom. iii. 24:

"Being justified freely by his grace, through the redemption that is in Christ Jesus."

Second:—The grace of adoption, John i, 12:

"But as many as received him (Christ) to them gave he power to become the sons of God, even to them that believe on his name."

Third:—The grace of the new birth, 1 John v. 1:

"Whosoever believeth that Jesus is the Christ, is born of God."

Fourth:---The grace of the Holy Spirit, Gal. iii. 13,14:

"Christ hath redeemed us from the curse of the law, being made a curse for us: for it is written, cursed is every one that hangeth on a tree: that the blessing of Abraham might come on the Gentiles through Christ Jesus; that we might receive the promise of the Spirit by faith."

Fifth:---The grace of righteousness, Gen. xv. 6:

"Abraham believed God, and it was counted to him for righteousness."

Sixth:---Grace to lead a holy life, Titus ii. 11, 12:

"The grace of God that bringeth salvation hath appeared to all men, teaching us that, denying ungodliness and worldly lusts, we should live soberly, righteously and godly in this present world."

And the inspired Apostle distinctly affirms that the Holy Scriptures are able to make the "man of God perfect, thoroughly furnished unto all good works," and "wise unto salvation through faith which is in Christ Jesus."

All this being true, then, is it not positively impious and wicked for Freemasonry to expel the Lord Jesus Christ from every part of its religious worship and, like the Romish Church, substitute for faith in Christ its degrading and profane ceremonies, and obedience to the obligations and precepts of the order? And is it not equally impious and wicked for a professing Christian, and more especially for a Christian minister, to swear to ever "maintain and support" this unscriptural and anti-scriptural doctrine?

Fourth:---*Freemasonry claims, under certain conditions, to free men from sin.*

In the "General Ahiman Rezon, or Freemason's Guide," by Daniel Sickles, Masonic Publishing Company, New York, p. 70, and "Hand Book," p. 86, we read:---

"The Common Gavel is an instrument made use of by Operative Masons to break off the rough corners of stones, the better to fit them for the builders' use, but we as Free and Accepted Masons are taught to make use of it for the more noble and glorious purpose of divesting our hearts and consciences of *all the vices and superfluities of life, thereby fitting* us as living stones of that spiritual building, that house not made with hands, eternal in the heavens."

Here it will be observed four things are very plainly affirmed. First, that man by nature is corrupt, his heart and conscience being full of "all the vices and superfluities of life." Second, that all these vices and superfluities must be removed. Third, that by removing or striking off all these vices and superfluities one is fitted as a "living stone for that spiritual building, that house not made with hands, eternal in the heavens," and Fourth, that we as Speculative Masons, are taught to make use of the common gavel for the more noble and glorious purpose of divesting our hearts and consciences of all these vices and superfluities, or in other words, man is sinful and corrupt by nature and by practice, he must be cleansed and purified, and Masonry alone, symbolized by the common gavel, is to effect his regeneration.

But the religion of Freemasonry, its pretended vicariousness and the great benefits to be derived from affiliation with its infidel system of lodge worship is more distinctly asserted in the

"Lexicon of Freemasonry," by A. G. Mackey, p. 16, under the word "ACACIAN:"

"Acacian—a term signifying a Mason who *by living in strict obedience to the obligations and precepts of the fraternity is free from sin.*"

It could not be possible to frame words so as to express a simple proposition in any clearer or plainer language than this. "Strict obedience to the obligations and precepts of the fraternity," it is guaranteed by Masonry will thoroughly "free a man from sin." Now let us examine this grand Masonic boast and see what comes of it. But let me first premise that no man is born into Masonry, all are initiated. Let us suppose then, the case of two men who are Masons, one a rum-seller and the other a minister or Methodist class-leader. The rum-seller, we will assume has been concocting and disposing of poisonous liquors, manufacturing drunkards, and preparing men and women for satan's kingdom for twenty years before he becomes a Mason. He is initiated, we will say when he is forty years old, and for twenty years thereafter, he lives in strict obedience to the obligations and precepts of the Masonic system, while at the same time he sells a great deal more gin and rum during this period, than he ever did before. Now, according to Masonic teaching this rum-seller is "free from sin." But here a very important question presents itself. Does Masonry free this rum-seller from the sins of the forty years of his life before he became a Mason, or does it simply free him from sin during his Masonic life only. If while he is a Mason he lives in strict obedience to the obligations and precepts of Masonry, and is "made free from the sins committed during that period of his life alone," how does he get free from the sins he committed during the forty years before he became a Mason?

Let Freemasonry answer, or perhaps some Christian Mason can do so?

And now how is it with the minister? He too, we will suppose, is made a Mason at the age of forty, and lives twenty years a Mason, strictly obeying all its precepts, and living up to all its obligations and requirements, and of course, like his brother, the rum-seller, he also is made free from sin during all that time. During the twenty years previous to his initiation, however, he has been dispensing the Word of Life, preaching the gospel to the best of his ability, and preparing men for the kingdom of heaven. He was brought into covenant relation with God through faith in Christ, and therefore had his sins forgiven through the blood of the atonement. But when he was made a Mason he was brought into covenant relation with Masonry, through the most horrible and villianous obligations imaginable. In the ministers' case then, have the precepts and obligations of Freemasonry taken the place of the blood of Christ? And is strict obedience to these precepts and obligations able to accomplish for him during the last twenty years of his Masonic life, what a steadfast living faith in the Lord Jesus Christ had affected during the previous twenty years of his ministerial life and before he had become a Mason? Obedience to Masonic obligations and precepts, as we have already seen, necessarily requires the "careful exclusion" of Christ, or any allusion whatever to his name, or any reference to the principles of his gospel from the whole Masonic system, and consequently the inference is unavoidable that in all the future Masonic life of the Minister or Class-leader obedience to Masonic obligations must take the place of faith in Christ, and consequently *justification by works* must supercede and become a substitute for *justification by faith.*

This is precisely the doctrine promulgated by the Church of Rome.

The Romish Church declares in Canon 9, Sess. 6, Council of Trent, as follows:—

"Whosoever shall affirm that the ungodly is *justified by faith only*, so that it is to be understood that nothing else is required to co-operate therewith, in order to obtain justification, and that it is on no account necessary that *he should prepare and dispose himself by the effort of his own will*; LET HIM BE ACCURSED." Also in Canon 11:—

"Whosoever shall affirm that men are justified solely by the imputation of the righteousness of Christ or by the remission of sin to the exclusion of grace and charity which is shed abroad in their hearts and inheres in them; or that the grace by which we are justified is only the favor of God, LET HIM BE ACCURSED."

And again, Sess. 7, Canon 8, Council of Trent:–

"Whosoever shall affirm that grace is not conferred by the (seven) sacraments of the New Law, *by virtue of the act performed* (*ex opere operata*) but that faith in the divine promise is all that is necessary to obtain grace, LET HIM BE ACCURSED."

In opposition to this false pernicious doctrine both of Freemasonry and Romanism the Word of God distinctly affirms. Rom. iii. 24:—

"Being justified *freely* by his grace, through the redemption that is in Christ Jesus."

Again in Gals. ii. 16.

"Knowing that a man is not justified by the works of the law, but by the faith of Jesus Christ even, we have believed in Jesus Christ that we might be justified by the faith of Christ and not by the works of the law, for by the works of the law shall no flesh be justified."

And again in Titus iii. 5.

"Not by works of righteousness which we have done but according to his mercy he saved us by the washing of regeneration and renewing of the Holy Ghost, which is shed on us abundantly through Jesus Christ, our Saviour."

And again in Eph. ii. 8, 9.

"For by grace are ye saved through faith and that not of yourselves; it is the gift of God. Not of works, lest any one should boast."

Freemasonry asserts that by strictly obeying the obligations and precepts of the fraternity we are saved. The Word of God declares that "by grace we are saved through faith," in the Lord Jesus Christ.

Freemasonry and Romanism both declare that what they term "good works" will save a man. The Word of God declares, "not of works, lest any one should boast," for "all our righteousness are but filthy rags." Eph. ii. 8, 9. Isa 64, 6.

And again in I. John i. 7.

"If we walk in the light as he is in the light we have fellowship one with another and the blood of Jesus Christ his Son cleaneth us from ALL sin."

The precious blood of the Son of God cleanses from all sin—original and actual—present past, and future—is the positive assertion of Divine Revelation. "Obedience to the obligations and precepts of the fraternity" will free from sin" is the equally positive declaration of Masonry.

Now both these cannot possibly be true and which therefore am I bound to believe? If the boastful *good works* of the Masonic system and the equally pretended *good works* of the Romish system will free a man from sin and insure his acceptance with God, then most assuredly the gospel of God is a fable and faith in Christ is vain.

But let us here enumerate a few of those precepts and obligations which as Masons, we are called upon to obey "right or wrong," and by living in strict obedience to which we are confidently assured shall free us from sin.

"All sectarian tenets must be carefully excluded from the system." Webb's Monitor, p. 285.

"Prayer in Masonic lodges should be of a

general character *containing nothing* offensive to *any class* of concientious brethren. Ibid.

The Jew, the Mahomedan, the Parsee, the Budhist, the Confucian, and the savage, would be offended at the bare mention of Christ's name in any Masonic prayer, or religious ceremony, and in order to please all these, and to render the religion of Masonry universal his name *must be* carefully excluded, and lodge prayers must be of a general character.

The word of God emphatically declares that "there is one God and one mediator between God and men, the man Christ Jesus," (Tim. ii. 5.) and Freemasonry as emphatically affirms that that mediator must be rejected.

But again:

"The religion of Masonry is pure theism." "Lexicon of Freemasonry," p. 404:—

"A Christian Mason is not permitted to introduce his own peculiar opinions with regard to Christ's mediatorial office into the lodge." "Lexicon," p. 404:—

"Right or wrong, your very existence as a Mason hangs upon obedience to the powers immediately set above you." "Webb's Monitor," p. 196:—

"If we would be Masons, we must yield *private judgment*." "Traditions of Freemasonry," p. 30.

"Masons must be of that religion in which all men agree." "Manual of the Lodge," p. 215.

"Always hail, ever conceal, and never reveal our little senseless secrets." "Hand Book," p. 74.

"If your wife, or child, or friend, should ask you anything about your initiation—as, for instance, if your clothes were taken off, if you were blindfolded, if you had a rope round your neck, etc., you must always emphatically deny everything; you must conceal---hence, of course, you must deliberately lie about it. It is part of your obligation, nevertheless. But you know 'if you live in strict obedience to your obligation, you'll be free from sin.'"

"Furthermore that I will obey all due signs and summons." "Hand Book," p. 183.

"Whenever you see any of our signs made by a brother Mason, and especially the *grand hailing sign of distress*, you must always be sure to *obey* them, even at the risk of your life. If you're on a jury, and the defendant is a Mason, and makes the Grand Hailing sign, you must obey it; you must disagree with your brother jurors, if necessary, but you must be very sure not to bring the Mason guilty, for that would bring disgrace upon our order. It may be perjury, to be sure, to do this, but then you're fulfilling your obligation, and you know if you 'live up to your obligations you'll be free from sin.'"

"Furthermore, that I will keep the secrets of a brother Master Mason as inviolable as my own." "Hand Book," p. 183.

"You must conceal all the crimes of your brother Mason, except murder and treason, and these only at your own option, and should you be summoned as a witness against a brother Mason be always sure to shield him. Prevaricate, don't tell the *whole* truth in this case, keep his secrets, forget the most important points. It may be perjury to do this, it is true, but you're keeping your obligations, and remember if you 'live up to your obligation strictly, you'll be free from sin.' "

"Furthermore, that I will not cheat, wrong or defraud a lodge of Master Masons or a brother of this degree." "Hand Book," p. 184.

"If you cheat, wrong or defraud any other society or individual, it is entirely your own business. If you cheat the government even, Masonry cannot and will not touch you, but be very careful not to cheat, wrong or defraud a brother Mason or a lodge, whoever else you may defraud; live up to your obligation, and you'll be free from sin."

"Furthermore, that I will not strike a brother Master Mason." "Hand Book," p. 184.

"Whether you quarrel with or strike other men is none of our business, but your obligations enjoin you not to strike a brother Master Mason. It may be wicked and sinful, to be sure, to strike any man, or to quarrel with anybody, but our rules make no provision except for the protection of Masons only, and if you live in strict obedience to your obligation, you'll be free from sin."

"Furthermore, that I will not violate the chastity of a Master's wife, mother, sister or daughter, knowing them to be such." "Hand Book," p. 184.

"This gives you full permission, my dear sir, to do as you please outside of the Masonic order, but you must always respect the female relatives of Masons. Adultery is a great crime under any circumstances, it is true; but so long as you live in strict obedience to your Masonic obligation, you'll be free from sin."

"Furthermore that I will not give the Grand Masonic word, except upon the five points of fellowship, and then only in low breath." "Hand Book" p. 184.

"Whether you swear or take God's name in vain don't matter so much. Of course the name of the Lord Jesus Christ, as you know, don't amount to anything, but *Mah-hah-bone*—O, horror! You must never, on any account, speak that awful name aloud. That would be a most heinous crime—unmasonic—unpardonable. You are *recommended*, it is true, not to take the name of God in vain, but to speak of him with reverence; but then, you know, you have *solemnly sworn* not to take Mah-hah-bone, the name of the great Masonic god, in vain, and you must be very sure to keep your obligation, for he who lives in strict obedience to his Masonic obligation is free from sin."

And lastly:

"Binding myself under no less a penalty than that of having my throat cut across and my tongue torn ont by its roots." "Hand Book," p. 74.

"When a brother reveals any of our *great secrets;* whenever, for instance, he tells anything about Boaz, or Tubalcain, or Jachin, or that awful Mah-hah-bone, or even, whenever a minister prays in the name of Christ in any of our assemblies, you must always hold yourself in readiness, if called upon, to cut his throat from ear to ear, pull out his tongue by the roots, and bury his body at the bottom of some lake or pond. Of course, all this must be done in secret, as it was in the case of that notorious man Morgan, for both law and civilization are opposed to such barbarous crimes, but then, you know you must live up to your obligation, and so long as you have sworn to do it, by being very strict and obedient in the matter, you'll be free from sin."

These my son are a few of the precepts and obligations of the Masonic institution, as we find them scattered up and down through our various monitors and in the ritual of the order, and all that's necessary to say, concerning them, is that if the majority of Freemasons do not strictly live up to them, it is because as men they are nobler and better than the villainous system which they have sworn to conform to and abide by, would make them.

Fifth:—*The Masonic philosophy affirms that every member within the precincts of its lodges is constantly in search of divine truth.*

This preposterous claim on the part of Freemasonry and this phase of its antichristian religion perhaps more than any thing else serves to brand this wicked system as the most brazen hypocrisy and the most consumate blasphemy that ever cursed the earth.

Remembering the unchangeable landmark on the "exclusion of all sectarian tenets," and the rejection of the name of Christ from all lodge prayers, we shall be better able to understand, and more fully to appreciate the true purport of the cunningly devised fable set forth by Freemasonry in the following extracts.

In "Mackey's Manual of the Lodge," p. 20, I read:—

"Search of *Truth*, the great object of all Masonic labor."

Again on p. 29:—

"The truth of God and the soul—the nature and essence of both—which constitute the chief design of all Masonic teachings."

Again on p. 48:—

"The Mason living and working in the world as his lodge, *must seek to raise himself out of it* to that eminence which surmounts it, where alone he can find DIVINE TRUTH."

Again on p. 88:—

"The whole design of Freemasonry as a Speculative science is the investigation of Divine Truth. To this great object everything else is subsidiary. The Mason is, from the moment of his initiation as an Entered Apprentice, to the time at which he receives the full fruition of Masonic light, an investigator—a laborer in the quarry and the temple—whose reward is to be *truth*, and all the ceremonies and traditions of the order tend to this ultimate design. In Speculative Freemasonry there is an advancement from a lower to a higher state—from darkness to light—from death to life—from error to *truth*."

Again on p. 93:—

"Now what are the wages of a Speculative Mason? Not money, nor wine, nor oil. All these are but symbols. His wages are *truth*."

Again on p. 94:—

"The Fellow Craft represents a man laboring in the pursuit of *truth*."

In the "Masonic Ritualist," by A. G. Mackey, M. D., I read:—

"The keystone of a Mark Master is therefore the symbol of a fraternal covenant among those who are engaged in the common search after Divine Truth."

And again in the "Symbolism of Freemasonry," by Mackey, p. 166:—

"Every Speculative Mason is familiar with the fact that the East, as the source of material light, is a symbol of *his own order which professes to contain within its bosom the pure light of truth*."

And now to cap, as it were, the very climax of the unparalleled hypocrisy of this whole system, we are furnished the following explanation of these wicked pretensions.

In the "Manual of the Lodge," by Mackey, p. 93, and in the "General Ahiman Rezon," by Sickles, p. 169, we read:—

"It is one of the most beautiful, but at the same time one of the most abstruse doctrines of the science of Masonic symbolism *that the Mason is ever to be in search of truth*, BUT IS NEVER TO FIND IT."

What a strange picture this presents! Ministers,

deacons and class-leaders, all represented as "searching after truth in the labyrinthine forests of Masonic falsehood, but all doomed "*never to find it.*"

How accurately St. Paul discribes this stupendous folly when in writing to Timothy he says. 2 Tim. iii. 1 7:—

"This know also, that in the *last* days perilous times shall come. For men shall be lovers of their own selves, covetous boasters, proud, blasphemers, disobedient to parents, unthankful, unholy, without natural affection, truce breakers, false accusers, incontinent, fierce, despisers of those that are good, traitors, heady, high-minded, lovers of pleasure more than lovers of God ; having a form of godliness, but denying the power thereof, *from such turn away.*"

And now mark the coincidence in verse 7:—

"*Ever learning and never able to come to a knowledge of the truth.*"

And

Lastly:—*Freemasonry claims to be the only true religion now in the world, that Divine Truth which guides man in his pilgrimage of life, and that which confers such inestimable benefits on its votaries that "nothing can be suggested more which the soul of man can require.*"

In the "Symbolism of Freemasonry," by Past Grand Master Mackey, p. 148, we read:—

"Freemasonry itself, anciently, received among other appellations, that of *Lux* or *Light* to signify that it is to be regarded as that SUBLIME DOCTRINE OF DIVINE TRUTH, by which the path of him who has attained it is to be illuminated in his pilgrimage of life."

What more can be said of the Gospel of Christ, than that it is "the sublime doctrine of Divine Truth?" And what higher claim can be made for it than that "it illuminates our pathway in life's pilgrimage."

And in the "General History Cyclopedia and Dictionary of Freemasonry," by Macoy and Oliver, p. 428, we read:—

"There is that latent in Freemasonry, which makes it exactly the institution THAT IS MOST NEEDED in this age."

And again in the "General Ahiman Rezon or Freemason's Guide," by Daniel Sickles, p. 196, it is stated that:—

"We now find man *complete* in morality and intelligence, with the stay of religion added to ensure him of the protection of the Deity and guard him against ever going astray. These three degrees thus form a perfect and harmonious whole, nor can it be conceived that anything can be suggested more, which the soul of man requires."

And in the "Book of the Ancient and Accepted Scottish Rite," by McClenachan, p. 575, we read:—

"Onward! and all earth shall aid us,
Ere our peaceful flag be furled,
Masonry at last shall conquer,
And its altar be the world."

Hence, according to all this, the religion of Masonry cannot possibly be excelled. It is the

"Divine Truth" itself, it is that which is "exactly most needed in this age," it confers such inestimable blessings and benefits that it is not possible to conceive how the soul of man can require anything more. And it is boastfully asserted that it shall go on conquering, and to conquer until at last it shall be the only religion in the world. And yet with all this superlative greatness and goodness, and with all these pretended advantages accruing from a knowledge of its divine principles it requires every one of its members, ministers and all, to take "a most solemn and binding obligation," never to lisp a single syllable concerning it, to father, mother, wife, child, or friend, it positively refuses admission within its sacred lodges to seventy-five or eighty per cent. of the human family, and it absolutely requires that every one who is fortunate enough to secure the right of initiation shall pay a large sum of money before entering one of its lodges. Talk of the arrogance, and the lying pretensions of Rome, but if Romanism can outdo Freemasonry in the impudence of its assumptions, in the falsehood of its doctrines, and in the chicanery and cunning, manifested in executing its vicious designs, then it must be very wicked indeed.

CHAPTER V.

Masonry and Romanism. — Private judgment.— Their secrecy and despotism illustrated.—Masonry and the Bible.—Square and Compass.— "Book of the Law."—Masonic covenant.— The Bible not the Masonic rule of faith— Only a Symbol. — Three great lights.— Three lesser lights. — Masonic and Romish coincidence. — Both false and unscriptural. — The Worshipful Master and Pope both gods.—Masonry and Leo XII.

Mr. Barton:—In our investigation of the Masonic philosophy thus far my dear Henry, we have made at least, I think, one very important discovery, namely: that as religious institutions, there is a most remarkable coincidence between Freemasonry and Romanism. We have found that both systems are based upon lying traditions; that both teach justification by works; that both prescribe the same remedies for purifying man's evil nature; that both claim universality and a vast antiquity; that both assert a divine origin; that both use altars and lighted candles in their religious worship, and that both claim an unchangeable or infallible perfection for all their decrees and landmarks.

But the similiarity between them is still more clearly manifested in the fact that both religions, positively and absolutely deny the right of private judgment. Neither the Mason on the one hand, nor the Catholic on the other, dare think and act for himself in matters pertaining to either system, and in this total subjugation of the will and judgment we discover the real secret of that terrible power which both Masonry and Romanism exercise over their members, and by means of which the latter are kept in such complete subjection and are made to accept as truth all the wicked absurdities and the stupendous mass of ridiculous fables found in the traditionary teachings of both institutions.

In the creed of Pope Pius IV. article 2, we read:—

"I also admit the Holy Scriptures *according to that sense which our Holy Mother, the Church has held*, and does hold, to which it belongs to judge of the true sense and interpretation of the Scriptures, nor will I ever take and interpret them otherwise than according to the unanimous consent of the Fathers."

In this article of the Romish creed, three things are plainly set forth:—

First, that every Roman Catholic is bound to admit the Scriptures, *only* in that sense in which the church has held and does hold them.

Second, that *none* but the Roman Church can

give the true sense and interpretation of the Scriptures. And

Third, that no Roman Catholic must ever take and interpret the Scriptures or any part of them except only in that sense which the church prescribes, and in which a score or more of Latin and Greek theologists are supposed to have interpreted them some sixteen or seventeen hundred years ago.

Summing all this up in a few words then, it simply means that no member of the Romish Church can exercise his *private judgment* in matters of faith, but must always submissively bow to the will and judgment of his priest or bishop.

Just think of a railroad Irishman, an Italian organ-grinder, a Spaniard, or a Portuguese, searching the Sacred Scriptures in the light of the Greek and Latin Fathers !

But Freemasonry imposes a like restriction, if not a weightier one on every member sworn into its infidel association.

Just as a Roman Catholic is bound to submit to the will of his priest or superior in the church, so a *Free*-mason is bound to submit to the will of the Worshipful Master or his superior in the lodge, and that even whether the Masonic decree be "right or wrong."

In the "Traditions of Freemasonry," by Pierson, p. 30, we read:—

"*We may not call in question the propriety of this organization,*" *i. e.* the despotic character of Masonry, "*if we would* be Masons WE MUST *yield private judgment.*"

Or in other words, so far as his Masonic standing is concerned, no member of the fraternity is allowed to exercise his own judgment, but must submit to the decrees of the order, and believe whatever the Masonic ritual teaches.

Again in "Webb's Monitor," by Morris, p. 169, we read:—

"*Right or wrong* his (a member's) very existence as a Mason hangs upon obedience to the powers immediately set above him. The one unpardonable crime in a Mason is contumacy or disobedience."

This is Masonic law, inflexible and unchangeable, and beyond this no Mason dare go. He must obey implicitly, whether he likes it or not, and whether the command given, or the statement made be "right or wrong," and like the Romanist, he has no redress. He "must yield his private judgment," and allow another man, less moral and less intelligent perhaps, to think and judge for him as regards Masonry. And if he refuses to do so, which is very seldom the case, he violates his obligation, and commits "the one unpardonable crime in a Mason."

In opposition to this wicked despotism, both of the lodge and chapel, the Scriptures very plainly teach us that our Lord and his Apostles always appealed to their hearers to exercise their own judgment upon the doctrines addressed to them.

What does our Lord say? Luke. xii, 57:—

"And why, even of yourselves, do you not judge that which is right?"

What does St. Paul say? I. Cor. x. 15:—

"I speak, as to wise men, judge ye what I say."

And again I. Thess. v. 21:—

"Prove all things; hold fast that which is good."

But apart from the coincidences which exist between Freemasonry and Romanism in their mock solemn ceremonies, and in their moral and doctrinal features there is also a very close similiarity plainly discernable in their construction, and in the vicious principle of secrecy so peculiar to both systems. This perhaps can scarcely be better exemplified than by reference to the diagram on the next page.

In Figure 1, representing the Romish system, are a number of concentric circles, with "Our Most Sovereign Lord God, the Pope" in the center. In the outer circle is the Congregation, with the Priest as center. In the next circle are the Priests, with the Bishop as center. In the next are the Bishops, with the Arch-Bishop as center. In the next are the Arch-Bishops, with the Cardinal Arch Bishop

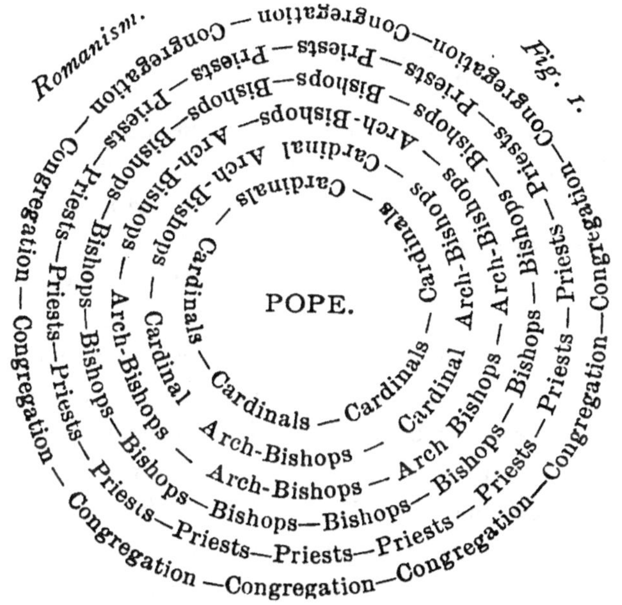

Romanism. *Fig. 1.*

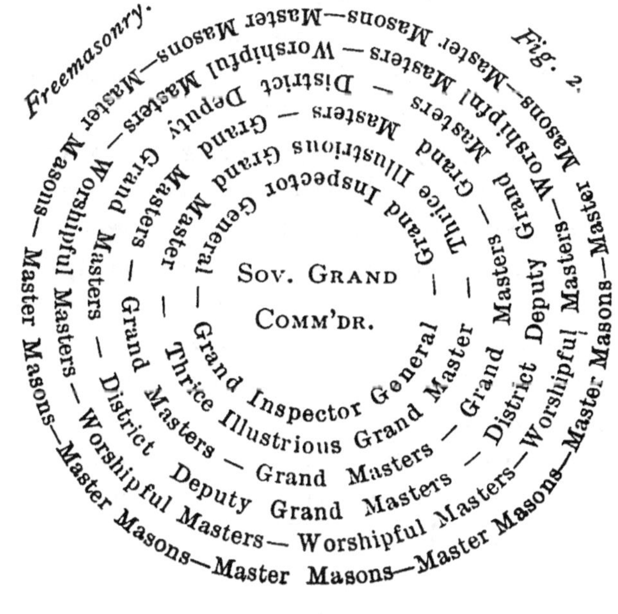

POPE.

Cardinals — Cardinals — Cardinals — Cardinals — Cardinals — Cardinals

Cardinal Arch-Bishops — Cardinal Arch-Bishops — Cardinal Arch-Bishops — Cardinal Arch-Bishops

Arch-Bishops — Arch-Bishops — Arch Bishops — Arch-Bishops — Arch-Bishops — Arch-Bishops — Arch-Bishops

Bishops — Bishops — Bishops — Bishops — Bishops — Bishops — Bishops — Bishops — Bishops — Bishops

Priests — Priests — Priests — Priests — Priests — Priests — Priests — Priests — Priests — Priests — Priests — Priests

Congregation — Congregation — Congregation — Congregation — Congregation — Congregation — Congregation — Congregation — Congregation — Congregation — Congregation

Freemasonry. *Fig. 2.*

Sov. Grand Comm'dr.

Grand Inspector General — Grand Inspector General — Grand Inspector General

Thrice Illustrious Grand Master — Thrice Illustrious Grand Master — Thrice Illustrious Grand Master

Grand Masters — Grand Masters — Grand Masters — Grand Masters — Grand Masters

District Deputy Grand Masters — District Deputy Grand Masters — District Deputy Grand Masters

Worshipful Masters — Worshipful Masters — Worshipful Masters — Worshipful Masters — Worshipful Masters — Worshipful Masters

Master Masons — Master Masons — Master Masons — Master Masons — Master Masons — Master Masons — Master Masons — Master Masons as center. In the next circle are the Cardinal Arch-Bishops, with the Cardinal as center, and in the inner circle are the Cardinals, with "His Holiness," the Pope, in the center of all.

Now, let it be remembered, that every man, woman and child in the Congregation, or outer circle, is bound under pain of eternal damnation to obey the Priest implicitly and without questioning; the Priests are bound under similar penalties to obey the Bishop; the Bishops are in like manner bound to obey the Arch-Bishop; the Arch-Bishops the Cardinal Arch-Bishop; the Cardinal Arch-Bishops the Cardinal; and all must implicitly obey the Pope. He claims to be infallible, and actually sits in the temple of God "exalted above all that is called God, or that is worshipped," and "showing himself as if he were God." 2 Thess. ii. 4.

Then again, all these various grades of church dignitaries are bound together by the most solemn obligations of secrecy, so that what one tells the other in the confessional, can never be revealed under pain of the most fearful penalties, and even should a Catholic priest be summoned as a witness in a criminal prosecution, and although the prisoner may have confessed to him all the particulars of the crime committed, yet he will positively refuse to testify, or else deny all knowledge of the facts. And should a husband and wife go to confession to the same priest, neither can tell the other what both had previously whispered into the ear of that strange man in the confessional. This is Rome.

And now let us look at Freemasonry.

In Figure 2, which represents the Masonic system, we have the same number of concentric circles as in the former case with the "Most Puissant Sovereign Grand Commander" in the center. In the outer circle are the Master Masons, with the Worshipful Master in the center; next are the Worshipful Masters, with the Deputy Grand Master as center; then the Deputy Grand Masters, with the Grand Master as center; and so on up to the "Most Puissant Sovereign Grand Commander," who occupies a position corresponding to that of the Pope.

In Freemasonry also, every Master Mason is bound to obey the behests of the Worshipful Master, "*right or wrong*," the Worshipful Masters are equally bound to submit to and obey the Deputy Grand Master; the Deputy Grand Masters are bound likewise to obey the Grand Master, and thus right through, up to the Most Puissant SOVEREIGN, who sits at the very head of the Holy Empire, and holds a sway over his subjects, not a whit inferior to that of the Pope, or the most despotic Monarch on earth.

Then remember again, that the members of all

these Masonic rings are likewise sworn to keep one another's secrets inviolable, to obey all Masonic laws, "right or wrong;" to give one another due and timely notice of all approaching danger, and to obey one another's signs and summons at any risk.

The Masonic husband has secrets in common with the rum-seller, or perhaps with a gambler, which he cannot and dare not communicate to his wife, and he may, and very often has confidential conferences with worthless characters, one word of which he must never lisp at home.

Both the lodge and the chapel are imperious, arbitrary and despotic in the extreme, and neither the laws of the church, the State, nor the family, not even the plain positive commands of Scripture, are permitted to interfere with, or obstruct the enforcement of their selfish enactments.

But perhaps the most striking coincidence of all, between Freemasonry and Romanism is, that both systems degrade, debase and reject the Bible.

Henry:—But my dear father, how can that be? I know that Romanism is at war with the Bible, and with our public school system, because, that in our public schools the Bible is read, but I have always supposed that Freemasonry paid the very highest respect to the Bible, and in fact, that it was an indispensible article in every lodge, and publicly carried in every Masonic procession.

Mr. Barton:—Yes, the Bible is an indispensible article in all American and English lodges, but only as an *article of furniture.* There must be a copy of the Bible on the altar, and so must there be a hat on the Master's head, and a sword in the Tyler's hand, and one is just as indispensible, and as much thought of as the other. The Bible is a piece of lodge *furniture* and no more.

On this point the Masonic ritual is explicit.

In the "Manual of the Lodge," by Mackey, p. 49, we read:—

"The *furniture* of a lodge consists of a Holy Bible, square and compass."

And as for carrying the Bible in all our Masonic processions, that is simply done with the view of blindfolding the Christian public, to the real design of Freemasonry, and to advertise the pretended goodness of the order. No my son, Freemasonry and the Bible have nothing in common.

Don't you remember that Masonic law which states so plainly that "Masonry has nothing whatever to do with the Bible, that *it is not founded on the Bible*, for if it was *it would not be Masonry, it would be something else*," (Digest of Masonic Law, p. 207 209.) and that "the moral law of Masonry is the "*lex naturæ*, or law of nature."

Ancient Masonry consisting of only three degrees, which is really the only legitimate Masonry in existance, is purely symbolic, and every Masonic implement in the lodge room, the Bible included, is but a mere symbol.

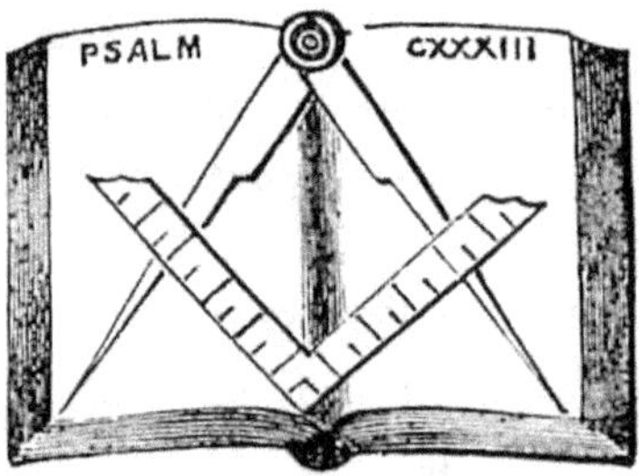

In the annexed figure you will notice that the Square and Compass are placed on top of the Bible, as we have them in the Entered Apprentice degree. Well, the Square is a symbol, the Compass a symbol, and the Bible a symbol — nothing more and nothing less. But Masonry regards the square and compass with far more veneration than it does the Bible; for the latter is only a mere local symbol, while the Square and Compass are *universal.* For instance, suppose we allow the pretended claim of Masonry to *universality*, and admit that there is a Masonic lodge in Constantinople among the Turks; in Calcutta or Madras among the Hindoos, in Pekin or Canton among the Chinese; in Teheran among the Persians, in Salt Lake City among the Mormons; or even in the camp of Sitting Bull among the American savages, will any one be simple enough to believe that in any of these places the Bible could be found on the Masonic altar, even as an article of furniture? Most assuredly not. The Koran, the

Shasters, the Vedas, the Book of Confucius, the Book of Mormon, or a piece of birch bark may possibly be found, but certainly no Bible. The Bible is the Magna Charta of heaven, the Christian's rule of faith, and consequently can form no part of the "*furniture*" of a lodge of Masons in any of the places or among any of the people just mentioned. But the Square and Compass must always and everywhere be displayed on the Masonic altar, and hence unquestionably Freemasonry regards the Square and Compass with more respect and reverence than it does the Bible. But hear what Masonic law has to say on this subject.

In the "Text-Book of Masonic Jurisprudence," by A. G. Mackey, p. 33 we read:—

"Landmark XXI:—It is a landmark that a "Book of the Law" shall constitute an indispensible part of the furniture of every lodge. I say advisedly a "*Book of the Law*" because *it is not absolutely required that everywhere the Old and New Testament shall be used.* The "Book of the Law" is that volume which by the religion of the country is believed to contain the revealed will of the Grand Architect of the Universe. Hence in all lodges in Christian countries the "Book of the Law" is composed of the Old and New Testaments; in a country where Judaism was the prevailing faith, the Old Testament alone would be sufficient; and in Mahomedan countries and among Mahomedan Masons, the *Koran* might be substituted."

This is the universal and immutable law of Masonry. This is one of the "Landmarks" concerning which it is positively stated on page 16, ("Text-Book of Masonic Jurisprudence.") "The landmarks of the order, like the laws of the Medas and Persians, *can suffer no change.*"

Here then we have the express declaration of an infallible, because unchangeable decree, that the Holy Bible, God's revealed will to man, is no better and no worse than the Koran, the Shasters, the Vedas, or the Book of Mormon, and that at best it is in the lodge room but a mere piece of furniture. "The Book of the Law" is that volume which by the religion of the country is believed to contain the revealed will of the G. A. O. T. U." is the plain, emphatic teaching of Masonry, and one of the *Bulls* of Leo XIII, might as well be this "book of the law" as any other so far as Freemasonry is concerned, and occupy the same position in the lodge that the Bible does.

In order to accommodate the Masonic philosophy, the Bible and the Koran must be placed on the same level. One must be considered just as good as the other. Masonry, like its twin sister Romanism, unchanged and unchangeable, the same everywhere, in Chicago, Constantinople, Calcutta, Pekin, and Salt Lake City, insists upon it that everything human and divine must give place to its landmarks, laws and edicts. The laws of heaven must be set aside, God's word must be debased, the Lord

Jesus Christ must be rejected, the Holy Spirit must be denied, repentance must be forbidden, heaven must be defied and despised, but Freemasonry must be honored and exalted. This is what the teaching of Masonry amounts to, when it places the Holy Scriptures on a common level with the philosophies of paganism, the writings of Joe Smith, or with the Square and Compass.

Henry:—But this is the Masonic law and usage perhaps, in countries where some other than the Christian is the prevailing religion. Now, is not the Bible highly respected as such, by Masonry, in all Christian countries, and is it not pointed out to the candidate, at his initiation, as his rule of faith ?

Mr. Barton:—Freemasonry claims to be a universal system, cosmopolitan in its nature, and with no special law for its government in one country more than another, and hence I utterly and positively deny that it shows any respect whatever to the Holy Bible as the Word of God anywhere, or on any occasion. It has the Bible on its altars in Christian countries and has it carried in all its public parades it is true, but that is done that Masonry may be honored and respected and not the Bible. Who, for instance, carries the Bible in all our Masonic processions ? Is he usually a man of known piety ? or is he always even a moral and good man ? Did you ever see a church deacon or elder, or any other church officer or member bearing along the Holy Bible in any of our public parades, whether at a funeral or corner-stone laying? If you have, I must say from long experience, and all candid Masons will bear me out in the assertion, that it is the exception and not the rule. On all such occasions the very worst and most rabid old infidel in the lodge, or among the local brotherhood is the one generally chosen to be the bearer in public of God's Word.

But again as you see, from the Masonic emblem, on page 124, although the Bible is open on the altar, yet the Square and Compass must always rest *upon* it. Now why not reverse this order and have the Bible rest *upon*, and be *above* the Square and Compass? Or why could not the Square and Compass be placed before, or beside, or behind the Bible? Why is it always necessary that the Square and Compass should be placed above the Bible? The reason for this is very plainly stated in the Masonic law book, as follows:—

In "Webb's Monitor," by Morris, p. 240, we read, under the word COVENANT:—

"The Covenant is irrevocable. Even though a Mason may be suspended or expelled, though he may withdraw from the lodge, journey into countries where Masons cannot be found or become a subject of despotic governments that persecute, or a communicant of bigoted churches that denounce

Masonry, *he cannot cast off or nullify his Masonicc ovenant.* NO LAW OF THE LAND CAN AFFECT IT. *No anathema of the church can weaken it.* IT IS IRREVOCABLE."

This is pure Masonic law, as inflexible as granite, as unchangeable as the decrees of fate. The Masonic covenant must be considered above, and be superior to every other covenant, human or divine; the laws of Masonry must be placed above every law; and hence the Square and Compass, the pure universal symbols of the order, must always be placed on top of the Bible, to signify that the covenants of Masonry, its laws and requirements, must be held as being paramount to, of more binding force, and therefore more to be honored, respected and obeyed, than all the laws and ordinances of God as revealed in the Bible, and all the laws and covenants of the realm, as recorded in the statute books of the nation.

But again, the Holy Bible is not set forth by Masonry as being man's rule of faith in any honest or true sense, and the teaching of its ritual on that point is simply a mockery. The Bible as we have seen, occupies no higher position in the Masonic philosophy than the Koran, the Shasters, or the Vedas, and speaking of the Bible, therefore, in a Masonic lodge, as a rule of faith under any circumstance, is the merest hypocrisy. Here in Chicago, for instance, we have "Chicago Lodge, No. 437," composed exclusively of Jews, and, I believe, reckoning among their number some of the most bignoted, the most bitter, and the most blaspheming against the name of Christ and Christianity of all the Jewish population in this city. Well, they have the Holy Bible (Old and New Testament) on the altar. Do you think the Worshipful Master of that lodge means anything by it, when he says, at the initiation of a Jewish candidate, "the Holy Bible is given to us as the rule and guide of our faith?" Or do you suppose the candidate himself pays the slightest attention to what is said? When a Roman Catholic is initiated into Masonry, does he accept the Bible as his rule of faith? Or when the Worshipful Master calls his attention to it in the words of the ritual, do you think he attaches any meaning to what he says?

Why, a Catholic's "rule of faith" is Scripture and *tradition*, and, therefore, to offer him the Bible alone as a "rule of faith" would be a positive insult to his belief, and in fact a direct violation by Masonry itself of its own part of the covenant, for the candidate is positively assured that there is nothing in the Masonic system that car conflict with his duty to God or to himself.

Suppose a Chinaman, or Japanese, or Mormon, or Spiritualist, were initiated in any one of our Chicago lodges, would the Holy Bible be his "rule of faith?" Most assuredly not. The Bible, therefore, on the Masonic altar, is a mere article of furniture and no more, and the language of the ritual in regard to it is a hollow mockery.

But the Square and Compass, being placed above the Bible on the Masonic altar, have another symbolic meaning. You will remember that the "moral law of Masonry" is defined as the "*lex naturæ*, or law of nature," and that this law, whatever it is, is the true basis of Masonic philosophy. The Mosaic decalogue is considered too "confined" and too "limited" to express all the grand requirements of Masonic morality, and hence it must be set aside and a more comprehensive and superior code adopted, and one that will more fully correspond with the boundless(?)universality of the system. These two laws then—the law of God as revealea in the Bible, and the "law of nature," represented or symbolized by the Compass and Square—are both displayed upon the Masonic altar. But as the latter is considered by Masonry superior to the former, so the representative of the greater law is always placed above the lesser, and hence the Square and Compass must always be placed above the Bible in all Masonic assemblies, and as these are but symbols of the "law of nature," so the Bible must be reckoned *only* as a symbol of the law of God. On this point the teaching of Masonry is clear and emphatic.

In the "Lexicon of Freemasonry," by Mackey, p. 62, under the word BIBLE, we read:—

"The Bible is used among Masons *as a symbol of the will of God*, however it may be expressed."

But what is a "*symbol*," as explained in the lodge philosophy? The definition of it is again furnished by the Masonic text-book.

In the "Lexicon of Freemasonry," by Mackey, p. 466, we read:—

SYMBOL.—A sensible image used to express an occult but analogical signification."

So then, according to the Masonic law, the Bible on the Masonic altar is nothing more or less than a mere "image" of God's will, and this "symbol" or "image" is of no more value than the rusty Square or the iron Compass which are always laid upon it; the law of God of no more value than the "law of nature," and the God of the Bible as no better than the god of the heathen.

Henry:—But, my dear father, at those public expositions which I recently witnessed I noticed that the Worshipful Master, after the hoodwink was removed from the candidate's eyes, called his attention to the Holy Bible as it lay open on the altar. What did the Master say at that time? And what is the meaning of the ritual used in that ceremony?

Mr. Barton:—As you observed, the hoodwink is removed by the Senior Deacon. The Worshipful Master then approaches the candidate, still kneeling at the altar, and says to him: "Brother Hunt," (or whatever his name may be) "on being brought to light in Masonry, you behold before you the THREE GREAT LIGHTS *of Masonry*, by the aid of the *three lesser lights.* The THREE GREAT LIGHTS of Masonry *are the Holy Bible Square and Compass.*" (See figure, p. 124, "Hand Book," p. 77:—

Here you will notice that Freemasonry recognizes *three great lights*, the Holy Bible, the Square, and the Compass. The three are equally great; there is no difference, according to the Masonic, ritual, between the degrees of greatness possessed by either, and, so far as being *lights*, the Bible is just as *great* as any one of the other two, and receives the same degree of veneration and respect from the lodge under the seal of the Masonic covenant.

This I think places the Word of God very low down indeed.

David says by the Holy Ghost: "Thy word is a lamp unto my feet, and a light unto my path." Psalm cxix.

The Son of God says: "Sanctify them through thy truth; thy word is truth." John xvii.

The Holy Ghost says: "Every word of God is pure." Prov. xxx. 5.

The Psalmist says: "Thou hast magnified thy word *above* all thy name." Psalm cxxxviii. 2.

But Freemasonry places "the Square and Compass above God's word," and consequently considers them equally worthy of being magnified above all his name; and, notwithstanding all this, as we have already seen, it is asserted of Freemasonry that it is the institution that is "exactly most needed in this age, and that it is not possible to conceive that anything can be suggested more, which the soul of man requires." "Sickles' Monitor," p. 196.

And here again another marked coincidence arises between Freemasonry and Romanism.

When the hoodwink is removed, the rite of illumination performed, and the new birth accomplished, according to the Masonic philosophy, the Worshipful Master directs the candidate's attention to the Masonic altar and its strange surroundings.

He says to him:—"Bro. Hunt, on being brought to light in Masonry, *you behold before you* the THREE GREAT LIGHTS of Masonry *by the aid* of the *three lesser lights.* The THREE GREAT LIGHTS of Masonry are the Holy Bible, Square and Compass. The *three lesser lights* are three burning tapers, placed in a triangular form near the altar, representing the SUN, MOON, and MASTER OF THE LODGE."

Now, what is the meaning of all this, and what

lesson does Masonry purpose here to convey to the candidate's mind?

On being brought to light we see that his attention is directed to six objects, the Holy Bible, Square and Compass on one side, and the "three burning tapers" on the other. We also find that these three burning tapers" represent the "*Sun, Moon, and Master of the Lodge*," the three manifestations of the Masonic god, and that *the Holy Bible is beheld only by the aid* of these "*lesser lights*," or in their symbolic reflection alone, and hence Freemasonry means to teach the candidate that, whoever or whatever has been his guide and counselor in the past, the Masonic philosophy alone, "that sublime doctrine of divine truth," must lead and guide him in the future. That hereafter he must receive the Bible only in that sense in which Masonry receives it, read it with Masonic eyes, and understand it with Masonic understanding. In a word, that for ever after he must, as a Freemason, interpret the Scriptures *only* according to that sense which Freemasonry may see fit to sanction, or according to the inspiration of the Master, or god of Masonry.

Now, compare this with the teaching of Rome. In the article of the creed already quoted, Creed of Pope Pius IV. article 2d, we read:

"I also *admit* the Holy Scriptures, *according to that sense* which our Holy Mother, the Church, has held, and does hold, to which it belongs, to judge of the true sense and interpretation of the Scriptures, and neither will I ever take and interpret them otherwise than according to the unanimous consent of the Fathers."

That is, the Roman Catholic promises and declares that he will "admit the Holy Scriptures," not according to his own judgment exercised upon them, but simply as the church admits them, and that he will never try to interpret them at all, nor any part of them, except "according to the unanimous consent of the Fathers." The Romanist promises to read the Scriptures through the eyes of the church represented by the priest, and to understand them only with his understanding. The Masonic minister, or professing Protestant Christian, solemnly swears that he will be obedient to all the laws of the Master Mason's degree, and hence that he will read the Holy Scriptures only through the eyes of Masonry, represented by the Worshipful Master, that he will understand them only with his understanding, and that, come what may, the landmarks of the order must never be infringed upon or changed.

How wonderfully consistent a man can act when once he has taken the Masonic obligations, and has experienced the Masonic new birth!

But again, the Worshipful Master, still addressing the candidate kneeling at the altar, goes on to say:—

See "Manual of the Lodge," by Mackey, p. 30

"Hand Book of Freemasonry," p. 77:—

"The Holy Bible is given to us as the rule and guide of our faith, the Square to square our actions, and the Compass to circumscribe our desires and passions within due bounds toward all mankind, and more especially toward our brother Masons."

And this portion of the ritual is clearly and authoritatively explained by Past Grand Master and Past General Grand High Priest, A. G. Mackey, as follows:—

In the "Manual of the Lodge," p. 30, he states that:—

"The Bible is the light which enlightens the path of our duty to God; the Square that which enlightens the path of our duty to our fellow-men; and the Compass that which enlightens the path of our duty to ourselves."

Here then we find that the plain, positive teaching of Freemasonry is, that the Holy Bible *enlightens*, the Square *enlightens* and the Compass *enlightens*. The Masonic initiate is taught to learn from the Bible, from the Square and from the Compass, and his mind is directed to all three in the same breath, each one being of equal importance. Now, if the Holy Bible were sufficient for man's instruction and enlightenment, of course no necessity could arise for the symbolic light reflected from the Square and Compass; but because in the wisdom of Masonry it is nothing but a mere "symbol" or "image" of God's will, just as the Square and Compass are symbols of the will of the god of nature, so the law of the latter is placed on an equality with, if not actually above the former.

In all the Mass-houses of Popery the Bible is supplanted by the Mass-book and the Missal, while in all Masonic lodges the Bible is degraded below the Square and Compass. In all the Roman Catholic chapels throughout the world you will find tub-fulls of *holy water*, boxes of holy oil, whole forests of candles, thousands of beads, millions of shrines, charms, agnes deii, holy bones, images and crosses, but no Bible. The word of God is displaced, and the senseless rites, customs and symbols of pagan Rome are substituted in its stead, while in all Masonic lodges, even in professedly Christian countries, the Holy Bible is also virtually ignored, and the "law of nature" and the false traditions of heathen philosophers are presented to the candidate for his future guidance and instruction.

And yet for all this, men professing Christianity, and claiming even to be Protestant ministers, will generally say what they know to be positively false, in order to support this villainous system, and be the most vehement in denouncing any one who dare separate himself from, and expose it. Could human perversity be better exemplified, or is it possible that such inconsistency has ever before been manifested in the history of the world? I firmly believe that in the manufacture of Freemasonry, Satan has even outdone himself.

In direct opposition to the false and pernicious teaching, both of the Masonic lodge and the Romish chapel, we have the clear emphatic declaration of God's word.

St. Paul says, 2 Tim. iii. 15–17:—

"From a child thou hast known the Holy Scriptures, which are able to make thee wise unto salvation through faith which is in Christ Jesus.

"All Scripture is given by inspiration of God, and is profitable for doctrine, for reproof, for correction, for instruction in righteousness: that the man of God may be perfect, thoroughly furnished unto all good works.'

But again, the Masonic ritual says:—

"Manual of the Lodge," by Mackey, p. 49.

"Hand Book of Freemasonry," p. 93.

"The Holy Bible is dedicated to God, the Square to the Master, and the Compass to the Craft."

Now, what is meant by this? We have seen that, as a Great Light, the Holy Bible is only a mere symbol of the law of God, while the Square and Compass are equally Great Lights, and symbols of the "law of nature," which is the moral law of Masonry. These three symbols then, the Bible, the

Square, and the Compass, are dedicated to the deities to which they respectively refer. That is, the Bible is dedicated to the true God, the Square to the "god of nature," who governs nature, and the Compass to Masonry in general, or "the Craft." But we see that the "Square is dedicated to the Master," and hence the Master is the representative or personification of the "god of nature," or the Sun in the East governing the Craft, and the Craft itself, or Masonry is the thing governed; and therefore it unquestionably follows that the true God, the Worshipful Master, and the Craft, or in other words, that God, Baal, or the Sungod and Masonry, are placed on the same level.

This is the same as Romanism conferring infallibility on the Pope and making him God and the vicar of Christ. But Jesus Christ alone is equal with the Father, and therefore both Masonry and Romanism dethrone Christ and substitute the Master and the Pope in their respective religious systems. And this is further confirmed by the fact that in Masonry an obligation taken on the Bible alone would be worthless; to render it binding the candidate's hands must rest on the Square and Compass.

And, lastly, the Masonic system itself does not claim that its principal tenets and requirements are contained in the Holy Scriptures. Hear what the Ritual says on this point.

"Hand Book of Freemasonry," p. 175.

As the candidate is led into the lodge in the Master Mason's degree he is met by the Senior Deacon, who places both points of the Compass to his naked left and right breasts, and thus addresses him:—

"Bro. Hunt, upon your first admission into a lodge of Master Masons it becomes my duty to receive you upon both points of the Compass extending from your naked left to right breasts, the moral of which is to teach you that, as the most vital parts of man are contained within the breasts, *so* are the most excellent tenets of our institution contained within both points of the Compass, which are Friendship, Morality, and Brotherly Love."

And again, after taking the obligation, p. 186:—

"You are never to lose sight of the moral and Masonic application of this highly useful and valuable instrument, (the Compass,) *which teaches* Friendship, Morality, and Brotherly Love."

So, then, according to the Masonic ritual itself, the very keystone, as it were, of the whole fabric—the "three most precious jewels" of a Master Mason, supposed to be Friendship, Morality, and Brotherly Love—are not derived by Masonry from the Bible, but from the pagan emblem of the Compass alone.

Freemasonry places the Authorized Version of the Scriptures on the same equality with the "*lex naturæ*, or law of nature." Now, let us hear what

Romanism has to say in regard to the same Bible.

In the Encyclical letter of Leo XII., dated at Rome, at St. Mary Majors, the 3d day of May, 1824, the following preamble occurs:—

"You are aware, venerable brethren, that a certain society, called the *Bible* Society, strolls with effrontery throughout the world, which society, contemning the Traditions of the Holy Fathers, and contrary to the well-known *decree of the Council of Trent*, labors with all its might, and by every means, to translate, or rather to pervert, the Holy Scriptures into the vulgar language of every nation; from which proceeding it is greatly to be feared that what is ascertained to have happened, as to some passages, may also oecur with regard to others; to wit: That by a perverse interpretation the gospel of Christ be turned into a human gospel, or what is still worse, the *gospel of the devil.*"

Hence, according to Pope Leo XII., after whom the present Pope is named, the very Bible which is insulted on the Masonic altar contains not the revelation of God, but simply the "gospel of the devil," while Freemasonry steps boldly to the front exclaiming: "Quite correct, Most Holy Father! Quite correct! My Square and Compass are every way equal to, if not superior to the Authorized Version of the Bible, and will "*enlighten*" mankind quite as well. Go on, my dear sir! Go on, Bro. Leo, and issue your *Bulls* and Encyclicals against the Bible with all the rancor of which your old heart is capable, and I'll keep right on in my peculiarly aggressive course, degrading and debasing God's

Word below my pagan emblems, and teaching my people that it is no better than the Koran, the Shasters, or the Book of Mormon. Go on, Mr. Pope! Make all the Roman Catholics you can, and I'll guarantee to manufacture quite as many infidels from among the Protestants, and between us, I think, we shall be able to neutralize the great work of the Reformation, and perhaps destroy Christianity altogether.

Now hear the words of the Son of God, John v. 39:—

"Search the Scriptures, for in them ye think ye have eternal life, and THEY ARE THEY WHICH TESTIFY OF ME."

Again, in Matt. xxii. 29:—

"Jesus answered and said unto them, YE DO ERR, NOT KNOWING THE SCRIPTURES, nor the power of God."

But Romanism emphatically declares that we err if we *do know* the Scriptures; while Freemasons, in the display of a spirit not a whit better than that of the most bigoted Roman Catholic, can use no milder expression than "perjured villain," when referring to a seceding Mason who strictly follows the teachings of the Scriptures by renouncing that "wicked imposture."

Hear again what Peter says, 2 Peter i. 19:

"We have also a more sure word of prophecy; *whereunto ye do well that ye take heed*, as unto a light that shineth in a dark place, until the day dawn, and the day-star arise in your hearts."

CHAPTER VI.

MASONRY AND ROMANISM.—The confessional.—Conflict of authority.—Masonic prayers.—Master opening the lodge.—The G. A. O. T. U.—Master closing the lodge.—Masonry idolatrous worship.—Master praying for candidate.—Masonic confession of faith.—Prayer at Hiram's grave.—Romish prayers.—Inconsistency of Protestant ministers.—Masonry and Romanism condemned by God's Word.

Henry:—My dear father, I know not whether I feel more pleasure or astonishment at the terrible revelation you have already made to me of the Masonic philosophy. I am certainly well pleased that I had the good sense to consult you in regard to my intention of becoming a Mason, but from the facts you have presented and the evidence adduced to show the absolute wickedness and the innate corruption of the thing, I am both pained and astonished that any Protestant Christian, and more especially that any Protestant Minister, could be found in this enlightened age who would even countenance, much less swear to "support and maintain" such a miserable imposture.

But there is one feature of the system which in all probability I would have never thought of, and one which is doubtless but very little understood. I mean the great similarity between itself and Romanism. I had always thought that the Church of Rome was ever an uncompromising enemy to Freemasonry, and yet you show that both systems are almost identical. Please explain how this happens.

Mr. Barton:—It is true, my dear Henry, that the Church of Rome is fiercely opposed to all secret societies outside of her own communion, and more especially to the Masonic, but her opposition to the latter arises not because of the antichristian and infidel doctrines of Freemasonry, for the religion of Rome is equally false and unscriptural. Neither has the antagonism between the two systems arisen because of the principle of secrecy, for Romanism is as much of a secret combination as Freemasonry is, if not more so. We know that the Jesuits, the Jansenists, the Carmelites, the Paulists and the various other orders of monks and ecclesiastics within the Romish church, not counting such organizations as the "Ancient Order of Hibernians," are all of them as much secret institutions as the Masonic fraternity, and hence the opposition to Masonry by the Church of Rome cannot have originated on the simple ground of secrecy alone. From the fact that the two are rival institutions, both being so much alike one would be almost led to suspect that perhaps jealousy has something to do with the conflict between them, and that Romanism is opposed to Masonry on the principle expressed in the old adage that "two of a trade can never agree;" but the real cause of their opposition to one another is the confessional.

That is the great machinery by means of which the Romish Church carries out all her plans and purposes. Every member of that stupendous system must visit his priest in the confessional at least once a year, and hence, in 1738—twenty-one years after the birth of Grand Lodge Masonry—because the Freemasons of France and Germany rebelled against the power of the confessional, and utterly refused to submit to the infliction of priestly penances, Pope Clement VIII. issued his famous *bull* against the institution, and from that time on the chapel and the lodge have been opposed to each other.

But the contention between them is not for truth and purity, but for power and supremacy. It is a mere conflict of authority and nothing more. The Pope, or Sovereign Pontiff, is the *Pontiex Maximus*, or the Jupiter of pagan Rome, and represents the god of Romanism, while the Worshipful Master is the personification of Hiram Abiff, or Osiris, or Baal, which was the name of Jupiter in Egypt and Phœnicia, whence the Masonic philosophy has come, and is the representative of the god of Masonry. But as every worshipper of the Rom-ism god must *reveal* or *coufess* to the priest, who alone is to be the custodian of all secrets, while every worshipper of the Masonic god must *conceal* and *never reveal*, but must himself be the keeper of all secrets, and is therefore exalted above the priest, both systems cannot harmonize, and hence the bitter antagonism which arose between them in 1738.

But notwithstanding this apparently wide gulf thus separating these two terrible powers of despotism and falsehood for the present, yet, should an emergency ever arise when it would become necessary for men to array themselves on the side of rlghteousness and to defend the pure principles of gospel truth and the full freedom of an open Bible, untrammelled either by Jesuit cunning or lodge duplicity, it is very greatly to be feared that, forgetting their petty differences for the time being, both Romanism and Freemasonry would make common cause and stand shoulder to shoulder, the very embodimeut of the works of darkness. We have every reason to thank God, however, for their present attitude towards each other, as two such terrible systems united would be well-nigh irresistible.

But, aside from their hostility because of the confessional, there is scarcely another doctrine or dogma in the whole theology of Rome which has not its exact counterpart in the religious philosophy of Freemasonry; and examining both systems in the light of God's Word, and witnessing the evil effects of their teachings in those communities where either is in the ascendency, and noting their direct opposition to the spirit and genius of the gospel of Christ, it is almost impossible to say which is the most corrupt and wicked. Romanism, it is true, acknowledges the Lord Jesus Christ as the Only Begotten Son of God and the Saviour of the World, but then it constitutes the Pope the vicar of Christ—infallible—and therefore equal with God himself in one of his greatest attributes; while the Virgin Mary is represented as the Queen of heaven—immaculate—the most powerful advocate the sinner can have; and her love and compassion and her ability and willingness to save are so magnified and extolled, that the love of Christ and salvation through his blood alone fade almost to insignificance.

Freemasonry, on the other hand, casts out the name of Jesus Christ altogether, and will not recognize him at all in any of its prayers or other acts of religious worship, while at the same time it exalts a Tyrian brass-finisher, a rude pagan mechanic, a priest of Bacchus, named Hiram Abiff, to the position of a god, magnifies his pretended virtues, extols his character, lauds his pagan piety and supposed fortitude, sings songs of praise to his name, substitutes this heathen deity for Christ, and offers freedom from sin and salvation in the "Grand Lodge above," through the mythical legend of his death and burial in the place of pardon for sin through the blood of Christ, and salvation through his name in the Heaven of God and of his saints.

In Romanism, prayers are offered to a multitude of deified men and women, canonized by the rescripts of Popes and the decrees of councils, and who are constituted so many mediators between God and man. In Freemasonry, prayers are offered to a myth, to a supposititious being called the "god of nature," the "G. A. O. T. U.," and it recognizes no mediator whatever.

In continuing our investigation, then, of the Masonic philosophy, we shall notice at the proper time this further coincidence of the purely antichristian character of both systems, but shall first examine the religious worship, or the devotional exercises of the lodge, and thus have a practical illustration of those landmarks, rules, and edicts, which declare so positively that "all sectarian tenets must be carefully excluded;" that all Masonic prayers must be of a "general character, and must contain nothing offensive to the conscientious scruples" of a Jew peddler, or a pagan idolater, and that the only recognized law of Masonry must be the "*lex naturæ*, or law of nature," as anything else would be too "confined" and "limited."

We have already seen the distinctness with which it is stated that "no lodge can be regularly opened or closed without religious services of some sort."

Let us now observe how this law is put in practice, and how rigidly the Masonic landmark in regard to lodge worship must be enforced and obeyed. And, first, to begin with the opening prayers.

In the "Freemason's Guide," by D. Sickles, 33°, p. 22, we read:—

"The lodge should always be opened and closed with prayer," And on the same page the following prayer is given:—

"Most holy and glorious Lord God, the Great Architect of the Universe, the Giver of all good gifts and graces! Thou hast promised that 'where two or three are gathered together in thy name, thou wilt be in their midst and bless them.' In thy name we have assembled, and in thy name we desire to proceed in all our doings. Grant that the sublime principles of Freemasonry may so subdue every discordant passion within us, so harmonize and enrich our hearts with thine own love and goodness, that the lodge at this time may humbly reflect that order and beauty which reign forever before thy throne. Amen."

Response by the brethren, "So mote it be."

(See also "Hand Book of Freemasonry," pp. 25-26.)

Concerning this prayer, as well as those that follow, we read in the "Manual of the Lodge," by Mackey, p. 13:—

"This prayer, although offered by the Master, is to be participated in by every brother, and at its conclusion the audible response of 'Amen. So mote it be,' should be made by all present."

Religious Services in Opening the Lodge.

The above figure represents the lodge as it is being opened with Masonic prayer. The Worshipful Master stands in the East, immediately under the letter "G," the symbol of the Grand

Geometrician of the Universe, or the god of Masonry, hat in hand, repeating either the foregoing, or one of the following so-called prayers, with the brethren standing before him.

Here are the good and the bad mixed in together. The Jew, the Chinaman, the Turk, the Materialist, and the Methodist—the rum-seller, the gambler, the profane swearer, and the minister of the gospel, all standing round the same altar, all engaged in the same common act of religious worship, all imploring the same blessings from the same deity, and at the close of the prayer all unanimously responding with equal reverence, and in the same breath, "So mote it be." But to whom is this prayer addressed? And what god can it be possible for Masonry to recognize under such circumstances?

The prayer as we see, is offered to the "Great Architect of the Universe," the "G. A. O. T. U," but who is this "G. A. O. T. U.?" And what attributes does he possess? It cannot possibly mean the God of Heaven, because he "at sundry times, and in divers manners spake in times past unto the fathers by the prophets," and gave man even a written law in which he has fully revealed both his *name* and *will*, but he has never styled himself an Architect. God also manifested himself on earth clothed as a man—"the Word made flesh"—tn the person of the Lord Jesus Christ, "who is the brightness of the

Father's glory, and the express image of his person," but our Blessed Lord never called his Father an Architect, nor is he ever called by any such name in any part of the Bible. An Architect is a man who furnishes plans for, and superintends the erection of a building made from material already prepared; but God created of nothing the heavens and the earth, and all the host of them, and hence he cannot be a mere Architect, and it would be a direct insult to call him such a nick-name.

The meaning of the expression, however, in the Masonic prayer is, that nature made itself; that there is some undefinable, unintelligible, unrecognizable power, or principle, or thing in nature, which produces of and by itself the vast results and mighty changes we daily witness around us, causing the variety of the seasons in their annual course, during which nature, as it were, dies and is buried in winter, and is again re-animated and resurrected in the summer. Or the constant succession of day and night, when, during one part of the twenty-four hours, the *sun* or *sun-god*, or light-giving principle, is *alive*, and light is triumphant, and then again the sun is *dead*, and darkness and gloom prevail. Life succeeded by death, figuratively represented by the life of nature in summer, and its death in winter, and by the life and triumph of the sun or sun-god by day, and his death by night, was the mythical basis of all the philosophies of paganism, and is the foundation of that celebrated legend of Hiram, in the third degree, as we shall find hereafter—where the death of the candidate represents the death of light, or truth, or nature, and then again his subsequent resurrection, the final triumph of day over night, of light over darkness, and of truth, or Masonry, represented by the letter "G," over the falsehood of creeds and sects. This is the Masonic idea, and it is this principle in nature, this incomprehensible something, this philosophic natural myth, which is addressed in the lodge as the "G. A. O T. U.," and to whom all Masonic worship is, and must be offered; for, as a matter of course, the worship of the true God through the Lord Jesus Christ would be too "sectarian," "confined," and "limited" to suit the pretended universality of Masonry. But how a minister or professing Christian can associate night after night with these lodge men, and join in this idolatrous worship, sanctioning the total rejection of Christ, approving of the prayers offered, encouraging by his example his brother Masons to continue in their present irreligious state, and confirming them in their opposition to the very gospel of which he himself professes to be a preacher; I say, how a minister can do this, and at the same time be a Christian, and *love* the Lord Jesus Christ in sincerity, is one of the greatest mysteries, or else one of the greatest inconsistencies of modern times.

Again, on page 23:—

"ANOTHER PRAYER which may be used at opening:"

"Great Architect of the Universe! In thy name we have assembled, and in thy name we desire to proceed in all our doings. Grand &c., &c., to the end, as before. Amen."

Response by the brethren: "So mote it be."

Again, from "Manual of the Lodge," by A. G. Mackey, p. 15:—

"PRAYER AT OPENING."

"Most holy and glorious Lord God the Great Architect of the Universe, the Giver of all good gifts and graces! Thou hast promised that where two or three are gathered together in thy name, thou wilt be in the midst of them, and bless them. In thy name we assemble, most humbly beseeching thee to bless us in all our undertakings, that we may know and serve thee aright, and that all our actions may tend to thy glory, and to our advancement in knowledge and virtue. And we beseech thee, O Lord God, to bless our present assembling, and to illuminate our minds, that we may walk in the light of thy countenance, and when the trials of our probationary state are over, be admitted into THE TEMPLE not made with hands, eternal in the Heavens. Amen."

Response by the brethren, "So mote it be."

From "Webb's Monitor," by Dr. Robert Morris, P. G. M., &c., of Kentucky, p. 11:—

"PRAYER AT OPENING.

"Supreme source of all wisdom, truth and love, look graciously down upon thy people here assembled, to pursue the peaceful avocations of Masonry, and grant us at this time a double portion of thy grace, that we may give higher honor to thy holy name, and more lovingly aid each other through the journey of life. Impress upon our hearts the shortness of life, the nearness of death, and the vastness of the work we are summoned here to do; that with freedom, fervency, and zeal, we may serve thee, with brotherly love,relief and truth we may honor thee, and so at last be found fitted as living stones for the House not made with hauds eternal in the Heavens. Amen."

"So mote it be."

And again, from the "New Masonic Trestle Board" by C. W. Moore, published by authority of the National Masonic Convention, held at Baltimore, 1843, p. 13:—

"Great Architect of the Universe! In thy name we have assembled, &c., as before. Amen. So mote it be."

ANOTHER.

"Supreme Ruler of the Universe! We would reverently invoke thy blessing at this time. Wilt thou be pleased to grant that this meeting, thus begun in order, may be conducted in peace, and closed in harmony. Amen." 'So mote it be."

This last prayer is that which was always used by J. H. Dixon, while he was Worshipful Master of Keystone Lodge, No. 639, in this city, in 1872, and when I was Senior Warden of the lodge.

From the "Freemasons' Monitor," by Z. A. Davis; edition of 1843, p. 141:—

"May the favor of Heaven be upon this our happy meeting. May it be begun, carried on and ended with order, harmony and brotherly love. Amen."

The foregoing are the "religious services" used at the opening of all Masonic lodges in the United States; and now let us glance at the prayers to be used at closing.

"General Ahiman Rezon or Freemason's Guide," by Sickles, 33°, p. 25:—

"Supreme Architect of the Universe, accept our humble thanks for the many mercies and blessings which thy bounty has conferred on us, and especially for this friendly and social intercourse. Pardon, we beseech thee, whatever thou hast seen amiss in us since we have been together, and continue to us thy presence, protection and blessing. Make us sensible of the renewed obligations we are under to love thee, and as we are about to separate and return to our respective places of abode, wilt thou be pleased so to influence our hearts and minds that we may, each one of us, practice out of the lodge those great moral duties which are inculcated in it, and with reverence, study and obey the laws which thou hast given us in thy Holy Word. Amen."

"So mote it be."

"Manual of the Lodge," by A. G. Mackey, Past Grand Master; Past Grand High Priest, &c., page 15:

"Supreme Architect of the Universe, accept our humble praises for the many mercies and blessings which thy bounty has conferred on us, and especially for this friendly and social intercourse. Pardon, we beseech thee, whatever thou hast seen amiss in us since we have been together, and continue to us thy presence, protection and blessing. Make us sensible of the renewed obligations we are under to love thee supremely, and to be friendly to each other. May all our irregular passions be subdued, and may we daily increase in Faith, Hope and Charity, but more especially in that charity which is the bond of peace and the perfection of every virtue. May we so practice thy precepts, that we may finally obtain thy promises, and find an entrance through the gates into the temple and city of our God. Amen."

"So mote it be."

Also "New Masonic Trestle Board," by C. W. Moore, p. 13:—

"Supreme Grand Master! Ruler of Heaven and earth! Now, that we are about to separate and return to our respective places of abode, wilt thou be pleased so to influence our hearts and minds that we may, each one of us, practice out of the lodge those great moral duties which are inculcated in it, and with reverence study and obey the laws thou hast given as in thy Holy Word. Amen."

"So mote it be."

Every religious assembly, or church meeting, is usually dismissed with a benediction, and as "the meeting of a Masonic lodge is strictly a religious ceremony," hence, of course, that must be closed with a benediction in like manner.

The following form is therefore prescribed in all the manuals, being always pronounced by the Worshipful Master, and none else is permitted.

"Manual of the Lodge," by Mackey, p. 16:—

"May the blessing of Heaven rest upon us and

all regular Masons! May brotherly love prevail, and every moral and social virtue cement us. Amen."

"So mote it be."

Religious Services in Closing the Lodge.

The above figure represents the lodge as it is closed with prayer and the benediction by the Worshipful Master, according to ancient usage. But suppose he should be a rum-seller, or irreligious, or a profane swearer, or even a scoffer at religion and religious matters, (and all such men are Masters of lodges, five times out of seven,) and that some of the lodge members present were professing Christians—

one or two deacons, a Sunday-school superintend- ent, and a couple of class-leaders—how very spiritual end edifying such prayers and benedictions must appear, and what a wholesome influence Freemasonry must necessarily exert in the community under these circumstances! But regard all these prayers and this whole lodge worship in any light you please, and they are simply and only an abomination, and a blasphemy throughout. Suppose it be denied that these prayers are addressed to the "god of nature," but that the "G. A. O. T. U." means the true God—the God of the Bible—the God and Father of our Lord Jesus Christ, then what? Our blessed Lord himself expressly declares in John xiv. 6:—

"I am the WAY, the *truth and the life;* NO MAN COMETH UNTO THE FATHER BUT BY ME."

Now, if the Son of God has uttered these words, and if they are the truth, as He declares they are, and that He is the only "way" to the Father, then most undeniably the Masonic prayers, by asserting a contrary doctrine, and presuming to reach God by a different way, are a falsehood, an insult to Jesus Christ, and an abomination in the sight of Heaven.

And again, in John v. 22, 23:—

"The Father judgeth no man, but hath *committed all judgment unto the Son*, that ALL MEN SHOULD HONOR THE SON, *even as they honor the Father.* HE THAT HONORETH NOT THE SON,

HONORETH NOT THE FATHER WHICH HATH SENT HIM."

"If this declaration be the truth of God, and that ALL MEN, *Masons* and non-Masons, are commanded to honor the Lord Jesus Christ by their faith, their prayers, their worship, their love, and their obediance, then most undeniably the Masonic philosophy is the antichrist, and every man who participates in lodge worship is guilty of a gross violation of God's law when he treats the name of Christ with the contempt implied in the foregoing prayers. And again, if by not honoring Christ, the Father himself is dishonored, then it is as plain as the sun-light, that all Masonic prayers are a dishonor and a direct insult to the true God, and that the religious services of Freemasonry are of the rankest idolatry.

In John iv, 24, it is written:—

"God is a spirit, and they that worship him must worship him in spirit and *in truth.*"

And again in Matt. xvii, 5, and Luke ix, 34, 35:—

"While he yet spake, behold a bright cloud overshadowed them, and behold a voice out of the cloud which said, this is my beloved Son in whom I am well pleased, *hear ye Him.*"

Now, even admitting that the "G. A. O. T. U." of Masonry means the true God, and that the names "God" and "Lord" mentioned in the Masonic ritual, allude to the God and Father of our Lord Jesus Christ, surely it cannot be claimed, even then, that lodge worship is a worship offered to God, "*in truth*." Almighty God expressly commands to *hear* his Son, but Freemasonry as positively commands, that that Son shall not, and must not be heard in any lodge or chapter of the order, and therefore, unquestionably every Masonic prayer is an abomination in the sight of God and all who engage in such worship approach Him with a lie on their lips.

Again in John xiv, 13, we read:—

"Whatsoever ye shall ask the Father IN MY NAME that will I do, that the Father *may be glorified* in the Son. If ye shall ask anything in my name I will do it."

And again, John xvi, 23, 24:—

"Verily, verily, I say unto you, whatsoever ye shall ask the Father IN MY NAME, he will give it to you. Hitherto have ye asked nothing in my name. Ask and ye shall receive, that your joy may be full."

Is it not very evident then, from these express declarations of God's Word that all our prayers should be addressed to the Father through Christ alone "that the Father may be glorified in the Son?" And consequently if the "Great Architect of the Universe" in the Masonic prayers means the true God, then these prayers are positively and absolutely a blasphemy, while if that expression does not mean the true God, then, without any question, the worship of the Masonic lodge is a wicked idolatry. Take whichever horn of the dilemma you please, if the Bible be the Word of God and diyine truth, Freemasonry is and must be demon worship.

But not only are solemn religious exercises performed at the opening and closing of all Masonic lodges, but every candidate in like manner must be Masonically prayed for at his initiation, and hence the form given below, like the closing benediction, is to be found in all the monitors and text-books, and is pronounced by the Master only, no other prayer being allowed. When the candidate is led into the lodge and the *rite of induction* is performed, he is conducted by the Senior Deacon towards the center of the room and "caused to kneel for the benefit of prayer." (See "Hand Book" p. 64.) The Worshipful Master than rises to his feet, gives three raps with his gavel, calling up the entire lodge, and repeats, for the special benefit of the kneeling neophyte, the following so-called prayer, from which of course, the name of Christ must be carefully excluded:

"Manual of the Lodge," by Mackey, p. 22.

"Hand Book of Freemasonry," p. 64.

"Vouchsafe thine aid, Almighty Father of the Universe, to this our present convention, and grant that this candidate for Masonry may so dedicate and devote his life to thy service that he may become a true and faithful brother among us. Endue him with a competency of thy divine wisdom, that by the secrets of our art he may be better enabled to display the beauties of godliness to the honor of thy holy name. Amen. So mote it be."

Worshipful Master praying for the Minister at initiation.

The above figure represents the candidate kneeling on the floor of the lodge, stripped of his clothing, dressed in an old pair of lodge drawers, blindfolded and with a rope round his neck, the Senior Deacon standing behind him and the Worshipful Master in the East as before, under the symbol of the "G. A. O. T. U." repeating over him this Christless prayer. The Master of the lodge perhaps is a gambler, a rumseller, a dancing-master or profane swearer, while the poor, denuded, kneeling candidate is the Rev. Dr. James Hunt, or some other minister or professing Christian. What a low, degrading position, surely, for any man to place himself in, and more especially for one who professes to be the spiritual guide of others! What a demoralizing effect his conduct on such an occasion must have on those around him, and what a fearful spectacle for all good men and angels, that he not only becomes a participant in such a wicked mockery of God, but that he actually returns to this same temple of Baal on a subsequent night and of his own free will and accord solemnly swears that he will "conform to, abide by and maintain and support" this fearful lodge idolatry for ever!

But there is yet something still more wicked to follow, if, indeed, anything can exceed this in wickedness. On being inducted into the religious philosophy of the "god of nature," as in joining the church of Christ, one must make a confession of faith, and here, while kneeling in the lodge room, is the proper time to make that confession.

After tne Master repeats his Masonic prayer ne resumes his hat, and approaching the kneeling, blindfolded candidate, places his right hand upon his head and demands in a loud voice, "in whom do you put your trust?"

Candidate making Confession of Masonic Faith.

The annexed engraving represents the candidate in this terrible situation, with the Master's hand upon his head. All eyes are upon him. He is surrounded by men, most of whom, perhaps, he has never even heard of, and of whose characters he absolutely knows nothing. The good and the bad, the deacon and the drunkard, the rough and the refined, are standing around him; and surely if the professing Christian, or Christian minister, ever had an opportunity and a most suitable one to confess Christ before men, this kneeling candidate has it now; and yet were he to do so in reply to the Master's question and adhere to that confession, he could not be initiated into Masonry any more than a woman or a blind man could. And as he kneels on the lodge room floor, should he reply "my trust is in the Lord Jesus Christ," or "my trust is in God, through Cnrist," the Master will still repeat his question, and so continue to do until Christ's name is dropped from the confession, and the general answer given "in God." And, further, should a minister or class-leader be Worshipful Master, and the name of Christ be confessed by a candidate, he must refuse to recognize it; he must adhere to the ancient usage, recognizing only the god of Masonry. Under these circumstances it is almost difficult to say which dishonors the God of the Bible most—the minister or Masonry.

As if in utter condemnation of this very act of gross infidelity on the part of his professed followers, our blessed Lord himself declares, Matt. xii. 8:

"Whosoever, therefore, shall confess me before men, him will I confess also before my Father which is in Heaven. But whosoever shall deny me before men, him will I also deny before my Father which is in Heaven."

And St. Paul, in Phil. ii. 2, distinctly asserts that:—

"Every tongue should confess that Jesus Christ is Lord, to the glory of God the Father."

But, in addition to the foregoing prayers, the following is also used in all Masonic lodges in this country, though omitted in Canada.

In the concluding portion of the legend of the third degree, the candidate, personating Hiram Abiff, lies on the lodge floor, wound up in a canvass, shamming death. The Master and brethren surround his pretended dead body, and make two ineffectual efforts to raise it, but fail each time by reason of its supposed decomposition. The Master then, pretending to be in great distress, demands, "brethren, what shall we do?" The Senior Warden suggests, "let us pray;" the Master then adds, "brethren, let us pray;" and they all kneel on one knee, in mock solemnity around the *sham* dead body of the candidate—minister or mock auctioneer—and the Master reads or repeats the following so-called prayer.

"Manual of the Lodge," by Mackey:

Thou, O God! knowest our down-sitting and our uprising, and understandest our thoughts afar off. Shield and defend us from the evil intentions of our enemies, and support us under the trials and afflictions we are destined to endure while traveling through this vale of tears. Man that is born of a woman is of few days and full of trouble. He cometh forth as a flower, and is cut down; he fleeth also as a shadow, and continueth not. Seeing his days are determined, the number of his months are with thee; thou hast appointed his bounds that he cannot pass; turn from him that he may rest, till he shall accomplish his day. For there is hope of a tree, if it be cut down, that it will sprout again, and that the tender branch thereof will not cease. But man dieth and wasteth away; yea, man giveth up the ghost, and where is he? As the waters fail from the sea, and the flood decayeth and drieth up, so man lieth down, and riseth not up till the heavens shall be no more. Yet, O Lord! have compassion on the children of thy creation, administer them comfort in time of trouble, and save them with an everlasting salvation. Amen.

Response—"So mote it be."

Prayer at the grave of Hiram, personated by the candidate.

The annexed engraving represents the candidate —minister, or dancing master—as he plays the part of dead Hiram in the lodge room, the brethren and Master kneeling around his supposed dead body, and the latter reading the above, so-called prayer.

Now suppose that God should say to this candidate, thus enacting such a deceptive mockery, as he once said to that avaricious planter, "thou fool, this moment shall thy life be required of thee," and so make him dead in reality, what would be the fearful consequence of his guilty conduct? And if he believes at all in the teaching of God's Word, how is it possible that a minister, or professing Christian, can retire from such a scene as this, and, kneeling in his closet, return thanks to God, through Christ, for the privilege afforded him of engaging in such a grossly, wicked abomination, and acting and personating such a lie?

And now, having thus briefly examined the prayers of the lodge and Masonic worship, and having seen it practically demonstrated that Freemasonry, if not antichristian, is nothing at all, let us now take a hurried glance at the prayers of the chapel and Romish worship, and see which is the most anti-scriptural and infidel, and who is the most consistent, an Irish Catholic or an American dlvine.

Like the manuals and monitors of Masonry, all the devotional books of Romanism are substantially the same, but here I shall use the latest publication.

In the "Ursuline Manual," recommended by "John, Cardinal McCloskey," and published in New York by Thos. Kelly, 17 Barclay St., I read on p. 27 as follows:—

"Hail, Queen Mother of mercy! Our life, our sweetness and our hope, hail! Exiles, children of Eve, we cry to thee; to thee we sigh, mourning and weeping in this vale of tears. Turn, gracious advocate, turn thou upon us the eyes of thy tender mercy; and after this our exile ended, show unto us Jesus, the blessed fruit of thy womb, O gentle, O tender, O sweet Virgin Mary. Make me worthy to praise thee, holy Virgin. Give me strength against thine enemies."

Again, on p. 60—"LITANY OF THE BLESSED VIRGIN:"

"We fly to thy patronage, O holy Mother of God; despise not our petitions in our necessities, but *deliver us from all dangers*, O ever glorious and blessed Virgin."

And again, on p. 66:

"Remember, Mary, tenderest hearted Virgin, how from of old the ear hath never heard that *he who ran to thee for refuge, implored thy help and sought thy prayers was forsaken of God.* Virgin of virgins, Mother, emboldened by this confidence, *I fly to thee, to thee I come*, and in *thy presence I, a weeping sinner, stand.* Mother of the Word Incarnate, O cast not away my prayer, but in thy pity hear and answer. Amen."

Now compare these prayers with the prayers of Masonry and say which contains the most idolatry, and which dishonors the Lord Jesus Christ the most?

The Romish priest prays to Mary, and "stands before her a weeping sinner," imploring her aid as the mother of Christ, while the Protestant minister, as the Masonic sinner, repudiates the name of Christ altogether, and addresses his worship to the "*god of nature.*"

And again, from the "Christian's Pious Address to Jesus, Mary and Joseph:"

"Most adorable Jesus, most admirable Mary, most amiable Joseph; wonderful trinity of three persons, the most holy that ever have been or ever shall be in this world, prostrate at your feet in union of all the humility and devotion of heaven and earth, I hail, honor and love you in every way in my power."

Here you will observe that Jesus, Mary and Joseph are mentioned in the same breath, and receive equal "honor and love" from the Roman Catholic worshiper.

Now compare this with the following from the Masonic ritual and manual.

At the opening of every lodge the Worshipful Master proclaims:

"Accordingly, in the name of God and the Holy Saints John, I declare ——— Lodge No. ——— open in form on the third degree of Masonry" (or first or second, as the case may be.) "Hand Book," p. 39:—

In the "Manual of the Lodge," by Mackey, p. 13, we read:—

"The lodge is then declared, in the name of God and the Holy Saints John, to be opened in due form on the first, second or third degree of Masonry, as the case may be. A lodge is said to be opened in the name of God and the Holy Saints John, as a declaration of *the sacred and religious purposes of our meeting*," &c.

Now if it is sinful and idolatrous for a Roman Catholic to put Jesus, Mary and Joseph on the same level, speaking of them with equal reverence, is it not just as sinful and idolatrous, to say the least of it, for a Freemason to place God and the Saints John on the same level and mention their names with the same degree of respect and with equal pious regard? Or how in this instance is Romanism wrong and Freemasonry right?

In direct opposition to all this wicked infidelity, and as if to specially condemn these idolatrous practices, both of the lodge and chapel, our blessed Lord himself declares, in John x. 1, 9:—

"Verily, verily, I say unto you, he that entereth not by the door into the sheepfold, but climbeth up some other way, the same is a *thief* and a *robber*. I am the door; by me, if any man enter in, he shall be saved."

And again, John xv. 23:—

"He that hateth me, hateth my Father also."

And 1 John ii. 23:—

"Whosoever denieth the Son, the same hath not

the Father; but he that acknowledgeth the Son, hath the Father also."

And again, St. Paul says, 1 Tim. ii. 5:—

"There is one God and one mediator between God and men, the man Christ Jesus."

And again, in Isaiah xlii. 8:

"I am the Lord; that is my name: and *my glory will I not give to another*, neither my praise to graven images."

And again, in Chap. xlviii. 11:

"For mine own sake, even for mine own sake will I do it: for how should my name be polluted? And *I will not give my glory to another*."

So, also, in 2 John, verse 9:

"Whosoever transgresseth and abideth not in the doctrine of Christ hath not God. He that abideth in the doctrine of Christ, he hath both the Father and the Son."

But how can it be claimed that Romanism "abideth in the doctrine of Christ," when the man-made laws and decrees of that church place the Virgin Mary above and before Christ? And, on the other hand, how can it be asserted with any degree of truth that a man can "abide in the doctrine of Christ," and still be a Freemason, when Freemasonry rejects the mediatorship of Christ altogether? Or, in this instance, which is the most erroneous and Christ-dishonoring system—Romanism or Freemasonry?

CHAPTER VII.

Masonry Mutilates the Bible.—Credibility of Masonic witnesses.—Christ's name expunged from the Scriptures.—Inconsistency of Masonic ministers.—Mutilation of the Bible expressly forbidden.—Masonic morality a caricature.—A trinity of thieves.—Worship of the Virgin Mary.—Rome mutilates the Bible.—Which is most to be condemned, a Catholic priest or a Masonic minister?

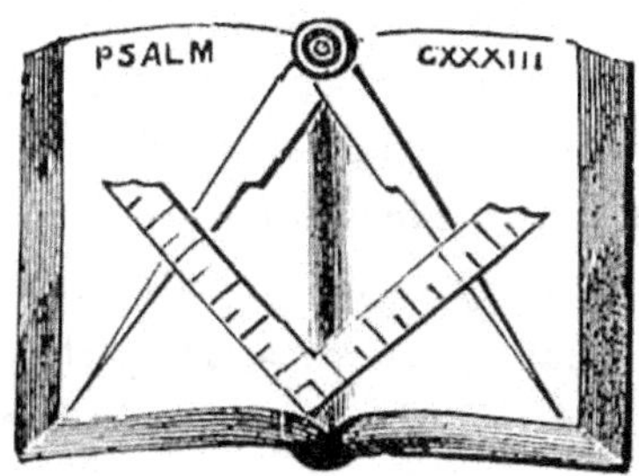

Considering what has been already advanced against the Masonic institution, one might think it scarcely possible to add anything more, or to adduce any further proof to show that, as a religious philosophy, it is a base, unscrupulous fabrication, and that in principle and practice it is diametrically opposed to Christianity. And yet we have still stronger evidence on this point. We have seen that its only moral code is the "law of nature," and the only god of its religion and worship the "G. A. O. T. U." We have found that it considers the Bible as no better than the Koran, nor as good as its Square and Compass, and that it places as much reliance, if not more, in the pretended revelations of paganism as in the Word of God. We have learned that its gavels and mallets are said to purify the heart, that its hoodwinks, cable-tows, and clownish buffoon ceremonies accomplish the "new birth," and that obedience to obligations and precepts, requiring a man to lie at every turn, will free one from sin, and to crown all, we have seen that it ignores and rejects the Lord Jesus Christ, "carefully excluding" his name from every prayer and religious ceremony of its pagan ritual. All this, one might suppose, ought to be enough to condemn any system to lasting infamy at least in the estimation of the Christian public, but Freemasonry commits one more act of sacriligious vandalism, which for the wickedness of its conception and the bare-faced impiety of its execution casts all its other works of damning darkness completely in the shade. It blackballs Christ, and admits the Jew, the pagan, the rum-seller, the profane and the gambler, but it manifests its antipathy to Christianity in a still more marked and positive manner, by ***knowingly, designedly and wickedly expunging His name even from the Bible itself.*** Not satisfied with excluding Him from all its religious worship, it absolutely steals His name from His own Word. And the ministers and church members of its connection not only approve of this willful degradation of the Lord Jesus

Christ, but they actually swear to "matntain and support it," and exert what influence they can to foist the blasphemous philosophy of Freemasonry upon the community for divine truth.

The Church of Christ is usually represented, in the Bible, under the figure of a temple, of which Christ himself is both the foundation and living head.

St. Paul, in writing to the Corinthians, says:—

"Ye are God's *building*."

And again, in Ephesians ii. 20, 21:

"And are *built* upon the foundation of the apostles and prophets, Jesus Christ himself being the chief corner-stone, in whom all the building, fitly framed together, groweth unto an holy *temple* in the Lord."

Freemasonry, as a counterfeit of the Church of Christ, refers in like manner to the symbolism of a *temple* which it pretends every Mason is erecting in his heart, pure and spotless, but of which, nevertheless, corrupt human nature is the only foundation. And in order to sustain this pretension at any risk, and to establish by some means the erroneous delusion that man can save himself and offer so-called spiritual sacrifices on his own merits alone, it has transferred into its ritual, and always uses in its degree work, what purports to be a portion of the Second Chapter of St. Peter's First General Epistle, from the first to the seventeenth verses inclusive, but from which, of course, in "strict obedience" to Masonic law, and in perfect harmony with an "ancient landmark," it knowingly and willfully expunges the name of Christ, and thus quotes the Scriptures as Satan quoted them about 1900 years ago. And yet the rulers and teachers of the craft, those who hold the reins of power in the institution, and whose edicts we are sworn to obey "right or wrong," cunningly attempt to cover up this transparent swindle by pretending that the Scripture passages incorrectly quoted in the earlier Masonic publications have in the later editions been "set right and corrected." This charge will be fully sustained by the following extracts copied from the "*Advertisement*" and "*Preface*" to the last edition of "Webb's Monitor," by Past Grand Master Morris, of Kentucky, and published by Past Grand Orator, J. C. W. Bailey, of Chicago, in 1872.

"To the Masonic Fraternity everywhere:—

"Dear Brethren—The preface to this Masonic Monitor attributes the origin of its compilation to Robert Morris, LL. D., who prepared it for John Sherer, of Cincinnati, and also sets forth its authenticity and its accuracy as a Masonic Monitor, as left to us by the original author, Thomas Smith Webb; the compiler having merely *corrected* the punctuation and the *Scripture passages incorrectly quoted.* * * * * * For these reasons I ask the continued patronage of this *excellent work*, whose cost I have reduced so that every Master Mason may purchase one for his special use." * * * * * * * *

Yours fraternally,

JOHN C. W. BAILEY.

And Robert Morris, the compiler above alluded to by Bailey, asserts in his preface to this work, in relation to Webb's original publication,("Freemason's Monitor," p. 6:)

"In this edition," he says, "the phraseology of that of 1816 and subsequent issues has been followed, correcting typographical errors and improving the punctuation. A few *Scripture passages incorrectly quoted* have been set right," &c.

From these extracts, then, it will be observed that R. W. Bro. John C. W. Bailey, and P. G. M. Bro. Robert Morris, LL. D., both affirm in language that cannot be mistaken that the "Scripture passages incorrectly quoted" by Thomas Smith Webb, the original author, "in the earlier editions of his work, and especially in that of 1816," have in this edition, published by Bailey, "been set right" and "corrected."

Let us now compare these two editions, that of 1816 and 1872, with one another, and with the Bible, and see what reliance can be placed on the pledged word of both these eminent Masons, one of them a deacon in one of our Chicago churches, and the other the Past Grand Master of a Grand Lodge, and a celebrated Masonic lecturer.

I shall place the Scripture passages as found in

both editions in juxtaposition, so that the truth or falsehood of our Right Worshipful and Most Worshipful teachers may be seen at a glance:—

From the "Freemason's Monitor," by Thomas Smith Webb; Cushing and Appleton, Salem, 1816, p. 76:—

"Charge to be read at opening the lodge:"—

"Wherefore, brethren, lay aside all malice, and guile, and hypocrisies, and envies, and all evil speakings."

"If so be, ye have tasted that the Lord is gracious, to whom, coming as unto a living stone, disallowed, indeed, of men, but chosen of God, and precious; ye, also, as living stones be ye built up a spiritual house, an holy priesthood, to offer up sacrifices acceptable to God."

From the "Freemason's Monitor," by Thomas Smith Webb; compiled by Robert Morris, LL. D.: John C. W. Bailey, Chicago, 1872, p. 73:—

"Charge to be read at opening the lodge:"—

"Wherefore, brethren, lay aside all malice, and guile, and hypocrisies, and envies, and all evil speakings."

"If so be, ye have tasted that the Lord is gracious, to whom coming as unto a living stone disallowed, indeed, of men, but chosen of God, and precious; ye, also, as living stones are built up a spiritual house, an holy priesthood, to offer up spiritual sacrifices acceptable to God."

Now, by reference to these passages, it will be noticed at once that they are substantially the same, and that the false quotations of Webb's earlier edition have neither been "set right," nor "corrected," but are precisely as he garbled them from the Bible in 1816, and, of course, precisely as they must remain until lodges and chapters of Freemasonry shall be no more. And by further comparing what is here purported to be a "correct" Scripture quotation with the text in the Bible itself, it will also be found that one whole passage—verse 2d—is entirely omitted, and that from verse 5 the name of Jesus

Christ is knowingly and designedly expunged. And yet Deacon Bailey and Dr. Morris have the wicked audacity to palm off this clumsy cheat upon their poor blindfolded dupes as "divine truth," while Masonic ministers and those "good men" to whom allusion is so frequently made, smilingly look on with marks of solemn approval from behind their little white aprons, and fraternally join hands with the rest of their fellow-conspirators in carrying out the base deception.

In 1 Peter ii. 5, the Masonic Monitor has it: "to offer up spiritual sacrifices acceptable to God;" while in the Scriptures it is "to offer up spiritual sacrifices acceptable to God, BY JESUS CHRIST."

Again:

From the "Freemason's Monitor," by Thomas Smith Webb, Salem, 1816, p. 232:—

"The following passage of Scripture is read at opening:—

2 Thessalonians, iii. 6 to 17:—

"Now, we command you, brethren, that ye withdraw yourselves from every brother that walketh disorderly, and not after the tradition which ye received of us."

Verse 12:—

"Now, them that are such, we command and exhort, that with quietness they work and eat their own bread."

From the "Freemason's Monitor," by Thomas Smith Webb; compiled by Robert Morris, LL. D., J. C. W. Bailey, Chicago, 1872, p. 102:

"The following passage of Scripture is read at the opening:

"Now we command you, brethren, that ye withdraw yourselves from every brother that walketh disorderly, and not after the tradition which ye received of us."

Verse 12:—

"Now them that are such we command, and exhort that with quietness they work and eat their own bread."

2 Thess. iii. 6, 16.

By referring once more to these extracts, we find both editions to be literally the same, not a single correction made, nor a wrong quotation "set right." Now compare them with the Scriptures, whence they were copied, and note the difference.

2 Thessalonians iii. 6 to 17:—

"Now, we command you, brethren, *in the name of our* LORD JESUS CHRIST, that ye withdraw yourselves from every brother that walketh disorderly and not after the tradition which he received of us." * *

Verse 12:—

"Now, them that are such, we command and exhort *by our* LORD JESUS CHRIST, that with quietness they work and eat their own bread." * *

Here again it will be found that from both monitors, the name of the Lord Jesus Christ is willfully and designedly expunged, and no correction whatever made by the impeccable Morris.

The "Masonic Text Book" puts it:—

"Now, we command you, brethren, that ye withdraw yourselves from every brother that walketh disorderly, "&c." 2 Thess. ii. 6.

While the Word of God has it:—

"Now, we command you, brethren, *in the name of our Lord Jesus Christ*, that ye withdraw yourselves, "&c."

And again, in the 12th verse, "Freemasonry," quotes:—

"Now, them that are such, we command and exhort, that with quietness they work and eat their own bread."

While the Bible says:—

"Now, them that are such, we command and exhort *by our Lord Jesus Christ*, that with quietness they work and eat their own bread."

And notwithstanding all this, these garbled quotations of the Masonic text-books are hypocritically designated as "the following passages of Scripture," thus pretending that they are correctly given, while Deacon Bailey and Robert Morris both unblushingly affirm that in the edition of Webb's Monitor, of 1872, the "Scripture passages" have been "set right" and "corrected." And if Bailey and Morris will thus *write* what they *must know* to be *false*, in order to sustain Masonry, why may not other men of less character and respectability *utter* a falsehood with the same design?

But not only is the Bible mutilated, and the name of Christ expunged from Webb's Monitor, in all its editions, from 1797 down to the present time, but the same thing is also done in *every* monitor and manual used by the Masonic fraternity everywhere, as the following Masonic text-books will abundantly testify.

I shall at first place the Holy Scriptures and one of the Masonic text-books in juxtaposition, that the difference between them may be seen at a glance; and as all the monitors are the same, and use identical language, this will suffice to mark the mutilation and the omission of Christ's name in each succeeding quotation.

"Sickles' Monitor," part ii., p. 4:—	Holy Scriptures, 1 Peter ii. 1 to 17 inclusive:
"Charge to be read at opening."	
Verse 5:—	Verse 5:—
"Ye, also, as living stones, be ye built up a spiritual house, an holy priesthood, to offer up sacrifices acceptable to God."	"Ye, also, as living stones, are built up a spiritual house, an holy priesthood, to offer up spiritual sacrifices acceptable to God BY JESUS CHRIST."

I simply quote here only those passages from which the name of Christ is expunged by Masonic authority, as the passage is already given in full on p. 180, from "Webb's Monitor;" but I desire to remark once more that verse 2d is excluded from all the text-books.

Again, Part ii, p. 51:—

2 Thess. iii. 6-16:—	Holy Scriptures, 2 Thess. iii. 6-16:—
"Now, we command you, brethren, that ye withdraw yourselves from every brother that walketh disorderly, and not after the tradition ye received of us."	"Now, we command you, brethren, in the name of our Lord Jesus Christ, that ye withdraw yourselves from every brother that walketh disorderly, and not after the tradition which he received of us."
Verse 12:—	Verse 12:—
"Now, them that are such, we command and exhort, that with quietness they work, and eat their own bread."	"Now, them that are such we command and exhort by our Lord Jesus Christ, tha with quietness they work, and eat their own bread."

Again, "New Masonic Trestle-Board," by C. W. Moore. Part ii. p. 9:

* * * * * verse 5. "Ye, also, as lively stones, be ye built up a spiritual house, an holy priesthood, to offer up sacrifices acceptable to God." * *

Again, on page 31, in the Royal Arch degree:—

"Charge at opening."

* * verse 6. "Now, we command you, brethren, that ye withdraw yourselves from every brother that walketh disorderly, and not after the tradition which he received of us."

* * verse 12. "Now, them that are such, we command and exhort, that with quietness they work, and eat their own bread."

"Freemason's Monitor," by Z. A. Davis, Philadelphia, 1843, p. 199:—

"Charge to be read in the lodge."

* * verse 5. "Ye, also as lively stones, be ye built up a spiritual house, an holy priesthood, to offer up sacrifices acceptable to God."

Again, on p. 226:—

"The following passage of Scripture is read at the opening."

2 Thess. iii. 6–17:—verse 6. "Now, we command you brethren, that ye withdraw yourselves from every brother that walketh disorderly, and not after the tradition that he received of us." * *

* * verse 12. "Now, them that are such, we command and exhort, that with quietness they work, and eat their own bread."

From the "Masonic Ritualist," by A. G. Mackey, Past Gen. Grand High Priest, &c., p. 271:—

"To be read at opening the lodge."

* * verse 5. "Ye, also, as lively stones, be ye built up a spiritual house, an holy priesthood, to offer up sacrifices acceptable to God."

Again, on p. 348:—

"The following charge is read at the opening of a chapter."

* * verse 6. "Now, we command you, brethren, that ye withdraw yourselves from every brother that walketh disorderly, and not after the tradition which he received of us."

* * verse 12. "Now, them that are such, we command and exhort, that with quietness they work, and eat their own bread."

And, lastly, from "Webb's Monitor," New York, 1802, p. 82, being the edition previous to that of 1816, mentioned by Bailey and Morris.

"Charge to be read at opening the lodge."

* * verse 5. "If so be ye have tasted that the Lord is gracious to whom coming as unto a living stone, disallowed indeed of men, but chosen of God and precious; Ye also as living stones, be ye built up a spiritual house, an holy priesthood, to offer up spiritual sacrifices, acceptable to God."

Again, on page 140:

"The following passage of Scripture is read at the opening."

2 Thess. iii. 6–17. "Now we command you brethren that ye withdraw yourselves from every brother that walketh disorderly and not after the tradition you received from us." * * verse 12: "Now them that are such we command and exhort that with quietness they work and eat their own bread."

These quotations could be easily multiplied rom all the Masonic text-books in the country, 6ut enough has been already furnished to demonstrate the fact that Freemasonry is willfnlly and designedly guilty of mutilating the Holy Scriptures, and of absolutely expunging the name of Christ from every part of the New Testament which is profanely used with such mock solemnity in the maeufacture of its pagan ritual.

We oftentimes see it making great parade of the Bible, just as the Pharisees used to parade their prayers and almsgiving, having it ostentatiously carried in all its outdoor processions, as a means of advertising itself in public estimation; but as a system of religious philosophy, and within the secret recesses of its lodges and chapters, we also find that it debases and degrades that Bible, mutilates its contents, despises and ignores its precepts, falsifies its teachings, dishonors its Divine Author; and, to fill up the measure of its infamy and infidelity, it absolutely steals the name of Jesus Christ out of his own Word.

And this horrible incubus of wickedness, deception and hypocrisy is lying to-day, like a hideous nightmare, across the very bosom of the church, while men, calling themselves ministers of Christ, and professing Christians—but slaves to Masonry—hug this terrible delusion to their souls, and, as though it were of some inestimable public benefit, they cherish and foster its extensive wicked growth in every nook and corner of our country. Too truly, indeed, may it be said in the language of the ancient prophet:

"A wonderful and horrible thing is committed in the land; the prophets prophesy falsely, and the priests bear rule by their means; and my people love to have it so: and what will ye do in the end thereof?" Jer. v. 30, 31.

The command of God in relation to his Word is positive and unequivocal. He declares expressly in Deut. iv. 2:

"Ye shall not add unto the word which I command you; neither shall ye *diminish aught from it.*"

And again, in xii. 32:

"What thing soever I command you, observe to do it; thou shalt not add thereto, nor diminish from it."

And in Rev. xxii. 18, 19, the Son of God expressly affirms:

"For I testify unto every man that heareth the words of the prophecy of this book, if any man shall add unto these things, God shall add unto him the plagues that are written in this book.

"And if any man *shall take away from the words* of the book of this prophecy, God shall take away his part out of the book of life, and out of the holy city, and from the things which are written in this book."

But, as a sort of an apology for, or vindication of, the willful and wicked mutilation of God's Word, and the absolute repudiation and rejection by Freemasonry of the name of Jesus Christ, Past Grand

Master Dr. Albert G. Mackey offers the following explanation:

He says in his "Masonic Ritualist," p. 272:—

"The passages are taken with *slight* but *necessary* modifications from the 2nd chapter of the First Epistle of Peter and the 28th chapter of Isaiah."

Hence, according to Masonic law, the mutilation of the Bible and the "handling of the Word of God deceitfully" are but "slight *modifications*," while to willfully ignore and dishonor the name of Jesus Christ, the Son of God, is absolutely *necessary*.

And yet this miserable counterfeit, by its Grand Masters and Grand Orators, has the bold effrontery to prate of its noble "tenets," and to boast of the high moral tone of its monitorial teaching.

It professes to exercise "brotherly love," but the "brotherly love" of Masonry is nothing but the flimsy bond produced by wicked oaths, cemented by selfishness, and enforced by death penalties of which a cannibal might be ashamed. It lays great stress upon "relief," but the "relief" of the lodge means "relief" for a recompense, and then only to him who is "clear on the books," and, at the very best, is but the bare fulfillment of a sworn obligation. It unblushingly speaks of "truth," while the whole vile system is nothing but one tissue of falsehood, from beginning to end; and if the term has any signification at all in Masonic text-books, it simply means that you must *lie* to parent, wife, child and friend, and even to God himself—falsifying his Word and rejecting Divine truth—in order to be true to Masonry. It alludes to "temperance" in its monitorial teachings, but the "temperance" of Freemasonry simply requires that a man must not get so drunk as to become foolish enough to reveal its mountebank jugglery. The "fortitude" it recommends reaches only so far as to enable a Mason to resist the importunities of friends to quit the institution, or of the demands of God and of conscience to denounce its hidden works of darkness. It alludes to "prudence," but it is only to be "*prudent*" in all strange and mixed companies, never to let fall the least *sign*, *token* or *word* whereby the secrets (?) of Masonry might be unlawfully obtained. And it refers to justice in its ritual, but, like all the rest of its moral code, it means favoritism to Masonry, to the lodge, and to a brother, but cunning trickery, deception and double-dealing towards the cowan and "profane" public.

The religious philosophy of Masonry is but a base caricature of the Church of Christ, and its moral code but a clumsy burlesque on the teaching of the New Testament; and hence, in order to obtain a correct idea of what the system really is and what it teaches, we must read it backward.

And now let us briefly examine the other side of this picture.

In the Romish Church the Ten Commandments run thus:—

1. "I am the Lord thy God; thou shalt have no other God but me."

2. "Thou shalt not take the name of the Lord thy God in vain."

3. "Remember to keep holy the Sabbath day."

4. "Honor thy father and thy mother," and so on.

Now by comparing this with the Twentieth Chapter of Exodus, where the Ten Commandments are written as God himself gave them, it will be found that one whole commandment—the second—is entirely omitted, and that almost all the others are more or less mutilated. God has said: "Thou shalt not make to thyself any graven image, nor *any* likeness of anything that is in heaven above or in the earth beneath or in the waters under the earth; thou shalt not bow down to them or worship them." And as the Church of Rome makes an extensive use of images in her religious services, and as her people everywhere bow down before and worship them, it would never do to have this Second Commandment in the Catechism for children to learn, and hence she actually steals it out of the decalogue, and then divides the tenth in two to makc up the number.

Again, in Rev. xxii. 8, 9, it is written:—

"And when I had heard and seen I fell down to worship before the feet of the angel which shewed me these things. Then said he unto me, *See thou do it not.*"

The Church of Rome also teaches the veneration of angels, and in order to prove by some means that such idolatrous worship is right, she quotes this Scripture, but she does it falsely and to suit herself. She omits the words "See thou do it not," and gives the foregoing part of the passage, pretending it to be the correct teaching of the Bible.

And again, in Luke iv. 9, 10, we read:—

"And he brought him to Jerusalem and set htm on a pinnacle of the temple and said unto him, If thou be the Son of God cast thyself down from thence; for it is written, He shall give his angels charge over thee to keep thee, and in their hands they shall bear thee up lest at at any time thou dash thy foot against a stone."

Now, by referring to Psalm xci. 11, 12, from which the devil quoted this Scripture, it will be found that he designedly omitted the very gist of the whole passage. The Psalmist says, "He shall give his angels charge over thee, *to keep thee in all thy ways.*" These words, "to keep thee in all thy ways," the devil very cunningly omits and makes a malicious attempt to pass off his own wicked counterfeit as truth.

Here then, we have Freemasonry mutilating the Scriptures and stealing the name of Christ. Romanism mutilating the Scriptures and stealing the Second Commandment and portions of other passages, and the devil mutilating the Scriptures and stealing the most important part of the text he quotes.

Now which of these three—Masonry, Romanism or the devil—think you, is the most wicked and the most villainous thief? I think it requires but little penetration to be able to award the palm of victory to the Masonic institution.

One of the most popular doctrines of the Romish Church is the "Invocation of Saints," and unquestionably the Virgin Mary is the only one being, who receives the greatest honor, and to whom is ascribed the greatest glory in the Romish system. Every Roman Catholic in the world prays to the Virgin Mary at least ten times for every one time he prays to God, and without her special intercession, no Romanist would consider himself sure of God's favor. In relation to this doctrine, the church of Rome teaches as follows:—

Creed of Pope Pius IV, article 7:—

"Likewise, that the Saints reigning together with Christ, are to be honored and invocated, and that they offer prayers to God for us, and that their relics are to be held in veneration."

The "Council of Trent," Session 25, teaches:—

"That those men hold impious sentiments, who deny that the Saints who enjoy eternal happiness in heaven are to be invoked, or who affirm that they do not pray for men, or that to invoke them to pray for us, even for each individual is idolatrous, and that it is contrary to the Word of God, and opposed to the honor of Jesus Christ, the mediator between God and man; or that it is foolish to supplicate verbally or mentally those who reign in heaven."

And agreeably to the doctrine laid down in these infallible authorities, a canonized saint of the Romish Church, St. Bonaventura, published a work in honor of the Virgin Mary, in which he paraphrases the Psalms of David, and from which he has expunged the names "God" and "Lord," and when convenient has substituted the names "Mary" and "Lady." This work is called the "Psalter of the Blessed Virgin," and is one of the most popular books of devotion in the whole Romish Church, especially among the priests and other ecclesiastics.

In Psalm ii, of this "Psalter of the Blessed Virgin" we read:—

"Come unto *her* all ye that labor, and are heavy laden, and *she* will give you rest in your souls."

In Psalm vi:—

"O Lady, leave me not to be rebuked in the indignation of God, nor to be judged in his displeasure."

In Psalm xv:—

"Blessed be thy paps, with which thou hast nourished the Savior, with God-making milk." (*lacte deifico.*)

In Psalm xix:—

"Forsake us not in the time of our death, but succour the soul when it shall have left its body. Send an angel to meet it, and to defend it from the enemy."

In Psalm xxi:—

"Blessed are they who love thee Virgin Mary; their sins shall be mercifully washed away by thee."

"O Lady, I have cried to thee day and night; thou hast had mercy on thy servant."

"Let the families of the nations adore thee, and let all the ardor of angels glorify thee, etc."

In Psalm xxx:—

"In thee Lady have I trusted, I shall not be confounded for ever; in thy grace uphold me."

Thus it will be observed that the Romish Church through one of the most honored of her deified saints, mutilates the Scriptures so as to reject Christ and substitute Mary, who occupies the same position in the pagan worship of modern Rome, that Venus Minerva, Isis, or Astarte, did in the pagan worship of the ancients, while Freemasonry mutilates the Scriptures in order to reject Christ from its prayers, and substitute Hiram Abiff, who is the Osiris, or Baal, or Jupiter, in the professedly pagan worship of the lodge.

One system worships the goddess, and the other the god of the old pagan idolatories.

Now, if Romanism is to be condemned and abhorred by our Protestant ministers and church members for mutilating the Word of God, and rejecting the Lord Jesus Christ, as the mediator between God and man, why do they not abhor and condemn Freemasonry for the same iniquity? Or does that which is a positive vice in Romanism, and when practiced by a priest in the chapel, become an exalted virtue in Freemasonry, and when practiced by a Methodist or Congregational minister in a Masonic lodge?

The great central figure of the Romish system is the Virgin Mary. While on the other hand, the great central figure of Freemasonry, is Hiram Abiff

Now, inasmuch as the non-sectarianism of Masonry is one of its fundamental principles, or in other words, that the name of Christ cannot be used in any Masonic prayer, nor even be quoted in the lodge, in any Scripture passage in which it occurs, which I would ask is the most anti-christian system of the two? Romanism, which honors Christ, even but a little, and that indirectly through Mary? or Freemasonry, who repudiates Christ altogether? And who is the most consistent? A Roman Catholic who was born into his faith, or a Methodist Minister, who swears himself half-naked into a lodge?

CHAPTER VIII.

Masonic Antiquity.—King Solomon never Grand Master.—The SS. John, not Masons.—Nor all the Presidents.—Arnold a Mason.—First meeting held in 1717.—Sprung up in a grog-shop.—The "Masonic fathers."—The Masonic religion and philosophy revived.—Signs, grips, passwords and lodge government invented.—Early seceding Masons.—Two conflicting Grand Lodges.—Masonry conceived in fraud and sustained by deception.—Mah-hah-bone, by whom invented and how.

Henry:—Well, father, you have given me a most startling insight into the real design and character of the Masonic philosophy. But now I am desirous of knowing how this vast system of deception and despotism first originated. Who invented it? Or was it invented at all? Can its history be traced back to any definite source? Or is there any truth in the popular assertion, that it was first organized at the building of King Solomon's Temple? And that King Solomon, himself, was its first "Most Excellent Grand Master?" What was the origin of Masonry? And why was it first established?

Mr. Barton:—The answer to these questions, my dear Henry, leads at once to a full investigation of Masonic antiquity, and fortunately for us, on this, as on all other matters pertaining to that institution, we are furnished by Masonic authors and historians themselves, with the most minute, and most reliable information.

To continue our researches then, we shall begin first of all with the Grand Mastership of King Solomon.

On this subject, the Masonic ritual speaks as follows. (I shall quote only from Mackey, as the monitorial teaching in all Masonic text books is the same.)

"Manual of the Lodge," by Mackey, p. 55:—

"Our ancient brethren dedicated their lodges to King Solomon, *because he was* our first Most Excellent Grand Master."

And again on p. 109, in reference to the temple, he says:—

"It was symbolically supported, also, by three principal columns, *Wisdom*, *Strength* and *Beauty*, which were represented by the three Grand Masters, Solomon, King of Israel; Hiram, King of Tyre; and Hiram Abiff."

Now, both the assertions contained in these

extracts stand unsupported by any other testimony in the world, and are historically untrue. King Solomon never was Grand Master of a Freemason society, and he knew no more about the little mallets, and plumb-lines, and hoodwinks, and little blue ropes, and white aprons of a lodge of Speculative Masons, than he did of the first battle of Bull Run, or the great Chicago fire. On this point we have the very clearest and most positive evidence, not only from the highest dignitaries of the order, but also from its Grand Lodge Reports, and other official documents. Of these, I shall only select a few.

In an address delivered by T. S. Parvin, Past Grand Master, and the present Grand Secretary of the Grand Lodge of Iowa, at the Grand Reception, given in 1876, by the Freemasons of Keokuk, as published in the "Voice of Masonry," No. 11, p. 63, he uses the following remarkable language:—

"Such oracles," (speaking of the Masonic grandiloquent orators,) "are always proclaiming as Masons, Enoch, the translated; Solomon, the wise; and the SS. John, of Christian sanctity. It is amusing to note how they always enroll among their numbers the noble, and the good of all nations, and all the time as carefully exclude the opposite class. Now, in all candor, and with all proper respect to the brethren to this audience, not overlooking my own self-respect as a Mason, and a man of mature age, I must declare, that *such stuff*, while it may possibly be "told to marines," certainly to all such heresies we may apply the injunction of David in his lament over Saul, and tell it not in Gath, publish it not in the streets of Askelon. *Such tales will surely, sooner or later, return to our hurt as they ever should.*"

> "'t is true, 't is pity,
> And pity 't is, 't is true,

that even *Solomon was no Mason.* With all his wisdom, great as it was, *he knew no more of the mysteries of Freemasonry than did the beautiful Queen of Sheba*, who came from afar to adore his wisdom and the temple he built, if not to love his person. Nor is there any evidence, however faint, to prove that either of the SS. John, the austere and the lovely followers of all that is good in heaven, or on earth were Masons, beyond the wish that it were so by the Christian portion of the Universal Brotherhood. Nor is it true that all the Presidents from Washington to Grant included, were, or are Masons. The first was, the last is not. And what would the spirits of those anti-Masons, the elder and younger Adams, and Van Buren, and Filmore say, to the cruel accusation, could they but wing their way to the earth and throw back the lie in the face of their falsifiers. It is true, however—and the truth must be told—that Arnold, the single traitor of his age and country, was a Mason, as is well attested by the records of his lodge in Connecticut, his native State. So much the worse, both for the traitor, and those who, without evidence or trial would exclude him from their associates."

This is the testimony of one of the most eminent Masons now living, and a man too, who can be confidently relied on for his accurate historical knowledge, being one of the most honored professors in the State University of Iowa, at Iowa City.

But the celebrated Dr. Dalcho, the compiler of the Masonic constitutions of South Carolina, in his work entitled "Ahiman Rezon," published in 1822, uses perhaps still stronger language. He says:—

"Neither Adam, nor Noah, nor Nimrod, nor Moses, nor Joshua, nor David, nor Solomon, nor John the Baptist, nor John the Evangelist belonged to the Masonic order, however congenial their principles may have been. It is unwise to assert more than we can prove, and to argue against probability. Hypothesis in history is absurd. There is no record, sacred or profane, to induce us to believe that these holy and distinguished men were Freemasons and our traditions do not go back to their days. To assert that they were Freemasons may "make the vulgar stare," but will rather excite the contempt than the admiration of the wise."

And the Grand Lodge Report of Illinois for 1873, emphatically affirms on p. 63:—

"And while it is true that the fools are not all dead, it may now be safely said that he who teaches that Adam, Seth or Solomon were Freemasons, *sins against* light and knowledge and ought to be excluded from the platform of instruction."

Also Cornelius Moore, of Cincinnati, a celebrated Masonic historian and lecturer and author of a text book on Freemasonry, called the "Craftsman," in the March number of the "Voice of Masonry" 1878, page 188, writing on this very same subject of King Solomon's Grand Mastership, expresses himself in the following forcible manner:—

"Every one who knows anything about it, is aware that the pretended charter of A. D. 926 is pure fiction, and that the effort to trace the history of the order to king Solomon, and make him "our first Most Excellent Grand Master" is an insult to every member of the order. If we must have a Grand Master of three thousand years ago, *do* let us have one who had some claims to morality and decency. Solomon was a disgrace to his nation as well as to the moral sense of the world. Such a man Grand Master of Masons! No, no, the whole averment, as I said before, is an insult to the moral sense of every intelligent Mason, and the utterer of such stuff can only plead ignorance as an excuse for his proclaiming it before the world."

But the question may be asked, is there not a manifest contradiction then between the ritual and these Masonic authorities just quoted, where one asserts that King Solomon was, and the other that he was not Grand Master? In reply to this it will only be necessary to say that Freemasonry is the science of religious symbolism. Everything done in the degree work, every name mentioned and every implement made use of in the lodge has a symbolic religious meaning. The allusion even to the temple of Solomon is merely symbolic, denoting a "spiritual temple in the heart," and hence the name of Solomon himself is used only in the same manner, as a symbol of authority, power, greatness, wealth and wisdom. On this point the

"Manual of the Lodge," by Mackey, p. 26, speaks as follows:—

"The fact is that in Masonry all allusions to

the temple of Solomon are simply symbolic, and while the great symbol of a material temple prefiguring a *spiritual* one is preserved, no care has ever been taken to obtain correctness of architectural details or even of strictly historical facts."

When we come to examine the symbolism of the lodge and to enquire into the reason for its government by a Master and two Wardens, we shall have occasion to refer again to the symbolic use of the name of Solomon in the Masonic philosophy, but for the present it is enongh for us to know, that as a "historical fact" he never was Grand Master of a Masonic Grand Lodge, nor was Freemasory first organized in Judea, nor at the building of the temple.

This being the case, then the question naturally arises, when and where did our present system of Grand Lodge Masonry, or as it is commonly called, "Speculative Freemasonry" first originate?

Unquestionably there was a time when all such vainglorious titles as Worshipful Master, Most Worshipful Grand Master, Most Excellent High Priest, Most Excellent King, Thrice Illustrious Grand Master, Thrice Puissant Grand Master, Grand Elect Perfect and Sublime Mason, and Most Puissant Sovereign Grand Commander, were entirely unknown. At what period then, did these extravagant soubriquets come to be applied to the tailors, cobblers, counter-jumpers, pothouse-politicians, dancing masters and *humble* (?) Christians who largely compose the Masonic institution? Masonic history itself furnishes on this point all the necessary information, and does it so accurately too, giving the names of persons and places, and describing what actually occurred, in such a clear and comprehensive manner, that no doubt can possibly remain as to the birthplace, the origin and the present age of Grand Lodge or Speculative Masonry.

In "The Digest of Masonic Law," by G. W. Chase, p. 10, we read:—

On the accession of George I., the masons of London (that is the stone masons) and its environs resolved to *revive* the communications and annual festivals of the society. With this view the lodges at the Goose and Gridiron in St. Paul's Church Yard; the Crown in Parker's Lane; the Apple-tree Tavern in Charles St., Covent Garden and the Rummer and Grapes Tavern in Channel Row, Westminter, (the only lodges existing in the South of England at the time) with some other old brethren met at the Apple-tree Tavern, above mentioned, in February 1717, and having voted the oldest Master Mason then present, into the chair, "*constituted themselves a Grand Lodge pro tempore.*"

This was the first meeting ever held, and this is the first time of which we have any record in the history of the world, either sacred or profane, when any mention whatever is made of a Grand Lodge, or any other lodge of Speculative Masonry.

At the very best then, we find that it is but a

self-constituted society, the offspring of a low grog-shop, and numbering among its first members about a score or more of the convivial, free-and-easy stone-masons who occasionally frequented the Apple-Tree Tavern, and other saloons in the purlieus of London as mentioned by George Wingate Chase. Viewing it to-day in its despotic attitude of self-righteousness, observing its impudent assumption of power and popularity, and its utter defiance of public opinion, and listening to the high-flown eloquence of its Grand Orators, Grand Kings, and Grand High Priests, one is forcibly reminded of that famous exclamation of the town-clerk of Ephesus, in reference to Diana, and that celebrated image which he pompously claimed had fallen down from Jupiter "Great is Diana of the Ephesians!" Great now is the Freemasonry of the "Apple Tree-Tavern!"

But again I read from the Law Book.

"Digest of Masonic Law," p. 11:—

"Accordingly on the 24th of June, 1717, the assembly and feast were held at the Goose and Gridiron Tavern, in St. Paul's Church Yard, (in compliment to the oldest lodge, which met there,) and the oldest Master Mason, and Master of a lodge, having taken the chair, a list of candidates for the office of Grand Master was produced, out of which 'by a majority of hands,' the brethren elected Mr. Anthony Sayer, Grand Master of Masons for the ensuing year. who was forthwith invested by the said oldest Master, and installed by the Master of the oldest lodge. The

Grand Master then appointed his Wardens, (Captain Joseph Elliot and Mr. Jacob Lamball,) and commanded the brethren of the four lodges to meet him and his Wardens quarterly in communication."

This is the first Grand Lodge of Masons and these are the first Grand officers that ever existed, or of which there is any account. Masonry can trace its history back from the present time to this June meeting at the Goose and Gridiron Tavern in 1717, and give the names of all the succeeding Grand Masters from that time to this, but prior to that, all is Egyptian darkness as regards Speculative Freemasonry *in its present form.*

We find that Anthony Sayer, of London, and not King Solomon, of Jerusalem, was its first Grand Master; Captain Joseph Elliot, and not Hiram, of Tyre, its first Grand Senior Warden; and that Jacob Lamball, a carpenter, and not Hiram Abiff, the brass-finisher, of Temple fame, was its first Grand Junior Warden.

But we have still further, and perhaps stronger testimony on this subject. Mr. A. T. C. Pierson, than whom no higher Mason, and no better authority can be found in the world, says in his "Traditions of Freemasonry," p. 253:—

"A. D. 1717, was a new epoch in the history of Freemasonry, immediately prior to which time, but few lodges were in existence. *The society was composed of working Masons*, the only exceptions were made in favor of men distinguished for rank, scientific attainments, or position in civil life. On St. John, the Evangelist's day, of the above-mentioned year, an annual feast was held for the first time in several years. Several new regulations were adopted, *one* of which authorized the *acceptance* of members without reference to occupation or pursuit."

"Previous to A. D. 1717 those who were *accepted* into the fraternity, and who were not *operatives*, were designated as *gentlemen* Masons; after the change in the regulation governing admission was made, we find the term *Speculative* Masonry used."

This places the birth of Speculative Freemasonry beyond a question, and not only so, but it fixes the exact time even, when the words "accepted" and "speculative" were first used in connection with the system. From all the foregoing testimony then, we learn three very important facts, which must materially aid us in understanding this subject:—

First, that up to the year 1717, the only form of Masonry existing in the world was Operative Masonry, and that the only Masonic organizations were "Stone Mason's Unions." Second, that into these "Stone Mason's Unions" or societies, some "distinguished" men who were not Masons, were occasionally admitted or *accepted*, and who were afterwards designated as "gentlemen Masons," and third, that in February, 1717, at a general meeting of those "Trades Unions," held in a saloon called the "Apple Tree Tavern," in London, a resolution was passed abolishing the hitherto exclusive character of these societies altogether, and *accepting* men to membership without reference to occupation or pursuit, and whether distinguished or not, provided only their moral character was not very bad, nor their pocket books empty.

This February meeting, as we are further informed, was composed of the scattered remnants of four lodges in the South of England, (being the only ones then in existence,) who constituted themselves a General Assembly, for the future regulation and government of the new organization, and this is the germ of what is to-day called "Ancient Masonry," and the origin of our present Grand Lodge system of Masonic government. Some time previous to this first meeting at the Apple-Tree Tavern, (of which, however, Masonic history furnishes no record,) among others, one James Anderson, a Scotchman, and John Theopholis Desauguliers, a French infidel refugee, were admitted as "gentlemen Masons." Desauguliers was afterwards elected Grand Master in 1719, as we learn from Pierson; Mr. George Payne was elected in 1720, and John Duke, of Montague in 1721, while Anderson published in 1723, the "Charges of a Freemason"—the first book on Masonry that ever saw the light—and these are the "Masonic Fathers," who subsequently became so active in connection with Sayer, Elliott, Lamball, and others, in compiling and perfecting the Masonic degrees, and in propagating the principles of the system, wherever British commerce or British influence could introduce the noxious pestilence.

And in relation to the wonderful zeal manifested in the prosecution of their self-imposed task, the rapidity with which new degrees were multiplied the number and quality of the various Masonic rites manufactured, the unprecedented popularity which the new fangled system suddenly acquired in England, France and Germany, the real design which the early managers of the institution had in view, and the only motives by which they were actuated in disseminating a knowledge of its wonderful mysteries Mr. Pierson furnishes the following graphic description in his "Traditions of Freemasonry," pp. 254, 323:—

"The fraternity became very popular, and designing men sought to make use of it for their own selfish purposes. NEW DEGREES *were created and became the rage everywhere*, but more particularly in France and Germany, which became the hot-bed as it were of so-called Masonic degrees whose number was legion. Many of these degrees were arranged in systems or rites, most of which had their day and died out; a few, however, became popular, and have continued to be cultivated."

"Soon after the REVIVAL in the south of England, the improved system was introduced into France and Germany by the English residents of both countries; here as in England, the society became very popular, but the caprice of the intriguing spirits of the times assumed a different phase and ***the rage was*** *for new degrees* with high-sounding titles and showy costumes." (This seems to be the rage even to the present day.) "The politician, the priest, the philosopher, the astrologer, the deist, the religionist and the ambitious, took advantage of the prevalent idea. Kings, princes, statesmen, clergymen, politicians, tailors, the men of science; in fact, men in all ranks of life became actively engaged in manufacturing degrees and arranging rites to advance their particular interests, theories, dogmas, or ambitious pretensions. *The lists enumerate upwards of three thousand degrees*, each claiming to be Masonic or analogous thereto, and *all* created within three quarters of a century after the revival."

From this testimony, furnished by one of the leading Masons of America, we learn the following important facts: First, that the work performed at the February and June meetings of 1717 was a REVIVAL of the Masonic philosophy. Second, that this newly revived philosophy, on being introduced into France and Germany, and being exactly suited to the spirit of infidelity and free thought prevailing in these countries, spread with amazing rapidity, and third, that the entire movement was controlled and managed by "intriguing spirits," who were almost constantly employed in "manufacturing *new degrees* and arranging rites," with "high-sounding titles and showy costumes," just such titles and costumes as are worn to-day by the "Most Puissant Sovereign Grand Kings," the "Most Excellent Grand High Priests," and by the "Thrice Illustrious Elect Perfect and Sublime

Masons," who almost daily strut our streets in democratic America. Fourth, that all these degrees and rites were manufactured for the sole purpose of advancing the interests, the ambitious pretensions, the theories or the dogmas of their different designing authors. And, lastly, that during the time which intervened from the first saloon meeting in February, 1717, until the last finishing touch was given to the Royal Arch degree, as we shall learn by and by, no less than three thousand Masonic degrees had been manufactured and sold for cash in England, France and Germany. What a startling history of the origin of Freemasonry this is, and what a singular commentary on the indifference, the subserviency, or the cowardice of society, that an institution, professedly organized by such cunning knaves, and for such base purposes, and which has been sustained by fraud, falsehood and deception, from the commencement of its career to the present time, should be permitted to-day to dictate to, if not virtually to rule the nation, and to create such a dread in communities that eyen some of the ministers of Christian denominattons who detest its vile philosophy, and who would like to see it swept from the face of the earth, are absolutely afraid to mention its name, either in the pulpit, the prayer meeting or the Sabbath school, lest its secret vendetta vengeance might, in some concealed manner, be wreaked upon them.

And now having accurately ascertained the exact date when and where Speculative Masonry was organized, the names and residence of its first officials, the very place even where its first meeting was held, and the circumstances attending its early history and rapid growth, the next question which demands attention is, where did Anderson, Desauguliers & Co. find the material from which its degrees were compiled, and how did those degrees come to be arranged into systems and rites as we now have them?

The Grand Lodge of Illinois gives the best answer on record to these questions.

In the "Grand Lodge Report" of 1873, p. 128, we read as follows:—

"The first of the 'Charges of a Freemason' is the landmark concerning God and religion. It cannot be urged that this 'charge' is to be interpreted by the light of the legend and ceremonies of the third degree, or that it is in any manner qualified by them, for THE THIRD DEGREE WAS NOT MANUFACTURED UNTIL ABOUT THE YEAR 1721, *when its legend was adapted to Masonry from certain idle tales taken out of the Jewish Targums, published in London in* 1715, from a MS. in the University Library at Cambridge."

And Dr. Mackey, in his "Encyclopedia of Freemasonry," claims that the third degree was not manufactured until about the year 1738.

So then we have it, on the express declaration of

a Sovereign Grand Lodge, that even the legend of the very best and most important of all the Masonic degrees has been "adapted from certain idle tales taken out of the Jewish Targums," and yet these same idle tales, and the sublime degree founded upon them, are claimed to be of divine origin—"that sublime doctrine of divine truth"—beyond which "it cannot be conceived that anything can be suggested more, which the soul of man requires." And professing Christians and Christian ministers pretend to believe this ridiculous absurdity, and solemnly swear to maintain and support it, "right or wrong."

And again, in the "Traditions of Freemasonry," by Pierson, p. 16, we read:—

"To found the Universality of Freemasonry upon the few traditional S.·. T.·. W.·. which we are taught in the initiatory degrees is flying in the face of Masonic experience, and of our universally spread doctrines, and is in opposition to the first principles of the craft. It is admitted that we are in possession of numerous legends which *are not found* in Holy Writ, but being of very ancient date are entitled to consideration, *although* the authenticity of some of them may be questioned; yet we regard it as interesting and useful to gather up the *traditional* notices of the Early Ages, which, floating downward on the stream of time, have been *arrested* and *preserved* for our meditation and instruction."

This is precisely what Anderson, Desauguliers, Montague, and the rest of their co-workers did in the period from 1717 to 1738. They "arrested and preserved" the "traditional notices," the "idle tales," of the pagan legends of the "early ages," which of course "are not to be found in Holy Writ," and these "traditional legends,"or"idle tales," "although of questionable authenticity,"they interspersed with mutilated and garbled quotations from the Bible, thus forming degrees, and which they afterwards arranged into a regular system or series, constituting what is called a *rite.* Of these Masonic rites or systems four still exist and are cultivated at the present time: Namely the "York Rite," of four degrees, in England and the British provinces; the "French or Modern Rite," of seven degrees, in France and Belgium; the "Ancient and Accepted Scottish Rite," of thirty-three degrees, in Europe and America, and the "American, or Webb Rite," of thirteen degrees, in the United States alone.

Symbolic or "blue lodge" Masonry, however, consisting of the Entered Apprentice, the Fellow Craft, and the Master Mason degrees, is the foundation of every system, and is the only pure Freemasonry in existence; all the other degrees, except about twelve of which are termed chivalric, being but so many developments or elaborations of the Master Mason's degree.

The chivalric degrees, such as the Knights Templar, Knights of Malta, &c., are not generally considered Masonic, although engrafted into the system, because none can take these who reject Christianity, and this rule destroys that principle of universality which constitutes the very essence, and is the constant boast, of the Masonic system. As a striking illustration of the manner in which the Masonic degrees were first manufactured, and the cunning and deception practiced in their introduction, it will only be necessary to examine the origin and early history of the "Royal Arch," and the final completion of the Master Mason's degree as furnished us by Past Grand Master Pierson.

In the "Traditions of Freemasonry," pp. 320, 322, he says:—

"About A. D. 1740, the Chevalier Ramsay appeared in London. He was a Scotchman by birth, but had long been a resident of France: a zealous partisan of the Pretender (Charles, son of James II.) he sought to advance the Stuart interest by the use of Masonry. *He brought with him several new degrees*, which he endeavored to introduce in the English lodges. Among these degrees was one which he called Royal Arch."

Previous to this, however, that is in 1736, a number of influential Masons, headed by one Lawrence Dermott, seceded from the irresponsible Apple-Tree Tavern concern and organized for themselves an opposition Grand Lodge, with their headquarters at a small town called York, in the North of England, whence they subsequently received the name of "York Masons." These "seceders," or York Masons, immediately styled themselves "Ancients;" hence the high sounding title of "Ancient York Masons," while to the London gang they derisively applied the term "Modern." And thus these two contending factions, who professed to inculcate so strongly the beatific tenets of *friendship* and *brotherly love*, continued to manifest towards each other the bitterest animosity, did everything that jealousy and self-interest could prompt to destroy one another's popularity, and mutually waged a most uncompromising warfare during the space of seventy-seven years; and were only reconciled at last, as recently as 1813, by the indefatigable efforts of the Duke of Sussex, who was elected Grand Master of Masons in that year. Bearing these facts in mind, we shall be better enabled to understand the full meaning of the remainder of Pierson's narrative.

"Rejected," he says, "by the Grand Lodge, (of the Apple-Tree Tavern,) he, *i. e.* Ramsay, next sought alliance with the Ancients; here, too, he was foiled so far as his ulterior objects were concerned."

The shrewd Lawrence Dermott, who was for many years the active spirit among the *seceders*, saw in this new degree a means of drawing attention to the Ancient Lodges, and to increase their popularity. After a time it was claimed and asserted that the "Moderns," (or Apple-Tree Tavern Masons) were ignorant of the Master's part, and that the Ancients alone—*i. e.* the seceders—"had that knowledge, and that there were *four* degrees in Ancient Masonry, whereas the Grand Lodge acknowledged and knew of but *three*."

You will not fail to notice that the very conception of this whole Masonic scheme is a fraud and a swindle from the beginning. But the story goes on:—

"Emboldened by success, in A. D. 1756, Dermott published his *Ahiman Rezon*, in which similar statements were made."

"Thomas Dunckerley, an illegitimate son of George II., a man of most brilliant intellect, was chosen Master of a regular lodge in A. D. 1770; he soon assumed a high position among the distinguished Masons of the age, and finally became Grand Master. Visiting the *Ancient* lodges, he became acquainted with the new degree, and, resolved that they should not appropriate to themselves a single pearl of any real value, towards the elucidation of the craft, he determined to introduce the degree into the regular lodges."

"Divesting the degree as practised by the *Ancients* of many of its crudities; in fact, remodeling it and revising the lecture, he presented the Holy Royal Arch Degree to the Grand Lodge. It was at once found that the practice of this new degree required a change in that of the Master Mason's degree—*a removal* and a *substitution*—a transfer, says Dr. Oliver, of the Master's word."

"The new degree having received the patronage of the Duke of Clarence, (brother of the king) united with his own influence, enabled Dunckerley to suceessfully carry his project through, and since A. D. 1779 the 'Holy Royal Arch' has been cultivated under the authority of the Grand Lodge of England, (Apple-Tree Tavern Grand Lodge) and the degree declared to be part of ancient Masonry."

And thus in 1779 the "*Holy* Royal Arch" and the *Sublime* degree of Master Mason were both perfected, and the revival begun by Anderson, Desauguliers, Sawyer & Co., in 1717, was fully effected. The necessary change was made, the "*re-moval*" and "*substitution*" took place, the word "Jehovah" was removed from the Master Mason's degree, transferred to Dunckerley's Royal Arch and *Mah-hah-bone*, as we now have it, was invented and *substituted* as the "grand Masonic Word" in its stead.

From this authority, then, furnished as it is by a Mason than whom there is none higher in the world, we at once learn that instead of the "Master's Word" being lost through the pretended death of Hiram at the building of the Jerusalem temple, it was simply transferred in 1779 to a new degree, and *Mah-hah-bone* substituted in its place; and we also learn that instead of Solomon, King of Israel, Hiram, King of Tyre, and Hiram Abiff being the principal founders and promoters of the Masonic system, that Ramsay, Dermott and Dunckerley were the chief manipulators of our saloon bantling, and hence that to these latter worthies alone must be ascribed all the glory for those finishing touches which have left the institution in the form in which we now find it.

CHAPTER IX.

Masonry and the Ancient Mysteries.—Adam the first man who wore an apron.—By whom invested.—Distinction between Masonic lodges and Masonic philosophy.—Origin of Sabaism or star-worship.—The sun-god.—Worshiped in secret.—Ancient mysteries.—Mysteries of Egypt and Eleusis.—Masonry and the mysteries identical.—Osiris, the sun-god of Egypt.—Hiram Abiff and Osiris one and the same.—Freemasonry, the old sun-worship revived.—Meaning of the term "god of nature."—Must believe Masonic testimony concerning itself.

Henry:—But another difficulty presents itself. If, as has been so clearly demonstrated, the Masonic institution has existed only since February or June, 1717—that is about 162 years—how comes it then that other Masonic authors, and even some of those from whom you have already quoted, claim for it a much greater antiquity, and attempt even to trace it back to the time of Adam?

Mr. Barton:—Well, it is quite true that Adam was the first man who wore an *apron*, but although it may haye been "the badge of a Mason," yet instead of being "the emblem of innocence," it was undoubtedly, then as well as now, the emblem of deception, selfishness and sin; Adam being in-invested with it by Grand Master Satan himself. But if we desire to have a correct understanding of Masonic antiquity, we must always draw a broad line of distinction between the Masonic philosophy and the Masonic lodges in which that philosophy is inculcated.

The religious philosophy of Freemasonry is as old as sin itself, while the lodges which disseminate that philosophy were only instituted during the period from 1717 to 1738; and hence one class of Masonic writers, speaking of it as a religious system, endeavor to trace it back to a remote antiquity; while another class, alluding only to its government as at present constituted into lodges and Grand Lodges, refer it to the period just mentioned. This view of the question is fully sustained by all our Masonic authors, but by none of them with greater clearness and accuracy than is found in the voluminous writings of A. G. Mackey, Past Grand Master, and Past General Grand High Priest. He says in his

"Symbolism of Freemasonry," p. 11:—

"If we seek the origin of the institution moulded into outward form as it is to-day, we can scarcely be required to look farther back than the beginning of the eighteenth century, and indeed not quite so far."

While, in the very same paragraph, he also declares, with equal plainness, that:—

"If we seek the origin and first beginning of the *Masonic* philosophy, we must go away back into the ages of remote antiquity, when we shall find this beginning in the bosom of kindred associations, where the same philosophy was maintained and taught."

And again, in his "Text Book of Masonic Jurisprudence," p. 95, he says:—

"The truth is that *Masonry is undoubtedly a religious institution*, * * * which, handed down through a long succession of ages *from that ancient priesthood* who first taught it, embraces the great tenets of the existence of God and the immortality of the soul."

Upon the evidence of this high Masonic authority, then, we learn two very important facts, namely: that Freemasonry, in its present "outward form" of Grand Lodge government, came into existence only in the beginning of the eighteenth century, while at the same time its religious philosophy, its legend and various symbols, previously existed in the bosom of "kindred associations," away back "into the regions of remote antiquity." And, bearing this distinction carefully in mind, we can more easily understand, and more readily appreciate the full extent of that celebrated *Masonic revival*, which we are authoritatively informed took place under the leadership of Anderson and Desauguliers, as already referred to. But what was it that these "Masonic fathers," and their co-laborers really revived? Where did they find the material for the Masonic philosophy? And what were these "kindred associations" so confidently alluded to by Bro. Mackey?

In searching for the "beginning of the Masonic philosophy," no matter how far back we may go "into the ages of remote antiquity," we can find only two kinds of religions or religious philosophies: the religion of God and the religion of paganism; and but two classes of priests, the priests of God and the priests of Baal. And as the Bible contains all that can possibly be known concerning the religion of the true God, his worship, and the priests by whom that worship was taught and conducted, and as "Freemasonry has nothing whatever to do with the Bible, and is not founded on the Bible," according to its own authorized law-books and manuals, therefore it must necessarily follow, even in the absence of any further testimony, that the religious philosophy now inculcated in Masonic temples is the very same that was anciently taught and practiced in the pagan temples of Baal and Osiris. But we are not left to conjecture upon this point. Every Masonic manual and monitor makes more or less mention of it, while all our best and most popular writers speak of it in the most unequivocal terms. In fact, Freemasonry, by all its accredited authorities, claims to be a REVIVAL of the ancient religious philosophy of Egypt, Phœnicia and other pagan nations, who practiced a secret worship in honor of the sun-god, whom they designated by various names according to circumstances; and, what is more, this very claim is boastfully asserted.

Before referring, however, to the direct Masonic testimony which conclusively proves this fact, let us glance for a moment at the causes which originally gave rise to the worship of this supposed sun-god of paganism, and to the establishment of those "kindred associations," in the bosom of which, we have been so confidently informed by Mackey, the Masonic philosophy had been discovered.

In the "Traditions of Freemasonry," by Eierson, p. 231, we read:—

"Egypt was repeopled after the deluge by the sons of Ham, and they made more rapid advances in recovering a knowledge of the arts and sciences, partially lost by that catastrophe, than any other people, until Egypt became to be looked upon as the mother of science."

These early Egyptian settlers, in their periodical observations from year to year, (as we learn from history), in search of some sign by means of which they could tell about what time the river Nile would overflow its banks, and so enable them to prepare for flight to the hill country, at last, as a reward for their continued watchfulness, beheld in the morning' near the stars of Cancer, though pretty far from the bands of the Zodiac, toward the south, and a few weeks after their rising, *one of the most brilliant* if not *the brightest star* of the whole heavens, ascending the horizon. It appeared a little before the rising of the sun, which had rendered it almost invisible for a month or two previous. This phenomenon becoming visible only a short time before the rising of the Nile, the Egyptians pitched upon the appearing of this magnificent *star* as the infaliible sign of the beginning of the inundation, and hence, it became the *public mark* on which every one was to keep a watchful eye, not to miss the instant of retiring to the higher grounds.

As it was seen but a very little time above the horizon, it seemed to show itself to the Egyptians merely to *warn* them of the overflowing which soon followed. They than gave this star two names, having a very natural relation to the helps they borrowed thereform. I *warned* them of the *danger*, whereupon they called it Thaaut or Thot, *the dog;* they called it also the *barker*, the *monitor*, in Egyptian *Anubis.* And it may be worthy of brief mention that this same Anubis or dog star of the early Egyptians, is now the "*Blazing Star*" of the Masonic philosophy and has the very same meaning for the Mason to-day, (as will be shown hereafter) that it formerly had for the dwellers in lower Egypt.

The veneration with which this magnificent star was at first regarded, gradually led to its worship, which, after a time, was followed by the worship of other stars and heavenly bodies, and then again by others, until at length the doctrine of sabaism or star-worship became the common religion of Egypt and the adjacent countries, and finally led to the polytheism which afterwards everywhere prevailed.

But while polytheism, or the worship of many gods, was the universal religion of the multitudes or the common people in all pagan nations, yet the sun or sun-god, under different appellations, was everywhere constituted as the chief deity.

Emblem of Sun-Worship.

And while the pagan masses offered their public devotions to their myriads of senseless idols, the pagan priests and philosophers and rulers had a different worship, which they practiced only in secret, which they conducted with the most imposing ceremonies, and which they always celebrated in honor of the chief deity, or sun-god. This *secret* worship of paganism in every country was termed the "Mysteries," and is that which was revived by the "Masonic fathers" in the beginning of the eighteenth century; so that what was called the "Mysteries" of Osiris, or Baal, or Bacchus, or Dionysius in ancient times, is to-day known as the mysteries of Masonry. On this point all our Masonic writers, as has been already mentioned, give such plain, positive, unqualified, affirmative testimony, that, if we do not believe what they say concerning their own pet philosophy, it is useless to receive human testimony on any subject. And for the purpose of illustrating this Baal worship, and as if to give emphasis to their teaching, the emblem of the sun, moon, stars, &c., on the preceding page, is found in all our lodges and manuals.

In the "Traditions of Masonry," p. 232, we read:—

"More pages of the writings of the ancients, that have been preserved to our times, are devoted to the MYSTERIES than to the development of empires. Hence *we have better* knowledge of the ceremonial and legend of many of the phases of the mysteries, than we have of the country in which they were practiced."

This being the case then, let us now see how clearly the Masonic philosophy and Masonic institution are shown to be identical in every feature with these pagan "Mysteries."

In the "Lexicon of Freemasonry," by Mackey, p. 125, we read:—

"EGYPTIAN MYSTERIES.—Egypt was the cradle of the mysteries of paganism. At one time in possession of all the learning and religion that was to be found in the world, it extended into other nations the influence of its sacred rites, and its secret doctrines."

And in describing the "Mysteries," Dr. Mackey again says, on p. 315:—

"This is the name given to those religious assemblies of the ancients, whose ceremonies were conducted in *secret*, whose doctrines were known only to those who had obtained the right of knowledge by a previous *initiation*, and *whose members were in possession of signs and tokens, by which they were enabled to recognize each other.*"

Is not this an exact description of Freemasonry? Or could any language be employed to portray the Masonic system more accurately?

But again:—

"Warburton's definition of the 'Mysteries' was as follows. Each of the *pagan gods* had (besides the public and open) a *secret worship* paid unto him, to which none were admitted but those who had been selected by preparatory ceremonies, called INITIATION. This *secret worship* was termed the mysteries." (Divine Legation, vol .i, p. 189.)

"The most important of the *mysteries* were those of Mithras, celebrated in Persia; of Osiris and Isis, celebrated in Egypt; of Eleusis, instituted in Greece, and the Scandinavian and Druidical rites which were confined to the Gothic and Celtic tribes."

And in further explaining the common origin of these mysteries and their indentity in everything except in the name of the hero-god alone, the Masonic text-book relates:—

"Traditions of Freemasonry," p. 233:—

"And the mysteries throughout the world *were the same in substance*, being derived from one source and celebrated in honor of the same deities, though acknowledged under different appellations."

From all this undoubted Masonic testimony, then, the following facts are apparent, namely: that among the ancient pagans a *public* and a SECRET worship were practiced; that this SECRET worship first originated in Egypt, and was everywhere known as "THE MYSTERIES;" that all these "Mysteries" were the same in substance, their religious philosophy, their legend, and their hero, or sun-god, being the same everywhere, only "under different appellations;" that a knowledge of these "Mysteries" was obtained only by initiation, and that, as secret "religious assemblies," their different members were in possession of "signs, grips and tokens," by which "they were enabled to recognize each other."

These are the "kindred associations" alluded to by Mackey, and all other Masonic writers, and in the "bosom" of which, they assert in such very positive language, that the Masonic philosophy was found; and it is to prove this fact, and to establish, beyond a doubt, the identity of those "Ancient Mysteries" with the Masonic institution, that they have taken such great pains to describe with minute exactness every particular incident connected with their celebration.

But again Freemasonry teaches us:

"Lexicon of Freemasonry," by Mackey, p. 315:—

"In all these various mysteries we find a singular unity of design, clearly indicating a common origin."

"The ceremonies of initiation were all *funereal* in their character. They celebrated the death and resurrection of some cherished being, either the object of esteem as a hero, or of devotion as a god."

"Subordination of degrees was instituted, and the candidate was subjected to probations varying in their character and severity * * * * *the rites were practiced in the darkness of night*, and the full fruition of knowledge for which so much labor was endured, and so much danger incurred, was not attained until the aspirant, well tried and thoroughly purified, had reached the place of wisdom and of light."

Here we find the system of Freemasonry, its degrees, initiatory ceremonies, and the legend of Hiram Abiff, described with an accuracy of detail which may possibly be equaled, but cannot be excelled. "The Mysteries," he says, "were all funereal in character;" so is Freemasonry. They had a "subordination of degrees;" so has Masonry. "The Mysteries celebrated the *death* and resurrection of some cherished being;" Masonry celebrates the death and resurrection of Hiram Abiff. who is cherished among the fraternity as a being of superior excellence, and whose name is ever sacred on their lips.

And again, on the "Eleusinian Mysteries," p. 183, we read:—

"These were among the most important of the ancient rites, and were hence often called emphatically '*the Mysteries.*'"

"In these mysteries was commemorated the *search* of Ceres after her daughter Proserpine. * * * The chief dispenser of the mysteries was called the Hierophant, or revealer of sacred things, (we call him Worshipful Master in Masonry;) to him were joined three assistants, the Daduchus, or torch-bearer, the Ceryx, or herald, and the Hoepibomo, or altar-server."

In Freemasonry, the Senior Warden, Junior Warden, and Senior Deacon are "joined" with the Worshipful Master in opening, closing, and conducting the various degree ceremonies. The Worshipful Master is the Hierophant, or the "revealer of sacred things;" the Senior Warden represents the "torch-bearer," being next in office to the Master, and whose chief business it is to assist him in the active duties of the lodge; the Junior Warden represents the "herald," whose station is always in the south, and makes proclamation to the brethren, when the lodge is about to be opened or closed, while it is always the constant duty of the Senior Deacon to wait upon the altar. And the *Search* of CERES for her daughter Proserpine, which was practiced in the initiatory ceremonies of the Mysteries of Eleusis, is most vividly represented in the Master Mason's lodge by the *search* of the twelve Fellow Crafts for Hiram's body, and for the Master's word.

But again:—

"The mysteries were of two kinds, the lesser and the greater."

The Masonic mysteries, also, are of two kinds, the *lesser mysteries* comprising the Entered Apprentice, Fellow Craft, and the first section of the Master's degree, and the *greater mysteries* which comprise the drama of "Hiram, or the Temple Legend." But, as if to place this matter of the identity of Masonry with "the Mysteries" beyond the possibility of a doubt,

Dr. Mackey informs us in his "Lexicon," p. 135:—

"In these regulations, as well as in the gradual advancement of the candidate from one degree to another, *that resemblance to our own institution* is readily perceived, which has given to these, as well as to the other 'Ancient Mysteries,' the appropriate name of Spurious Freemasonry."

And again, in the "Symbolism of Freemasonry," by A. G. Mackey, p. 15, it is stated:—

"These mysteries existed in every country of heathendom, in each under a different name, and to some extent under a different form, but always and everywhere with the same design of inculcating, by allegorical and symbolical teachings, the great *Masonic doctrines* of the unity of God, and the immortality or the soul. This is an important proposition, and the fact which it enunciates must never be lost sight of, in any inquiry into the origin of Freemasonry; for the pagan mysteries were, to the spurious Freemasonry of antiquity, precisely what the Master's lodges are to the Freemasonry of the present day."

Again, in the "Traditions of Freemasonry," p. 8, A. T. C. Pierson declares:—

"The writings of the ancient sages afford many coincidences in ceremonies, customs, usages, symbols, and allegories, between the ancient mystic, or religious associations, (the Mysteries,) and that which is now termed Freemasonry."

And hence, if words have a meaning, it is undeniably demonstrated, by the very highest Masonic authority in the land, that the "ancient usages and established customs" of the secret worship of paganism, are to-day reproduced and enforced in all our Masonic lodges, and consequently that, when a candidate in the "*preparation room*" "seriously declares upon his honor" that he "will cheerfully conform to all the ancient usages and established customs of the fraternity," he simply pledges beforehand, that he will conform to all the ancient usages and established customs of the "*Secret Mysteries*" of the old sun-god of Egypt. And all his subsequent obligations, and every oath administered to him afterwards on the "Square and Compass," are but so many solemn pledges, swearing him, that he must forever after "conform to, and abide by, and maintain, and support" that wicked idolatry.

But Masonic audacity and infidelity go even still further than this. Freemasonry must be proved, by some means, to be of Divine origin, and as the "Ancient Mysteries," or Baal Worship, and the Masonic mysteries are one and the same, therefore nothing remains to be done but to assert the Divine origin of the former, and that, of course, vouches for the latter, while, at the same time, it proclaims, as loudly as the devilish ingenuity and the positive antichristian principles of Masonry can utter the words, that the teaching of the Bible is but a mere fable, and the gospel of Christ a base delusion.

In the "Traditions of Freemasonry," by Pierson, p. 13, we read:—

"The order known as Freemasonry appears to have been instituted as a vehicle to preserve and transmit an account of the miraculous dealings of the Most High with his people, in the infancy of the world."

"The identity of the Masonic institution with the 'Ancient Mysteries,' is obvious, from the striking coincidences found to exist between them."

And the "General Ahiman Rezon, or Freemason's Guide," by D. Sickles, p. 57. informs us that:—

"In Egypt, Greece, and among other ancient nations, Freemasonry, (that is the '*Mysteries*') was one of the earliest agencies employed to effect the improvement and enlightenment of man," while

In the "Manual of the Lodge," p. 12, it is declared that:—

"The 'Ancient Mysteries' were *those sacred rites, which have furnished so many models for Masonic symbolism*," and that "the opening ceremonies were of the most solemn character."

But however convincing all these various testimonies may be, and however undeniably they may establish the identity of Masonry with the "Ancient Mysteries," yet our Masonic authors are by no means satisfied to allow the matter to rest even here. In addition to all this they give a critical analysis of the legend, which was common to all the "ancient initiations," and make such a close comparison between that legend and the legend of Hiram in the Master Mason's degree, that no doubt whatever can remain, even in the mind of the most skeptical, that the *secret worship of paganism* was revived under the deceptive name of Freemasonry from 1717 to 1738, and that Hiram and Baal are one and the same characters. But, lest this should not be enough, and in order, if possible, that nothing might be left unsaid to connect the Hiram of the Masonic philosophy with the hero-god or sun-god of the old pagan "Mysteries," in specifying the different countries in which the "Mysteries" were practiced, and giving the names of their various founders, it is specially mentioned that Hiram Abiff himself introduced them into Judea, and hence, that there can be no mistake made in the third degree, when his name is substituted for that of Osiris, Baal, Bacchus, Dionysius, Brahma, or any other of the hero-gods of the ancient pagan worship. On these points we read as follows:

"Traditions of Freemasonry," p. 159:—

"The legend and traditions of Hiram Abiff form the consummation of the connecting links between Freemasonry and the ancient mysteries, and sustain beyond peradventure the theory that Freemasonry (the mysteries) dates anterior to the deluge and the strong probability of its (their) divine origin."

And again,

The "Lexicon of Freemasonry," by Mackey, p. 195, speaking of the Masonic legend, says:—

"There are characters impressed upon it which cannot be mistaken. It is thoroughly Egyptian, and is closely allied to the supreme rite of the Isianic mysteries."

Also in the "Traditions of Freemasonry," by Pierson, p. 240:—

"The Masonic legend stands by itself, *unsupported by history* or other than its own traditious; yet we readily recognize in Hiram Abiff the Osiris of the Egyptians, the Mithras of the Persians, the Bacchus of the Greeks, the Dionysius of the fraternity of the Artificers, and the Atys of the Phrygians, whose passion, death and resurrection were eelebrated by these people repectively."

"For many ages, and everywhere, Masons have celebrated the death of Hiram Abiff. Everywhere among the ancient nations there existed a similar allegory."

And, referring directly to the legend of Hiram in the third degree, Mackey, in his "Manual of rhe Lodge," p. 99, uses the following language:—

"The idea of the legend was undoubtedly borrowed from the ancient mysteries, where the lesson was the same as that conveyed now in the third degree of Masonry."

So also the "Freemasons' Guide," by Sickles, in explaining the Egyptian or Osirian legend and referring it directly to that of the Master Mason's degree, affirms in the following emphatic manner, p. 196:—

"The Egyptian rite was a dramatic representation. This myth is the antetype of the temple legend. *Osiris and the Tyrian Architect, i. e.* Hiram Abiff—ARE ONE AND THE SAME—not a mortal individual, but an immortal principle."

And lastly, in the "Traditions of Freemasonry," p. 233, speaking of the early introduction of these "*Mysteries*," or Baal worship, into different nations, it is unequivocally affirmed that:—

"The mysteries were introduced, (so says tradition,) into India, by Brahma; into China and Japan, by Buddha; into Egypt, by Thoth, the son of Mizraim; into Persia, by Zeradhurst; into Greece, by Melampus, or Cadmus; into Bœotia by Prometheus and his son; into Crete, by Minos; into Samothracia, by Eumospos, or Dardanus; into Messene, by Caucon; into Thebes, by Methapus; into Athens, by Erecthus; into Etruria, by Philostratus; into the city of Arene, by Lycus; into Thrace, by Orpheus; into Italy, by the Pilasgi; into Cyprus, by Cinyras; into Gaul and Britain, by Gomer; into Scandinavia, by

Sigge, or Odin; into Mexico, by Vitzliputzli; into Peru, by Manco Capac and his wife, and into Judea, by Hiram Abiff."

And now the last question which it is necessary for us to examine in relation to this matter, and in establishing the coincidence between the Osiris of the Ancient Egyptians, and Hiram of modern Masonry is, Who was Osiris? And what did he represent?

In the "Lexicon of Freemasonry," I read again on p. 130:—

"This legend (that is of Osiris) was purely astronomical. OSIRIS WAS THE SUN, *Isis the moon.* Typhon was the symbol of winter, which destroys the fecundating and fertilizing power of the sun, thus, as it were, depriving him of life. *This was the catastrophe* celebrated in the mysteries, and the aspirant was made to pass fictitiously through the sufferings and death of Osiris.

Here then, we have a brief, but very clear explanation of what is meant by the god of nature. It is the "fecundating and fertilizing power of the sun," and this "immortal principle," being represented by the name Osiris in the Egyptian mysteries, and Osiris and Hiram Abiff being one and the same, it must unqestionably follow, that the "fecundating and fertilizing power of the sun" is the god acknowledged and worshipped by Masonry, under the name of the "G. A. O. T. U.," Supreme Ruler of the Universe, &c., and it is further evident that the words "Lord" and "God" referred to in the Masonic ritual, allude only to this same "immortal principle," or this natural "power of fecundating and fertilizing." This is symbolized in the lodge by the letter "G,"and the supposed destruction of this power by *winter* or by *night* and *darkness*, is represented in the pretended death of the candidate in the Master's degree, as was done in all the "*Mysteries*," This was the philosophy of the ancient sun-worship, and it is the philosophy today in Masonry, as we learn from the foregoing extract; and therefore, without any controversy, the Speculative Masonry of the present day, revived in that London grog-shop, is the old Baal, or sun-worship of the ancients. But we have still stronger testimony on this point.

In the "Traditions of Freemasonry," by Pierson, p. 34, this question of Masonic sun-worship is placed beyond the possibility of a doubt. Pierson says:—

"Bazot tells us in his *Manuel de Franc Macon*, —Manual of Freemasonry—p. 154,that the veneration which Masons entertain for the east confirms an opinion previously announced, that the *religious system of Masonry*"—mark that—"comes from the east, and *has reference* to the *primitive religion* whose first occupation was *the worship of the sun*."

Also in the "Symbolism of Freemasonry," pp. 27, 28:—

"Among the Egyptians, too, the chief deity, Osiris, was but another name for the sun, while his arch-enemy and destroyer, Typhon, was the typification of night and darkness."

And again:—

"Many, indeed all of the Masonic symbols of the present day, can only be thoroughly comprehended and properly appreciated by *this reference to sun-worship.*"

And lastly, in the "Symbolism of Freemasonry," by Mackey, p. 20:—

"One thing at least," he says, "is incapable of refutation, and that is, that we are indebted to the Tyrian Masons for the introduction of the symbol of Hiram Abiff. The idea of the symbol, although modified by the Jewish Masons, is not Jewish in its inception. IT WAS EVIDENTLY BORROWED from THE PAGAN MYSTERIES, where Bacchus, Adonis, Proserpine and a host of other apotheosized beings play the same role that Hiram does in the Masonic Mysteries."

And now, in the face of all this vast accumulation of undisputed Masonic testimony, what other course is there left for us to pursue, but to believe what Freemasonry so confidently affirms concerning its own identity? When the Grand High Priests and the Sovereign Grand Kings of the institution positively declare that its religious philosophy, its worship, and its god, are precisely the very same as existed in the "Mysteries" of Baal, in Samaria, and of Osiris, in ancient Egypt, are we prepared to deny it, and to sustain our denial with proof? Most assuredly not. We must admit, whether we like it or not, that the Freemasonry of America to-day, both in whole and in part, is identical in every particular feature, with the secret worship of the sun-god as it was anciently practiced among pagan nations, the only difference being that the name of the hero-god is changed from Baal, or Osiris, to Hiram Abiff, and hence we must conclude, whether we will, or no, that every Masonic minister is doing as much, if not more, to paganize the community and to introduce men to the idolatrous worship of Hiram, as he is to Christianize it and to bring men to the Lord Jesus Christ.

And, it is a sad commentary on the efficiency or those churches whose ministers are "unequally yoked together with unbelievers," in pagan lodges, that they are spiritually dead, that no genuine revival of true, heartfelt religion, is ever known among them, and consequently that they exert but very little influence for real permanent good in any community where they exist. Search America to-day, and you cannot find a church organization of any name whatever, whose minister is a Freemason, or an Odd-Fellow, but what is, to all intents and purposes, a dead, inactive or lukewarm institution. It is precisely in the condition of the Church in Sardis, and to its minister and members the message of Christ is just as applicable at the present time as it was when first delivered through John in Patmos. Rev. iii, 1,2.

"I know thy works, that thou hast a name that thou livest and art dead. Be watchful, and strengthen the things which remain, that are ready to die: for I have not found thy works perfect before God."

CHAPTER X.

PREPARATION OF CANDIDATES.—Masons ignorant of Masonry.—Guilt of Masonic ministers.—Why lodges meet in "upper chambers."—Purging the lodge.—Initiation in darkness.—The Cable Tow.—"Neither naked nor clad."—"Neither barefoot nor shod."—Floor of the lodge, holy ground.

Mr. Barton:—And now, at last, we have arrived in the ante-room of the lodge, and are prepared to witness how our ministers and church members are made Masons, and to examine in detail the origin and meaning of every ceremony through which the candidate must pass before being permitted to take part in that secret mock-worship which is nightly offered in Masonic lodges to the "G. A. O. T. U." or the "god of nature."

Henry:—But my dear father, in view of all the evidence furnished by the accredited teachers and Grand High Priests of Masonry, there is one thing more I do not understand. If it be true, as it undoubtedly must be, that the Mysteries of Masonry and the "Mysteries of Baal or Osiris" are one and the same, how does it happen that intelligent, well-educated men will remain connected with such a system? Or do they really understand the true nature of the Masonic philosophy, and the source whence it originated?

Mr. Barton:—In answer to your question, my dear Henry, I will at once reply, and without any qualification whatever, that those who know the least about Freemasonry are the Masons themselves. As a general thing they never study it, except once in a while, as they attend lodge, and even then only as the ritual gives expression to its meaning. At home they must always maintain *silence* and *secrecy* on the subject, while in their various places of business and during business hours, even the most intelligent of the craft have neither the time nor inclination to throw away upon the study of what must appear at first sight to be but routine jugglery. Then, again, it must be remembered that the greater part of those who join the lodge do so from the idea that it will sooner or later be of advantage to them, in some way, and hence all they ever learn about it, or, in fact, all they ever care to learn, is what is called the "secret work," or the signs, grips, passwords and lectures, by means of which they can make themselves known as Masons, or visit a strange lodge, when necessary.

But while all this is undoubtedly true, so far as the rank and file of Masonry are concerned, what excuse can be made for the Masonic minister? And what explanation can be given of his inconsistent conduct in not only participating in the mock worship of the lodge himself, but also in encouraging others, by his example, to commit the same sin, as well as by indirectly using his influence to induce outsiders to join that notorious system of deception and folly? A Masonic minister understands the nature and history of the different ceremonies through which he has passed in being made a Mason, or else he does not. If he understands them, and therefore knows that they are pagan in their origin and principle, then it is scarcely possible to find language in which to express his guilt for supporting and propagating such a glaring outrage against God; while at the same time, if he does not understand the real meaning of these ceremonials, then he is equally guilty, because he has all the opportunity and necessary means at his disposal, to become thoroughly informed on the subject. A very slight study of any of the popular Masonic manuals will convince any one, (if he is only open to conviction) that the Masonic philosophy was borrowed directly from the ancient religion of the pagans, and hence on this point none need remain ignorant, except through the most wicked carelessness or neglect.

Let us then continue our further discussion of these different lodge ceremonies, and see what more our Masonic teachers have to say in regard to them.

LODGE MEETINGS IN UPPER ROOMS.

Lodge meetings are always held in the upper rooms of buildings, and the reason for this peculiar custom is therefore the first question which naturally presents itself for our investigation.

Now, why could not a Masonic lodge be opened on the ground floor, or in any other part of a building, except in the uppermost room? The reason, of course, is furnished by our Masonic teachers, and found in the Masonic manuals, and inasmuch as Freemasonry is the *secret* worship of Baal or sabaism *revived*, of course, it necessarily follows that everything pertaining to lodge worship, as well as its peculiar location, must have had its origin in, and be directly borrowed from the "*Ancient Mysteries*." The explanation, therefore, which Freemasonry offers for holding its lodge meetings in the upper rooms of buildings, is given as follows:

In the "General Ahiman Rezon," by Sickles, p. 75, we read:—

"Lodge meetings at the present day are usually held in upper chambers," and the reason for this custom is, that "Before the erection of temples *the celestial bodies were worshiped on hills* and the terresital ones in valleys."

The only reason, therefore, according to Masonic teaching, why lodge meetings are usually held in "upper chambers," is because in ancient times, sabaism, or the worship of the heavenly bodies, was conducted on high hills, or, as the Scriptures call them, "high places."

And as very clearly explaining the term Baal, and this ancient custom of worshiping on high hills as well as the consequent reason for the elevated position of our lodges in modern times, the following extract from the Bible Cyclopedia may be profitably quoted. The writer says:—

"Originally Baal was the *god of the sun*, the ruler and vivifier of nature, and Astarte, the goddess of the moon. In the later star-worship of the Western Asiatic nations, Baal was the name of Jupiter, the planet of fate, or, as some suppose, of Saturn. The proper Phœnician name, however, of Baal was Melkart, Melkrat, or Melchrat, which is usually supposed to mean 'King of the city,' *i. e.* Tyre, but others consider it a contraction of two words signifying 'King of the earth.'"

In Freemasonry, he is called and worshiped as the "Supreme Ruler of the Universe—the Great Architect of the Universe," &c.

"Baal was, perhaps, the same god as the Phœnician Moloch. The Greeks, for the purpose of distinction, termed him the '*Tyrian Hercules.*' (Freemasonry calls him the '*Tyrian Architect.*') From the earliest foundation of Tyre he seems to have been the tutelar god of that city, and his worship apparently extended thence, until it was prevalent in all the towns of the Phœnician Confederation, and was established in their remotest colonies, such as Malta, Cadiz and Carthage. It also overspread the neighboring countries of Egypt and Assyria. Each country, or locality, had its Baal, or chief god. According to Scripture, the temples of this idol (at least in Phœnicia and Assyria) were built on the *tops of hills*, or more frequently in solemn groves, and sometimes altars were erected to *him* on the *roofs of houses.*"

Symbol of High Hills.

The accompanying figure is depicted in all our lodges as representing the "high hills and low vales," where the religious services of Masonry are supposed to have been anciently practiced. In explaining this symbol to the candidate, on the night of his initiation, the following language is used, and, when compared with the above from the Bible Cyclopedia, will give us a further appreciation of the true reason why lodge meetings are always held in upper chambers.

In the "Manual of the Lodge," by Mackey, p. 43, we read:—

"Our ancient brethren met on the highest hills, and in the lowest valleys, the better to observe the approach of cowans and eaves-droppers, and to guard against surprise."

Now, no Mason, however slight may be his knowledge of history, will presume to assert that a Masonic lodge has ever been held on the top of a hill, or in the bottom of a valley, since Freemasonry was revived in 1717. And neither do the Masonic monitors set forth any such foolish notion. On the contrary, it is distinctly affirmed that this is the wrong meaning of the symbol, and that the truth concerning it, points directly to the ancient custom of sun-worship.

On this head, the "Manual of the Lodge," p. 44, declares that:—

"The reason assigned in the lecture for this assembling on high places, is the modern, *but not the true one.* The fact is, that mountains and other high places, were almost always considered as holy and peculiarly appropriate to religious purposes."

So then, because our "ancient brethern,"—the old sun-worshippers—met on the *highest* hills to worship Baal, or the sun-god, and Freemasonry being that same worship *revived*, it must necessarily follow, that Masonic lodges must be held in the highest rooms of buildings, to carry out the coincidence.

Being assembled in the lodge room, then the next ceremony performed is the

PURGING OF THE LODGE,

which is done in the following manner:—

Worshipful Master:—"Bro. Senior Warden, are you satisfied that all present are Masons?"

Senior Warden:—"I will ascertain by my *proper officer*, and report. Bro. Junior Deacon, proceed to satisfy yourself that *all* present are Masons."

The Junior Deacon, taking his rod under his

right arm, proceeds around the lodge room, stopping in front of any brother whom he does not recognize, and rapping with the end of his rod on the floor; that brother, thus challenged, if not vouched for by some well-known member present, must retire into the ante-room and there await (if he sees fit) the action of an examining committee. The Junior Deacon, in this manner, having made the entire circuit of the lodge, returns in front of the Senior Warden's station, and reports to that officer "All present are Masons." (See "Hand Book," p. 17.)

This ceremony, from its great importance, is never omitted, and the reason for its performance is given as follows, by the text-books of Masonry.

In the "Manual of the Lodge," by Mackey, p. 12, we read:—

"In the 'Ancient Mysteries,' (those sacred rites *which have furnished so many models for Masonic symbolism,*)"—mark that—"the opening ceremonies were of the most solemn character. The sacred herald in the 'Ancient Mysteries' commenced the ceremonies of the *greater* INITIATIONS by the solemn formula of '*depart hence, ye profane,*' to which was added a *proclamation*, which forbade the use of any language which might be deemed of unfavorable augury to the approaching rites."

This is precisely what is done in the Masonic lodge, only on a smaller scale. Every one not a Mason is termed "a profane," and the Junior Deacon ordering the "profane," or those not properly vouched for, from the *sacred* precincts of the lodge room, corresponds exactly with the *sacred* herald in the "Mysteries," ordering the profane from the presence of the *greater* INITIATIONS. The ceremonies in both cases are the same, only in Masonry we call the officiating officer Junior Deacon, while in the "Mysteries" he was called "the sacred herald." And as was done in opening the secret worship of the "Mysteries," so also, in opening the same worship in a Masonic lodge, a proclamation by the Worshipful Master is added similar to that made by the "sacred herald."

"Accordingly," he says, "in the name of God and the Holy SS. John, I declare Keystone Lodge, No. 639, opened in form, on the first degree of Masonry, (or the second, or third, as the case may be,) at the same time forbidding all immoral or unmasonic conduct, whereby the peace and harmony of the lodge might be disturbed, binding the offender under no less a penalty than that prescribed by the by-laws, or as a majority of the brethren present may see cause to inflict." (See "Hand Book," p. 26.)

By comparing this with the proclamation added, at the opening of the "*greater initiations*" in the "*Mysteries*," you will find them precisely the same.

THE TYLER.

The brethren being assembled in their lodge room, or "high place," and the lodge being *purged* in the manner already described, the next business is to place the Tyler outside the door "to keep off all cowans and eaves-droppers."

Now, why is there a Tyler placed in that position, and what are his duties.

The use of the word "Tyler," in the Masonic ritual, distinctly marks the birth-place of Grand Lodge, or Speculative Masonry. In England, as a general thing, the houses are roofed with slate, and along the ridge of the roof, tyles are placed to protect, or guard the building from destructive elements, and the mechanic, who puts on these tyles is called a "*Tyler*." In reviving the "Ancient Mysteries," therefore, in the beginning of the last century, and in borrowing the name "Masonry," with which to designate the new philosophy, the "Masonic fathers," also borrowed the term "Tiler," or "Tyler," which they applied to him, who *protects* or *guards* the lodge from ali outward elements dangerous to its pretended secrets. But the *Tyler* is stationed outside the inner door, and armed with a sword, scimitar shape, because a similar officer, performed precisely similar duties, and occupied a like position in the "*Ancient Mysteries*."

In the "Traditions of Freemasonry," by Pierson, p. 31, we read:—

"In every country under heaven, the initiations *i. e.* into the Mysteries, were performed in caverns, either natural, or artificial. The *entrance* to these caverns *was guarded* by a *Janitor*, *armed* with a *drawn sword*, to prevent unlawful intrusion."

This is precisely the reason why a *Tyler* sits

outside the lodge-room door armed with *his* drawn sword.

PREPARATION OF CANDIDATES.

The next business demanding attention in the regular order of lodge "work" is the "preparation" of candidates for "initiation." This is a very important rite, and must be examined thoroughly.

The Hierophant, or Worshipful Master, orders the Junior Deacon to "take with him the stewards, retire, prepare and present the Rev. Dr. James Hunt, for initiation." ("Hand Book," p. 60.)

Accordingly these officers repair to the "preparation room," where the candidate is in waiting, and the ceremony of "preparation" is at once proceeded with.

The candidate is deprived of all offensive and defensive weapons, divested of all his clothing, shirt excepted, and dressed in an old pair of drawers, having bone buttons, if any, as no metallic substance must be allowed on his person.

The whole of these preliminary ceremonies are briefly, but fully described by the Masonic ritual in the following manner. ("Hand Book," pp. 107, 159, 259.

Q.—"How were you prepared to be made a Mason?" *A.*—By being divested of all metals, neither naked nor clad, barefoot nor shod, blindfolded, and with a cable-tow once round my neck,"

In the second, or Fellow Craft degree, the cable-tow is twice round the naked right arm, and in the

Master Mason's degree, it is three times round his body, and both feet, legs, knees and arms are bare. (See p. 84.)

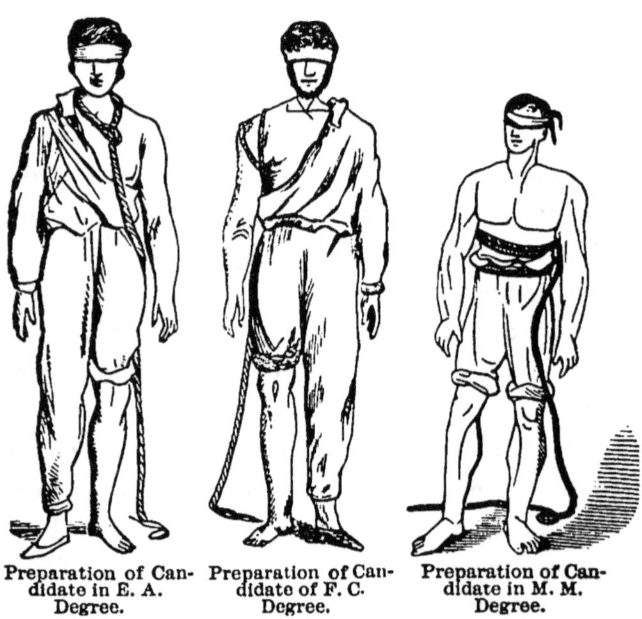

Preparation of Candidate in E. A. Degree. **Preparation of Candidate of F. C. Degree.** **Preparation of Candidate in M. M. Degree.**

The above engravings represent as correctly as can be, the manner of preparing candidates for the Masonic mysteries, and it will be observed in relation thereto that four conditions must always be complied with. First, the candidate must be *initiated in darkness*; second, he must be *invested with a girdle or cable-tow;* third, he must be *neither naked nor clad;* and fourth, he must be *either barefoot*, or else "*neither barefoot nor shod.*" Now what is the meaning of this singular proceeding, and why is it that there can be no deviation from this strange usage? Where did Freemasonry find these "preparation" ceremonies, and what authority is there for their adoption and continued use in all Masonic lodges?

They were all borrowed by the "Masonic fathers" from the old Baal worship of the "Ancient Mysteries," as the following authoritative teaching of Masonry will abundantly testify. We shall examine each one in the order in which they are here enumerated, beginning with the "hoodwink" or

INITIATION IN DARKNESS.

On this head we read in the "Manual of the Lodge," by Mackey, p. 38:—

"In the *Ancient Mysteries* (or *secret worship* of the pagan gods) the aspirant (or candidate) was always kept for a certain period in a condition of darkness. Hence darkness became the symbol of initiation."

Again in Pierson's "Traditions of Freemasonry," p. 31:—

"In every country under heaven the INITIATIONS were performed in caverns, either natural or artificial, and *darkness* was honored with peculiar marks of veneration, by reason of its supposed priority of existence." Again on p. 39:— "The candidate has represented man when he had sunken from his original estate and like the ***rough ashler*** is unfit to form a part of the spiritual temple. He maintained the same character in the *mysteries*. Emphatically *a profane*, *enveloped in darkness*, poor and destitute of spiritual knowledge and emblematically *naked*. The material darkness which is produced by the *hoodwink* is an emblem of the darkness of his soul."

Everywhere the "*Mysteries*" is the model of Masonry. Because candidates were initiated "in a condition of darkness," in "the *secret worship* of the pagan gods," so candidates are initiated "in a condition of darkness" in the mysteries of Masonry, and hence a hoodwink must be used.

And again in the "Symbolism of Freemasonry," by Mackey, p. 155, we read:—

"In all the ancient systems of initiation, (into the Mysteries) the candidate was *shrouded in darkness* as a preparation for the reception of light. The duration varied in the different rites. In the Celtic mysteries of Druidism, the period in which the aspirant was immersed in darkness was nine days and nights; among the Greeks at Eleusis it was three times as long and in the still severer rites of Mithras in Persia, fifty days of darkness, solitude and fasting were imposed upon the adventurous neophyte, who by these excessive trials was at length entitled to the full communication of the light of knowledge."

And on p. 136, he adds, that:—

"Darkness was the symbol of initiation."

The duration of darkness in the Masonic Mysteries, or in the revived form of these old pagan systems, is not quite so severe. The Entered Apprentice is *hoodwinked* for about the space of an hour; the Fellow Craft for about an hour and a-half, while the Master Mason, in the greater, or Sublime Mysteries of Osiris, is compelled to remain in darkness for at least three hours.

And lest any connecting link in the wonderful chain of evidence, binding the "Mysteries of Masonry" and the "Mysteries of Baal" together, might be wanting, the reason why lodge meetings are always held in the night time, is stated as follows:—

In the "Symbolism of Freemasonry," by Mackey, p. 157, we read:—

"Darkness like death, is the symbol of initiation. It was for this reason that *all the ancient initiations were performed at night.* The celebration of the mysteries was always *nocturnal.* The same custom prevails in Freemasonry and the explanation is the same."

This language is so plain that it needs no comment. Because the Osirian Mysteries were celebrated at night, so the Masonic Mysteries must in like manner, be celebrated at night.

And again in the "History of Initiation," by Dr. Oliver, than whom a greater Masonic writer has never lived; on p. 19, we read:—

"There was also another quality of the mind, which served to recommend the *Mysteries*, that strange attachment to the marvellous, by which every grade of human nature is swayed. To excite this sentiment in all its sublimity of horror, the ***initiations were performed at the dead of night.***"

"THE CABLE-TOW."

Our next question is where did Masonry find its "Cable-tow?"

Turning to p. 29 of Pierson's "Traditions of Freemasonry," we find that:—

"In the Mysteries of India," (that is in *the secret worship* of the pagan gods of India,) "the aspirant, (or candidate,) was invested with a consecrated sash, or *girdle*, which he was directed to *wear next his skin*. It was manufactured with many mysterious ceremonies, and said to possess the power of preserving the wearer from *personal danger*. It consisted of a cord composed of *three times three* threads twisted together and fastened at the end with a knot and was called *Zennar*. HENCE COMES OUR CABLE TOW."

Here then, we have it on the very highest Masonic authority that the *Zennar* of the Hindu initiations, and the *cable-tow* of the Masonic initiations are one and the same thing, and their coincident features are so distinctly marked that none can fail to understand their identity. It is said of the Indian *Zennar*, that it was worn *next the skin*; the cable-tow is also worn *next the skin*. The *Zennar* was twisted together, and fastened at the end with a knot; so is the cable-tow, the *Zennar* was composed of *three times three* threads, referring to the cable-tow of the Royal Arch degree, where the question is asked "How do you know yourself to be a Royal Arch Mason? By *three times three*. And lastly it is said of the *Zennar* that it possessed the power of preserving the wearer from *personal danger*, with the words "personal danger," strongly emphasized, doubtless to convey the impression that he who wears the *Zennar*, or *Cable-Tow* of Masonry round his neck, will have a very great many chances of escaping the hangman's rope, and be otherwise aided by Masonic cunning.

"NEITHER NAKED NOR CLAD."

The next point in the "preparation" ceremonies demanding our attention is, why is the candidate "neither naked nor clad?" Why is he divested of his clothing?

By remembering the fact that Freemasonry, as has been proven over and over again, is the old Baal, or secret sun-worship revived, the philosophy of this particular ceremony might appear self-evident. The members of the lodge are engaged in devotional exercises, with the Worshipful Master leading in prayer to the sun-god—the G. A. O. T. U.—or the god of nature. (See pp. 151 to 159.) Now, in order to carry out the true symbolism of the *sun*, and to indicate the wonderful powers and attributes of the god which is worshiped, there is nothing more natural than that the candidate should appear with part of his clothing off. If he was about to be initiated into the secret worship of the god of ice, or cold, if any such existed, he would naturally be warmly muffled up, but being about to be initiated into the *secret worship of the sun-god*, he must be "neitner naked, nor clad." He presents himself in darkness to indicate, that from the sun-god proceeds all light, and so he must present himself semi-nude, to indicate, that from the same sun-god proceeds all warmth and protection.

This is the true symbolic meaning of this ceremony, and it can bear no other construction, for by no other process of reasoning, can the analogy between the various initiatory rites be maintained intact, and the reason offered by Webb for the degrading custom, is as Bro. Mackey expresses it, in his "Manual of the Lodge," "absolutely beneath criticism."

NEITHER BAREFOOT NOR SHOD.

The last of the strangely debasing ceremonies of the Masonic "preparation room" is what Freemasonry terms the *rite of discalceation*, or baring the feet, and, like all the others, has been borrowed directly from the "Ancient Mysteries," or the "Secret Worship" of Baal.

"Symbolism of Freemasonry," by A. G. Mackey, p. 126.

"The direction of Pythagorass to his disciples, was in these words:—'Offer sacrifice and worship with shoes off.'"

"In another place he says:—'We must sacrifice and enter temples with the shoes off.'"

This Pythagoras is claimed by Masonic authorities to have been initiated into the mysteries of Osiris in Egypt, and is highly esteemed among the craft as "an ancient friend and brother."

And again, on p. 127, Mackey says:—

"The Druids practised the same custom whenever they celebrated their sacred rites, and the ancient Peruvians are said laways to have left their shoes at the porch, when they entered tne magnificent temple consecrated to the worship of the sun."

And again, on p. 128:—

"The rite of discalceation, therefore, is a symbol of reverence. It signifies in the language of symbolism that the spot which is about to be approached in this humble and reverential manner, is consecrated to *some holy purpose.*"

This, I think, establishes beyond a question the religious character of Masonry. "The spot" where secular or "profane" societies hold their meetings cannot be very well said to be "consecrated to holy purposes."

Again, on p. 129:—

"And into the Master Mason's lodge—that holy of holies of the Masonic temple * * * * the aspirant should remember, with a due sense of their symbolic application, those words that once broke upon the astonished ears of the old patriarch, 'put off thy shoes from off thy feet, for the place whereon thou standest is *holy ground.*'"

And lastly, in the "Traditions of Freemasonry," by Pierson, p. 29:—

"Among the ancients the ceremony of discalceation, or pulling off a shoe, indicated reverence for the presence of God."

From all this vast accumulation of undisputable evidence, then, it is absolutely undeniable that every ceremony of the "preparation room"—the hoodwink or darkness—the cable-tow—the rite of discalceation—the removal of the clothing—the purging of the lodge—the position, arms and duty of the Tyler, and even the very location of the lodge itself, are borrowed, without the slightest change (except in the names of persons) from the old defunct demon mythology of the pagan world; and yet the Grand High Priests and the Grand Chaplains of this rampant idolatry have the cool assurance to affirm in their manuals, monitors and text books that, after all, Freemasonry is of so sanctified a character that even the "floor of the lodge is holy ground."

Without question, to these men may be very appropriately applied the words of Isaiah, v. 20:—

"Woe unto them that call evil good, and good evil; that put darkness for light, and light for darkness; that put bitter for sweet, and sweet for bitter."

CHAPTER XI.

INITIATORY CEREMONIES.—Pitiable condition of Masonic ministers.—Rite of Induction.—Rite of Circumambulation.—Rite of Secrecy.—Masonic idols.—Masonic penalties.—An idolatrous system.

Mr. Barton:—Behold, now, the candidate—Deacon,Doctor of Divinity, or Jew-peddler—as he stands in the ante-room, "duly and truly prepared to be made a Mason." The "Manual of the Lodge," p. 20, describes him in his present unenviable position, as follows:—

"There he stands, without our portals, on the threshold of his new Masonic life, *in darkness, helplessness and ignorance.* Having been wandering *amid the errors*, and covered over with the pollutions of the outer and profane world, *he comes enquiringly to our door*, seeking the new birth."

This, under any circumstances, is a most lamentable picture of a minister of the gospel, however suitable the humiliating description might be to a rumseller or dancing-master, and yet, strange as it may appear, he acknowledges that every word of it is literally true.

The Junior Deacon leads him forward, and, taking him by the right hand, causes him to close his fist and with his knuckles to give three loud and distinct knocks upon the door. The Senior Deacon from within is sent to ascertain who gives the alarm, and, when he opens the door, demands in a loud voice, and somewhat sternly, "Who comes here?"

The ministerial candidate, not knowing, of course, what suitable reply to make, the Junior Deacon, who, perhaps, is a Jew, or a scoffer at the very religion which this same minister preaches, answers for him, that he is "the Rev. Dr. James Hunt, who *has long been iu darkness* and now seeks to be brought to light."

The figure on the previous page is a true representation of the candidate, as he stands in the open doorway of the lodge, and thus tremblingly acknowledges his past and present condition of spiritual ignorance and mental and moral blindness. Inside, and regarding him with the closest attention, are infidels, Jews, rationalists, profane swearers, rum-sellers and rum-drinkers, and yet in the presence of them all, this man, who is the pastor of a church, publicly confesses that all along he has occupied a false position; that his Christianity has been an utter failure; that up to the present moment he has been wandering in darkness and "covered over with the pollutions of the outward and profane world," and that now, at last, he comes to seek and to receive the true "light of divine truth," as it is imparted, for a certain cash value, in a Masonic lodge room. Now this voluntary confession on the part of this Masonic Minister is either true or false. If true, then most unquestionably he is a hypocrite in the church, and ought either to resign or be suspended from the ministry; while, if it be false, then it is equally certain that he is attempting to become a Mason under false pretences, and consequently must be a hypocrite in the lodge, and ought at once to be expelled from the order.

But while the Junior Deacon answers for the candidate at the door, he must answer for himself during all time to come, and in precisely the very same words, as will be seen from the following portion of the ritual: ("Hand book," p. 108.)

Q. "Being hoodwinked, how did you know it to be a door?"

A. "By first meeting with resistance, and afterwards gaining admission."

Q. "How gained you admission?"

A. "By three distinct knocks from without, answered by a like number from within."

Q. "What was said to you from within?"

A. "Who comes here?"

Q. "Your answer?" (And now observe carefully the minister's reply:)

I. "I, James Hunt, *who have long been in darkness*. and now seek to be brought to light."

Now, if this confession be literally true, the candidate who makes it cannot possibly be a Christian at the time, while, if it be not true, it is equally evident that no truly pious Christian would even think of uttering such a wicked falsehood; and hence the inevitable conclusion is that no man can be a true Christian and a true Mason at one and the same time.

Well, after a while the candidate is admitted "in the name of the Lord," and then the initiatory ceremonies at once begin. These consist of six distinct and separate *rites*, namely, the "rite of induction"—"rite of circumambulation"—"rite of secrecy"—"rite of illumination"—"rite of intrusting"—and "rite of investiture," and like all the preceding ceremonies of the "preparation room," every one of these different rites without a single exception, has been "*revived*" from the "Ancient Mysteries," and are precisely the very same, and performed, too, in the very self-same manner, as were practiced in the secret worship of Baal, when Ahab fed from Jezebel's table those priests, or Worshipful Masters, who promulgated that wicked philosophy. In establishing this fact, the teachers of Masonry seem to be uncompromising. They will have it that the Masonic system and the system of religion inculcated in the "ancient initiations," or secret worship of the sun-god, are identical in every feature, and hence they describe these various initiatory rites of Masonry so clearly, and refer to the manner in which they were formerly practiced with such minute accuracy, that none can fail to understand their meaning. This will appear self-evident as we proceed with our investigation.

RITE OF INDUCTION.

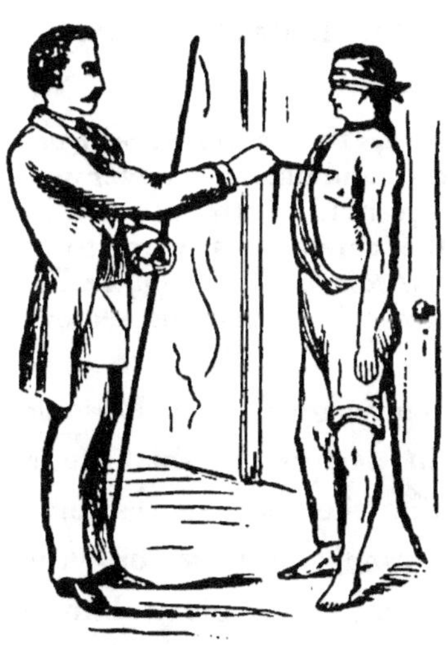

When the candidate is led into the Lodge room, by the Junior Deacon, he is met inside the door and about six feet from it, by the Senior Deacon, who presses the sharp point of an iron Compass to his "nk ed left breast," and thus while he repeats the following formula, performs the "rite of induction."

Senior Deacon:—"Dr. James Hunt, on your first admission into a lodge of Masons, it becomes my duty to receive you upon the point of a sharp instrument, pressing your naked left breast," (he then presses the sharp point of the Compass a little harder against the naked breast,) "the moral of which is to teach you, that as this is an instrument of torture to the flesh, so should the recollection thereof be to your mind and conscience, should you ever presume to reveal any of the secrets of Freemasonry unlawfully." "Hand Book," pp. 63, 64.

The figure on p. 265 represents the Senior Deacon and candidate as this ceremony is being performed; and its true origin, and the reason assigned for its performance in the lodge, is given by Masonry as follows:—

In the "Manual of the Lodge," by A. G. Mackey, p. 39, I read:—

"In the ancient initiation, (that is the ***secret worship*** of the pagan gods,) the candidate was never permitted to enter on the threshold of the temple, or sacred cavern in which the ceremonies were to be conducted, until, by the ***most solemn warning***, ***he had been impressed with the necessity*** of caution, secrecy and fortitude."

By referring to the language of the Masonic ritual, as before quoted, in performing this rite, it will at once be observed that the very same "solemn warning" is given the candidate now on "the threshold" of the lodge room, as was given him in ancient times on the "threshold of the sacred caverns," where the initiations into the "Mysteries" were conducted, and that in fact this particular Masonic "rite of induction" has been "revived" from that ***ancient secret worship*** without a single change.

Again in Pierson's "Traditions of Freemasonry," p. 31:—

"The probation of a candidate in ancient times" —*i. e.* in the "Mysteries"—"embraced many important particulars; but principally his fortitude and constancy were severely tried by the application of—sometimes an iron instrument, heated red—hot—at others, the point of a sword or *other sharp instrument, while he himself was deprived of all means of defense and protection.*"

This is precisely what is done in a Masonic lodge. The candidate—deprived of all means of defense or protection—is received on the "point of a sword," (as in English lodges,) "or other sharp instrument," and this act, when coupled with the "solemn warning," contained in the formula used by the Senior Deacon, completes this Masonic ceremony, just as it used to be practiced in the "Mysteries."

But the celebrated Masonic writer, Dr. George Oliver, in describing the Persian initiation of the "Mysteries," places the origin of this *rite of induction* beyond a question. He says, in his "History of Initiation," p. 68, that:—

"The successful probationer, at the expiration of his novitate, was brought forth into the cayern of initiation where he *entered on the point of a sword presented to his naked left breast* by which he was slightly wounded, and then he was ritually prepared for the approaching ceremony."

In this extract, we have not only a literal description of the "rite of induction," as it was performed in the old Persian Mysteries and elsewhere, but it also contains a correct account of the manner in which candidates for these "Mysteries," used to be prepared for initiation, and proves, with almost infallible certainty, that the ceremonies of the Masonic lodge, and especially this particular "rite," have been directly borrowed from that idolatrous worship.

RITE OF CIRCUMAMBULATION.

The next ceremony through which the candidate is made to pass is called the "rite of circumambulation," or the "symbolic pilgrimage" in search of light. Before entering upon this dark and fruitless journey, however, two important preliminaries must always be observed—he must kneel, that prayer may be offered for him to the "G. A. O. T. U.," by some infidel, or saloon-keeper, and while kneeling he must also publicly acknowledge his confidence in the god of the lodge, as he has already at the door publicly declared the uselessness of faith in the God of the Bible.

This prayer and confession of faith have already been discussed on pages 164 and 166, and need not be further referred to here, except merely to add that ths Worshipful Master "takes him by the right hand, orders him to arise, follow his conductor, and fear no danger."

The Senior Deacon now takes him by the right arm, as you see in the accompanying figure, and conducts him *once* round the lodge room in the first degree, *twice* round in the second degree, and *three times* round the lodge in the third degree; the Master, or Chaplain, in the meantime reading Psalm 133, Amos vii. 7, 8, and Eccles. xii., respectively.

The dotted lines in the figure on the following page represent the course they pursue. Starting at the point A, where the candidate has been kneeling, they pass towards the East, and thence by way of the South to the West, and so round by the North to the East again, stopping in front of the Junior Warden's station in the South at B. This is termed the "rite of the symbolic pilgrimage," or "rite of circumambulation," and its origin is accouned for as follows, by the manuals and text books of the order.

In the "Manual of the Lodge," by Mackey, p. 24, we read:—

"The *circumambulation* among the pagan nations

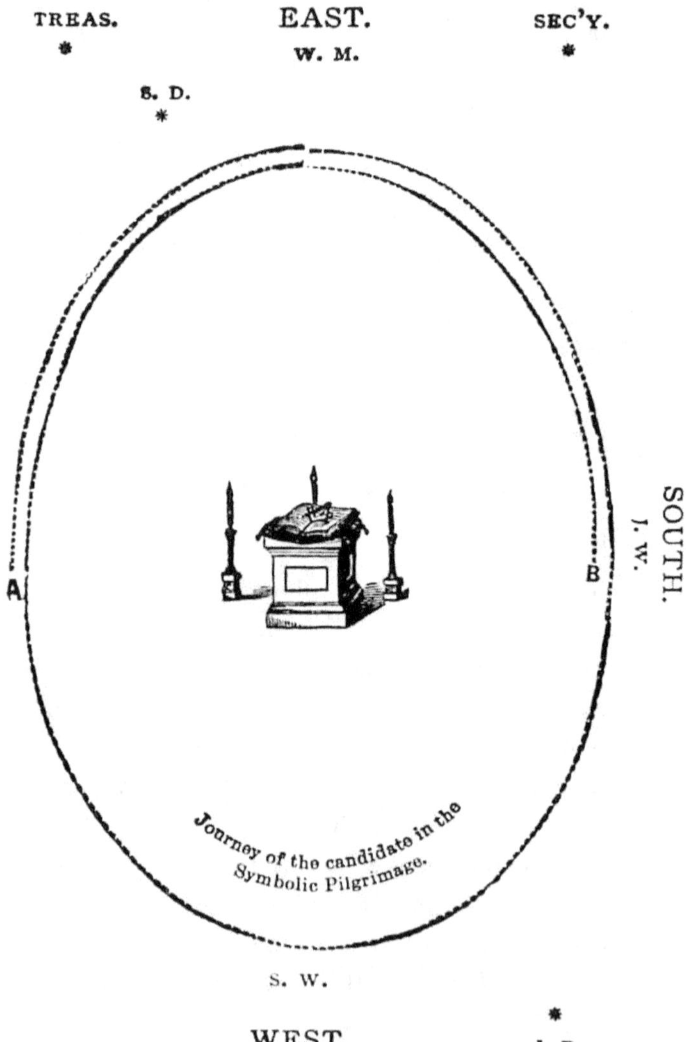
TREAS.
EAST.
W. M.
SEC'Y.
S. D.
A
B
SOUTH.
J. W.
Journey of the candidate in the Symbolic Pilgrimage.
S. W.
WEST.
J. D.

referred to the great doctrine of Sabaism, or sun-worship. Freemasonry *alone has preserved the primitive meaning*, which was a symbolic allusion to the sun, as the source of physical light and the most wonderful work of the 'Grand Architect of the Universe.' The lodge represents the world; the three principal officers represent the sun in her three principal positions—at rising, at meridian, and at setting. The *circumambulation*, therefore, alludes to the apparent course of the solar orb, through these points around the world."

This proves beyond the shadow of a doubt, that Masonry is the religious philosophy of the old Baal, or sun-worshipers, *revived*, and that the sun-god is constantly referred to in this, as in all the other ceremonies of initiation.

Again, in Pierson's "Traditions," p. 32:—

"In the rite of circumambulation, we find another ceremony *borrowed* from the ancient Freemasonry, that was practiced in the MYSTERIES. In ancient Greece, when the priests were engaged in the rite of sacrifice, they and the people always 'walked' three times round the altar, while singing a sacred hymn. In making this procession, great care was taken to move in imitation of the course of the sun. For this purpose, they commenced at the east, and passing by the way of the south to the west, and thence by the north, they arrived at the east again."

This is an exact description of the Masonic "rite of circumambulation," and in the absence of any further testimony, even, is sufficient of itself to establish the identity of Freemasonry, with the "Ancient Mysteries," or the "secret worship" of Baal or the sun-god.

Again, on the same page, we read:—

"Among the Romans, also, the rite of circumambulation was always used in the rites of sacrifice of expiation, or purification."

And again, on p. 33:—

"Among the Hindoos, the same rite of circumambulation has always been practiced. A Brahmin, upon rising from bed in the morning, having first adored the sun, while directing his face to the East, then walks toward the West, by the way of the South, saying at the same time, 'I follow the course of the sun.' The same ceremony was in use in the Druidical rites. The priests always made three circuits from east to west, by the right hand around the altar, accompanied by all the worshipers."

And, Mr. Grand Captain General Pierson, in explaining the number of revolutions to be made, and the particular line of march which the candidate must pursue, explains very clearly the true import and the origin of this particular rite. He says,

In the "Traditions of Freemasonry," p. 33:—

"It will be well for the Masonic student, in tracing out these analogies,"—*i. e.* the analogies between Freemasonry and the Ancient Mysteries,—"to constantly bear in mind that in the 'rite of circumambulation' the number of revolutions may, and does vary, according to different contingencies, although, of course, the number *three* is most important as a mystic and sacred number, but that *at all times the ceremony must be performed with the course of the sun*, turning to the *right*, and having the *altar* on the *right* hand."

This is precisely the manner, as will be seen from the above figure, in which this particular rite is performed now, and from the minute description given of it as it existed in the secret worship of Baal, it will be observed at once, how anxious our Masonic teachers are to prove that it has been *revived* without any material change, and that it occupies the very self-same position to-day in Freemasonry that it formerly did in the "Ancient Mysteries."

"RITE OF SECRECY."

The next ceremony demanding our attention is the *rite of secrecy*, which is performed in the following manner:

The candidate having passed through the rite of the "symbolic pilgrimage," and having made the same public confession before the three principal officers of the lodge, in the South, West and East respectively, as he made at the door, he is ordered by the Worshipful Master, or "Chief Hierophant," to be reconducted to the Senior Warden in the West, where he is taught how to approach the East, by *one*, *two*, or *three*, upright regular steps, as the case may be, and then caused to kneel at the *altar* in "*due form.*"

The figure on next page represents the candidate in this "*due form*" in the Entered Apprentice degree kneeling on his naked left knee, his right forming a square, his left hand supporting the Holy Bible, Square and Compass, and his right resting thereon, in which due form he takes the obligation of a

Mason, and which constitutes the "rite of secrecy." Before him stands the Worshipful Master, administering the obligation, and behind him the Senior Deacon or Conductor. (See "Hand-Book," p. 73.)

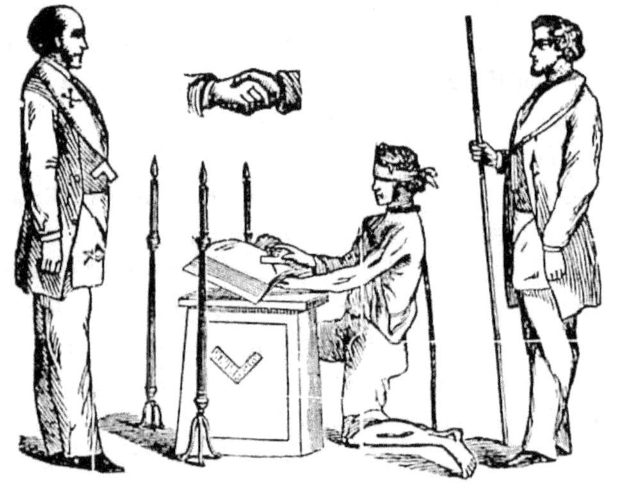

Rite of Secrecy and Goddess Fides.

The "due form," of course, like the "rite of induction" and the "rite of circumambulation," varies in the different degrees, and is correctly represented in the two remaining figures on page 280.

And now what is the origin of this ceremony? And why are Masonic candidates sworn, and in this peculiar manner?

The "Freemason's Guide," by Sickles, p. 62, gives us the reason in the following language:

"Among the ancients—*i. e.* in the Mysteries—

silence and *secrecy* were considered virtues of the highest order. The Egyptians worshiped Harpocrates, the god of secrecy, raised altars in his name, and wreathed them with garlands of flowers. Among the ancient Romans, too, these virtues were not less esteemed, and a distinguished Latin poet tells us, 'for faithful silence also there is a sure reward.'"

But in performing this "rite of secrecy," it will be remembered, and also may be noticed from the figure on the opposite page, that the candidate must always face the east and place his right hand upon the Bible, Square and Compass; and in explaining this ceremony, the Masonic authors refer to these two peculiar features of the rite as identifying it, beyond the possibility of a doubt, with similar customs which prevailed in the old Baal worship.

"Traditions of Freemasonry," by Pierson, p. 34:

"An oath taken with the face toward the east"—*i. e.* in the mysteries—"was deemed more solemn and binding than when taken with the face toward any other cardinal point."

In the "General Ahiman Rezon," by Sickles, p. 73, we read:—

"The right hand has in all ages been deemed an emblem of fidelity and the ancients worshiped deity under the name *Fides*, or Fidelity, which was sometimes represented by two right hands joined and sometimes by two human figures holding each other by the right hand." (See "Hand Book," p. 89.)

In the engraving on p. 274, illustrating this particular rite, a small figure will be noticed at the top—"two right hands joined." This represents Fides, *the goddess of secrecy*, as this idol is displayed in every Masonic lodge and chart and manual of any note in the world.

The accompanying figure also of "two human figures holding each other by the right hand," to which the above ritual refers, is another representation of the god of secrecy, and is copied from "Webb's Monitor," by Dr. Robert Morris.

Past Grand Master Pierson in his "Traditions," *p.* 37, in explaining the use of the right hand in the Masonic obligations refers to this idol as follows:

"The temple of this goddess (*Fides*) was first consecrated by Numa, and when they promised anything of old they gave the right hand to pledge it, as we do, therefore she is represented as giving her right hand and sometimes her two hands conjoined. Chartarius," he says "more fully describes this by observing that the proper residence of faith or fidelity was thought by the ancients to be in the right hand. And therefore, this diety was sometimes represented by two right hands joined."

And in the "Manual of the Lodge," by Mackey, p. 41, we read:—

"Numa was the first who erected an altar to Fides, under which name the goddess of *oaths* and honesty, was worshipped. Obligations taken in HER

NAME, were considered as more inviolable than any other."

And so Freemasonry has not only "borrowed" or "revived" the *rite of secrecy* from the "Ancient Mysteries" of Baal, but it has actually borrowed, and regards with religious veneration, the idol goddess, in whose name the obligations, or oaths of secrecy were always administered.

THE MASONIC PENALTIES.

But there is another peculiar feature of the rite of secrecy, to which all our Masonic writers very minutely refer as connecting it even still more closely with the "Ancient Mysteries" of pagan worship.

Attached to every Masonic obligation, is a most terrible and barbarous death penalty. In the first degree, it is to have the throat cut across, and the tongue torn out by its roots; in the second, it is to have the left breast torn open, and the heart plucked out, and in the Master Mason's degree, it is to have the body *severed* in twain, the bowels taken *from thence and burned to ashes.* These horrible penalties, under which every Masonic candidate must bind himself for the disclosure of a stupid, foolish sign, or grip of the thumb on a particular knuckle, are too revolting to demand any comment, and as a celebrated Chicago detective, himself once a Mason, truthfully expresses it, "are but simply the wicked consummation of outrageous brutality."

But why are these sanguinary penalties attached to the Masonic degrees? And why are Masonic candidates bound by such abominable imprecations?

We find the answer as usual in the text books and manuals of the lodge.

In the "Traditions of Freemasonry," by Pierson, p. 35, we read:—

"A most solemn method of confirming an oath *i. e.* in the "Mysteries," was by *placing a drawn sword across the throat* of the person to whom it was administered, and invoking heaven, earth and sea to witness the ratification. Among the Druids it was a necessary duty of the bards to *unsheath the sword* against those who had forfeited their obligation by divulging any of the secrets of the order. In this respect, their custom was the same as that of all other nations."

The italics in these extracts are Pierson's own, and are evidently intended to terrify the Masonic reader into the belief, that he in like manner forfeits his life should he ever dare to divulge any of the buffoon jugglery of the lodge.

And lastly, in describing the "secret initiations of Greece," the venerable Dr. Oliver, in his "History of Initiation, p. 82, gives a clearer insight, perhaps, than any hitherto furnished, for the reason why Masonic obligations are administered, and why death penalties are attached:—

"These rites, he says, "were known under the high and significent appellation of *the Mysteries*, and even in them a sub-division had been made, because it was thought dangerous to entrust the ineffable secrets to any but a select and chosen few, who were prepared for a new accession of knowledge by processes at once seductive and austere, and *bound to secrecy* by FEARFUL OATHS and *penalties* of the most sanguinary character. Death shall be his penalty, who divulges the mysteries."

From all the foregoing Masonic testimony then, we learn two undeniable facts: First, that every rite and ceremony of the lodge room, so far, has been wholly and literally revived from the "Ancient Mysteries," and second, that all the so-called oaths of Masonry, the mode of their administration, the position, or *due form* in which they must be assumed the fearful sanguinary death penalties attached to each, and even the very images of the *idol* in whose name these obligations are taken, are simply so many pagan customs, borrowed from the secret worship of Baal, by the "Masonic fathers" during the period from 1717 to 1738, and therefore, without entering further into any lengthened argument against the legality, or validity of these obligations, it will at once be apparent to every honest mind, that being sinful and idolatrous from beginning to end, they not only are not binding on the conscience of any candidate, but that the very fact of assuming such horrid oaths from the first, was a gross violation of the law of God, and ought at once to be repented of.

In assuming the oligation in the Fellow Craft degree, the candidate has his right hand on the

Bible, Square and Compass, and his left forming a right angle as in Fig. 2, while in the Master's and all subsequent degrees, both hands rest upon the "three great lights" as represented in Fig. 3.

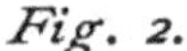

Fig. 2.

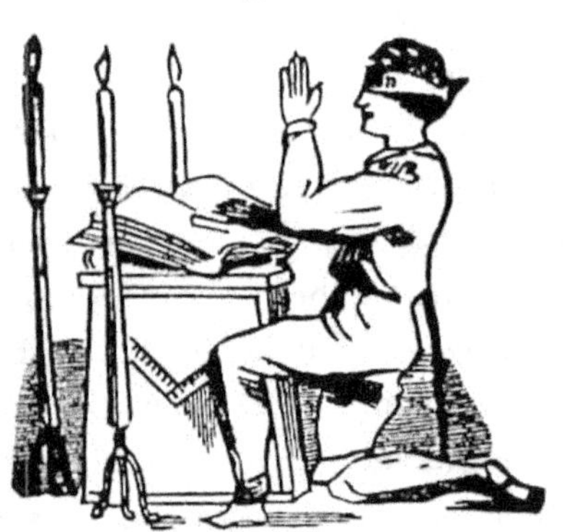

Fig. 3.

CHAPTER XII.

Rite of Illumination.—Virtues of a hoodwink.—Rite of Intrusting.— Rite of Investiture.—Masonry undoubtedly the worship of Baal.

The initiatory ceremonies of Freemasonry, in any of its degrees, might be properly divided into three separate periods: First, the period of *preparation* in the ante-room, concluding with the admission of the candidate into the lodge; secondly, the period of *darkness* and *gloom*, or the *hoodwink period*, during which, the first three religious rites of "Induction," "Circumambulation," and "Secrecy," are performed, and lastly, the period of *light* embracing the three remaining ceremonies of "Illumination," "Intrusting," and "Investiture," and during which also, the pretended secrets of the order are communicated to the candidate, and the symbolic philosophy of the system is explained. We are now entering upon a discussion of the ceremonies and symbols of the last period.

"RITE OF ILLUMINATION."

The "rite of secrecy" being concluded, as already described, and the initiate having been kept during all this time, in a wretched condition of darkness, symbolizing the darkness of his mind, to which he has several times already made public confession, he has now arrived at that particular stage in the initiatory ceremonies when he must be Masonically restored to light, which is done in the following manner:—

The Worshipful Master resumes his hat, and stepping back a few paces, demands of the candidate· "Bro. Hunt, in your present condition, what do you most desire?"

The newly obligated minister, prompted by the Senior Deacon, very mildly answers, "Light in Masonry."

The Master then continues, in a sort of serio-comic tone: "Bro. Senior Deacon and brethren, stretch forth your hands, and assist me in bringing this brother from darkness to light in Masonry. In the beginning, God created the heavens and the earth, and the earth was without form, and void, and darkness was upon the face of the deep, and the Spirit of God moved upon the face of the waters; and God said: Let there be light, and there was light. And now, in humble commemoration of which ancient events, I Masonically say: Let there be light." ("Hand Book, p," 76.)

Just as this word "light" is pronounced by the Master, both himself and all the brethren, whc are arranged in two rows on either side of the altar, bring their hands in front of the body to the due-

guard of a Mason, as represented in the annexed figure; at the same time the Senior Deacon, who is standing behind the candidate, swiftly snatches the hoodwink from off his eyes, and the Master concludes: "and there is light."

In some lodges at the word "light" the Master and brethren clap their hands and stamp loudly on the floor, representing a shock, and hence, this ceremony is sometimes also called "the shock of enlightenment."

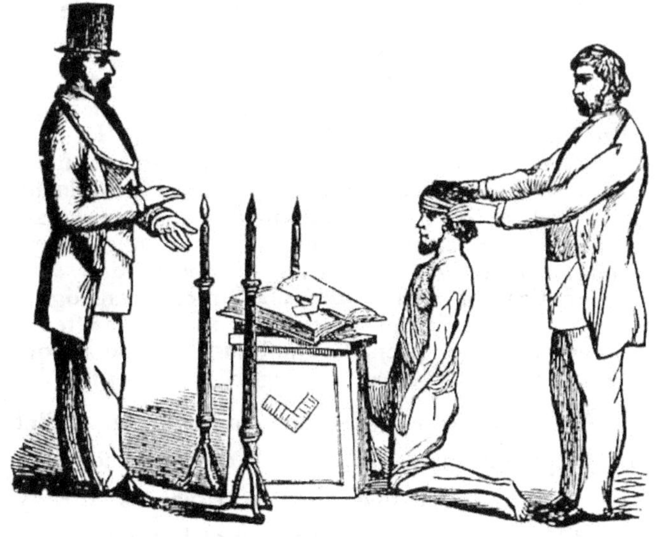

The above figure correctly represents the performance of this wonderful Masonic ceremony. The

Worshipful Master in front of the candidate under the due-guard of a Mason—the Senior Deacon behind him, snatching off the hoodwink, the altar before him, the Holy Bible, Square and Compass, the three burning tapers, and last of all, himself, a half naked, shivering wretched forsworn sinner.

And now, our next inquiry must be, whence did this ceremony come? And why has it a location and a name in the Masonic system? We are authoritatively answered, as usual, by the accredited teachers of the lodge.

In the "Freemason's Guide," by Sickles, p. 64, we read:—

THE RITE OF ILLUMINATION is a very ancient ceremony, and constitutes an important feature *in all the mysteries* of the early ages. In the Egyptian, Cabirian, Sidonian, Eleusinian, Scandinavian and Druidical *rituals* it held a prominent place, and in them all represented the same ideas. It marked the termination of the mystic pilgrimage through gloom and night, (or darkness,) and was emblematical of that moral and intellectual light, which pours its divine radiance on the mind after it has conquered the prejudice, and passion, and ignorance, with which it has so long been struggling."

And Dr. Albert G. Mackey, in finding a parellel for the pretended demand of the candidate for Masonic light, as explained in the ritual, as already quoted, declares in his "Symbolism of Freemasonry," p. 149:—

"He craves an *intellectual illumination*, which

will dispel the darkness of mental and moral ignorance, and bring to his view, as an eye-witness, the *sublime truths of religion*, philosophy and science, which it is the great *design of Freemasonry to teach*. In all the *ancient systems*, this reverence for light, as the symbol of truth, was predominent in the mysteries of every nation; the candidate was made to pass through scenes of utter *darkness*, and at length terminated his trials by an admission to the splendidly illuminated sacellum, or sanctuary, where he was said to have attained pure and perfect light, and where he received the necessary instructions, which were to invest him with that knowledge of the divine truth, which it had been the object of all his labors to gain, and the design of the institution into which he had been *initiated* to bestow."

From this description, we are enabled to form a pretty accurate idea of the very high estimation in which this particular ceremony was formerly held in the "Ancient Mysteries," and the wonderful benefits so boastingly claimed for it in the Masonic system, are fully set forth in the following brief extract from the lodge Manual.

In the "Freemason's Guide," by Sickles, p. 63, we read:—

"The material light which is thus afforded him is *succeeded* by an *intellectual illumination* which serves to enlighten his path on the journey from this world to the next." And Past Grand Master Mackey adds that this "rite of illumination," or 'shock of enlightenment,' "is a symbol of the birth of intellectual light and the dispersion of intellectual darkness." "Manual of the Lodge," p. 29, 30.

What an extraordinary ceremony this pagan rite of illumination is, to be sure! And what astonishing virtue there is in an old hoodwink after all! Why, it is a hundred fold better than anything to be found in the Romish Church, with all her boasted apostolical succession and pretended sanctity. In Romanism a man must go to confession quite often and get the priest's absolution, he must do a large amount of fasting — use immense quantities of holy water, walk on his knees from image to image in the chapel, doing penance, pay at least from nine to a dozen visits to the most popular Churches in any of our large cities, saying so many prayers at each, to secure a few years' indulgence from the Pope, wear charms, beads, crosses, agnes deii and a host of other silly trinkets on his person, and when dying, he must have holy oil rubbed on his body, with the priest's thumb, and all this to "enlighten his path on his journey from this world to the next." But pshaw! That's all miserable superstition! Let him only go into a Masonic lodge, dressed in an old pair of drawers, a slipper, a hoodwink, a cable-tow and with nearly one-half his body naked, and let him trot round there for an hour or so, like a schoolboy playing at blind-man's-buff, and then, when the old hoodwink is removed, he becomes "intellectually illuminated," his mind becomes thoroughly enlightened, the darkness of his soul is all dispelled, the "new birth" is fully accomplished and do what he will thereafter, except to secede from Masonry, he has secured for himself a safe passport to the "Grand Lodge above." And yet, with all this, we are positively assured by our Masonic teachers, as in the above quotation, that this ceremony of the "shock of enlightenment" has been wholly borrowed from the secret worship of the "Ancient Mysteries."

"Pah! 'Tis rank! It smells to heaven."

RITE OF INTRUSTING.

The "rite of intrusting" next demands our attention and is performed as follows: The hoodwink being removed, as above explained, and the "shock of enlightenment" completed with all its intellectual accompaniments, the Worshipful Master approaches the altar, before which the candidate is still kneeling, and points out to him the *three great* and the *three lesser lights* as already explained (on page 133). He then steps back a few paces and advancing again towards the altar, by "one upright regular step" with his left foot, brings the heel of the right foot to the hollow of the left, forming what Masonry very scientifically calls "the angle of an oblong square," making at the same time the due-guard and sign of a Mason. ("Hand Book," p. 39.)

He then approaches the altar a second time, and taking the candidate by the right hand as in ordinary hand shaking *entrusts* him with the wonderful secrets of this degree as follows:—

"Bro. Hunt," he says "in token of friendship and brotherly love, I have now the pleasure of presenting you with my right hand, and with it the *grip* and *word* of an Entered Apprentice Mason, but as you are yet uninstructed, brother Senior Deacon will answer for you."

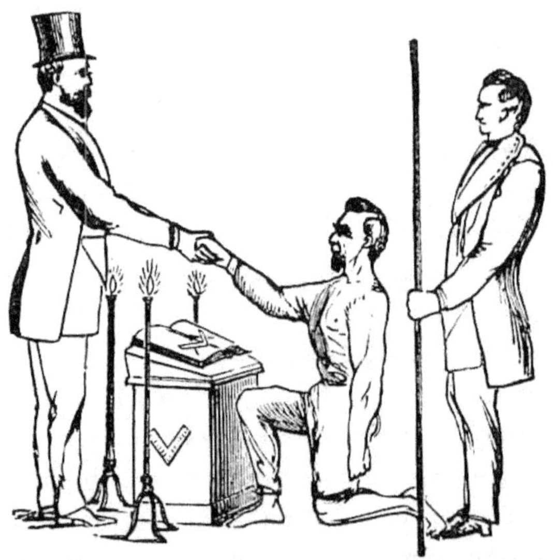

Q.—I hail. *A.*—I conceal. *Q.*—What do you conceal? *A.*—All the secrets of Masons in Masonry to which this token alludes. *Q.*—What is this? (pressing his thumb-nail on the first knuckle.) *A.*—The grip of an Entered Apprentice Mason. *Q.*—Has it a name? *A.*—It has. *Q.*—Will you give it to me? *A.*—I did not so receive it, neither will I so impart it. *Q.*—How will you dispose of it? *A.*—I will letter and syllable it. *Q.*—Letter it and begin. *A.*—Begin you. *Q.*—Nay you must begin.

Senior Deacon:—*A.*
Worshipful Master:—*B.*
Senior Deacon:—*O.*
Worshipful Master:—*Z.*
Senior Deacon:—*Az.*
Worshipful Master:—*Bo.*
Senior Deacon:—*Boaz.*

This constitutes the "rite of intrusting," and is correctly represented in the figure on p. 288. What a very dignified position this is for a Doctor of Divinity to occupy! And how exceedingly intellectual it must be to go over all the foregoing miserable stuff in a Masonic lodge room, with a saloon keeper, or gambler!

And now let us hear what Freemasonry teaches in regard to the antiquity of this *rite*, and what explanation it gives of its present position as a Masonic ceremony of vast importance.

In the "Symbolism of Freemasonry," by Mackey, p. 147, we read:—

"The *rite of intrusting*, to which we are now to direct our attention, will supply us with many important and interesting symbols. There is an important period in the ceremony of Masonic initiation, when the candidate is about to receive a full communication of the mysteries through which he has passed, and to which the trials and labors which he has undergone can only entitle him. This ceremony is technically called the *rite of intrusting*, because it is then that the aspirant begins to be intrusted with that for the possession of which he was seeking. IT IS EQUIVALENT TO WHAT IN THE ANCIENT MYSTERIES WAS CALLED *the autopsy*, or the seeing of what only the initiated were permitted to behold."

Thus, it will be noticed, we are not left in any doubt as to the origin of this rite. In the "Ancient Mysteries," or secret worship of the "sun-god," it occupied the same position that it does in Freemasonry to-day.

But hear again what General Grand High Priest Mackey says on p. 148:—

"This *rite of intrusting* is of course divided into several parts or periods, for the *aporreta*, or secret things of Masonry, are not to be given at once, but in gradual progression. It begins, however, with the communication of LIGHT, which, although but a preparation for the development of the mysteries, which are to follow, must be considered as one of the most important symbols in the whole science of Masonic Symbolism."

And again, on p. 149, he further explains:—

"In all the Ancient Mysteries this reverence for *light* as the symbol of truth was predominant. Light was in accordance with this old religious sentiment, the great object of attainment in all the Ancient (religious) Mysteries."

But Dr. Oliver, perhaps more than any other Masonic writer of modern times, has given the best description of the mode of initiation into the "Mysteries," the internal arrangement of the caverns in which the ceremonies were performed, the positions of the various officers in conferring the degrees, and especially the important part which this identical "rite of intrusting" was made to occupy in those "ancient secret initiations." He relates in his "History of Initiation," p. 74, in describing the "Mysteries of Persia," and the inner cavern where the secrets or aporreta were communicated, that:—

"This consecrated place was brilliantly illuminated and sparkled with gold and precious stones. A splendid sun and starry system emitted their dazzling radiance and moved in order to the symphonies of heavenly music. Here sat the Archimagus *in the east*, elevated on a throne of burnished gold, crowned with a rich diadem, decorated with myrtle boughs, and habited in a flowing tunic of bright cerulean tincture; round him were arranged, in solemn order, the Presules, or dispensers of the Mysteries, forming altogether a reverend assembly, which covered the awe-struck aspirant with profound feelings of veneration, and by an involuntary impulse, frequently produced an act of worship. Here he was received with congratulations, and after having entered into the usual engagements for keeping secret the sacred rites of Mithras, the sacred WORDS were *intrusted* to him, of which the ineffable Tetractys, or name of God, was the chief."

This is an exact representation of the interior of any of our aristocratic lodges of Freemasonry at the present time, with the single exception of the ornamentation of gold and precious stones.

In the "Archimagus seated in the East," and gorgeously attired, we find the prototype of our own

Worshipful Master, clothed in his gaudy regalia, and occupying a similar station in the Masonic lodge. "The Presules, or dispensers of the Sacred Mysteries," are aptly represented by the Wardens and Deacons, "the splendid sun and starry system" are reproduced by the illuminated figure of the sun, displayed behind the Master's chair, and by the clouded canopy decked with stars, which adorns the ceilings of our lodge rooms. The "congratulations" on being admitted; the solemn engagements to keep secret the sacred mysteries, and lastly the ***intrusting*** of the ***sacred words*** after the obligation of secrecy had been administered, are all as faithfully represented to-day in any well-governed lodge of Masons in the United States, as they ever were in the brilliantly lighted ***sacellum*** of the ancient Persian, or Egyptian initiations.

"RITE OF INVESTITURE."

The last ***rite*** of the Masonic initiatiory ceremonies, and the one which next demands our attention is called the "RITE OF INVESTITURE."

The candidate having received the ***new birth*** in the ***rite of illumination***, and having been mentally and morally enlightened through the "***rite of intrusting***," he is now presented with the *lamb-skin*, or WHITE LEATHER APRON, and this presentation of the apron, and teaching him how to wear it, is called the "***rite of investiture.***"

The annexed engraving represents the Worshipful Master presenting the candidate with "lamb-skin apron," and which he orders him to carry to the Senior Warden in the West, who in showing him how to wear it uses the following formula. "Hand Book," p. 82.

Senior Warden:—Brother Hunt, Masonic tradition informs us that at the building of King Solomon's temple there were various classes of workmen, each of whom, as a distinctive badge, wore their aprons in a peculiar manner. Entered Apprentices being bearers of burden, wore theirs with the bib turned up, to prevent their clothes from being soiled, but as stains upon the apron of the operative workman would bring credit, rather than disgrace, yet you being a Speculative Mason, are expected to keep yours unspotted from the world. You are therefore entitled to wear yours in this manner while working with us on this degree. (He turns up the bib of the apron.)

This concludes the "rite of investiture" and its origin, and the reason for its performance is fully explained as follows in the text books of Freemasonry.

In the "General Ahiman Rezon," by Sickles, p. 74:—

"The apron in ancient times—*i. e.* in the 'Ancient Mysteries'—was a universally received emblem of Truth. Among the *Grecian Mysteries*, the candidate was invested with a white robe and apron. In Persia, the investiture was exceedingly splendid, and succeeded to the commission of light."

In Mackey's "Manual of the Lodge," p. 32, we read:—

"In the Persian Mysteries of Mithras, the candidate was invested with a white apron. In the Brahminical initiations of Hindostan, the Zennar, or Sacred Corn, was substituted for the apron. Even the Japanese in their rites of initiation invest their candidate with a white apron."

Again, in the "Symbolism of Freemasonry," by Mackey, p. 130:—

"The *rite of investiture* called in the colloquially technical language of the order, the *ceremony of clothing*, brings us at once to the consideration of that well-known symbol of Freemasonry, the LAMB-SKIN APRON. This rite of investiture, or the placing upon the aspirant some garment as an indication of his appropriate preparation for the ceremonies in which he was about to engage, prevailed *in all the ancient initiations*."

And referring to its ancient use in the Scandinavian Mysteries, he adds:—

"In the Scandinavian rites, where the military genius of the people had introduced a warlike species of initiation, instead of the apron we find the candidate receiving a white shield, which was, however, always presented with the accompaniment of some symbolic instruction not very dissimilar to that which is connected with the Masonic apron."

And again, in the "Traditions of Masonry," pp. 43, 44:—

"There is no one of the symbols of Masonry more important in its teachings, or more interesting in its history, that that of the *lambskin* or *white leather apron*."

"The apron, or girdle, in ancient times was a universally received emblem of truth and *passive duty*." "Among the primitive Masons,"—*i. e.*, the ancient sun-worshipers—"this badge received a characteristic distinction from its peculiar *color* and *material*, and was, indeed, an unequivocal mark of superior dignity. The investiture of the apron formed an essential part of the ceremony of initiation, and was attended with rites equally significant and impressive."

Again, on p. 45, we read:—

"When a candidate was initiated into the 'Ancient Mysteries,' he was esteemed *regenerate*, and he was invested with a WHITE garment and apron as a symbol of his newly attained purity."

"Among the Greeks, the garment of initiation was *white*, because, says Cicero, white is a color most acceptable to the gods."

"The Japanese, for among them we find the Mysteries, present the candidate with a loose tunic and *white apron*. And in the last degree of the Druidical rites the candidate was solemnly invested with a flowing robe of the purest *white*."

It may perhaps be worthy of remark, that in alluding here to the Japanese "Mysteries," Past Grand Master Pierson uses the present tense, thus indicating that sun-worship is still the prevailing religion of that country, and this being the case, how, it may be asked, can a Masonic Missionary consistently request a Japanese pagan to forsake the practice of his secret pagan ceremonies, when he himself has been initiated into the very self-same rites and has absolutely sworn to "conform to, abide by, and maintain, and support" the very same idolatry forever.

And referring to the *apron* as being "in primitive times rather an ecclesiastical than a civil decoration," Mr. Pierson goes on to say in his closing remarks on the "rite of investiture"—"Traditions of Freemasonry," p. 47:—

"This is a collateral proof of the fact that Masonry was originally incorporated with the *various systems* of divine worship used by every people in the ancient world. * * If Masonry retains the symbol or shadow, it cannot have renounced the reality or substance."

And hence, unquestionably, the Masonic philosophy must be one in form and substance with those various systems of divine worship—the "Ancient Mysteries"—with which it was "originally incorporated," and so true is it that Freemasonry and the "Ancient Mysteries" are identical in every feature, and so persistently do all our Masonic teachers insist upon establishing this identity beyond any possibility of dispute, that Past Grand Master Mackey affirms of the North East Corner ceremony in the Entered Apprentice degree, that it is the only one of all the ceremonies of initiation which cannot be traced back to any pagan origin.

In the "Symbolism of Freemasonry," p. 175, he says:—

> "It may be noticed in conclusion that the corner-stone seems to be peculiarly a Jewish symbol. *I can find no reference to it in any of the ancient pagan rites* and the EBEN PINAH, the *corner-stone* which is so frequently mentioned in Scripture, appears in its use in Masonry to have had *unlike almost every other symbol of the order* an exclusively temple origin."

The foregoing quotations might be indefinitely multiplied from the various manuals and monitors of the lodge as well as from the authorized teachings of those who mould and fashion Masonic thought, both in Europe and America. But enough, and a great deal more than enough, has already been said, to prove with the force and accuracy of a mathematical demonstration that every rite and every ceremony through which the Masonic candidate is made to pass on the night of his initiation, from the time he enters the "preparation room" in the "upper chamber" of the building where the lodge is held, until he again reaches the sidewalk, the sworn slave of Masonry, have all been borrowed from the secret worship of the sun-god of the ancient pagans, and that the religious philosophy of Speculative Freemasonry, and the religious philosophy of the Baal worship of Samaria, are identically the same.

CHAPTER XIII.

The Master's Carpet.—Why so called.—Masonic Emblems.—Form of the lodge.—Its supports.—Covering.—Furniture.—Ornaments.—Lights.—Jewels.—Situation.

Mr. Barton:—Having now disposed of all the initiatory ceremonies, and having satisfactorily accounted for the existence of each one of them as a Masonic rite, the next subject demanding onr attention in the regular order of lodge work, is the discussion of the symbols and emblems on the "Master's Carpet." In the early days of Speculative Freemasonry, when its pagan philosophy was only yet in its infancy, and long before it carried itself so haughtily and defiantly as it does to-day, the symbols and emblems of the different degrees used to be rudely sketched with chalk or, charcoal on a certain part of the lodge room floor, on the night of initiation, and as that particular spot was always reserved for the exclusive use of the Worshipful Master, it came to be called the "Master's Carpet," and from that the name has long since been applied to all the Masonic emblems in general, as well as the charts and manuals in which they are now universally delineated.

The symbols of the Entered Apprentice degree to which our attention must now be mainly directed, are nine in number, having direct allusion to the Form of the lodge; its Supports, Covering, Furniture, Ornaments, Lights, Jewels, Situation and Dedication, and, like all the preceding ceremonies of initiation, every one of these emblems, without any exception, has been "borrowed" from the "Ancient Mysteries," or secret worship of Baal, and their former position in that idolatrous system is distinctly pointed out in the monitors and standard works of the institution.

On the night of his initiation, however, the candidate is given a far different explanation of these emblems, by the Worshipful Master. Freemasonry is but a wicked system of sworn deception, fraud, and "cunning craftiness," from beginning to end; and hence the promoters of its antichristian philosophy are always very careful, at first, to keep the real meaning of its pretended mysteries in the background, or, at least, until such time as the initiate has taken the Master Mason's obligation, when it is presumed he is *bound* so fast that he dare not revolt against the terrible bondage into which, perhaps, he has been unsuspectingly insnared. This peculiar feature of the Masonic institution furnishes one more proof of its pagan origin, have been borrowed like all its other elements of corruption in a direct line from the "Ancient Mysteries." As relating to the manner in which a similar practice of fraud and deception was carried out in the "Ancient initiations," we have the following truthful statement from the pen of that eminent Mason, Dr. George Oliver.

In his "History of Initiation," p. 80, he says:—

"The Mysteries being connected with the services of religion, the *miserable jugglers*, who profited by magnifying the absurd fears of superstition, *carried on the deception* to its utmost extent, and to the latest moment of their powers."

The "miserable jugglers" of the "Mysteries," profited by the deception of *their* candidates, the miserable jugglers of Freemasonry derive their power and profit from a similar source, and in precisely the same manner, and between both classes of hierophants there is also this further marked coincidence that in the Masonic institution the deception is knowingly practiced and to its fullest extent.

We shall now examine these different emblems in detail, representing each one precisely as it is on the chart or "carpet," and giving its true origin and the meaning it conveys in the religious philosophy of Masonry, as furnished us by the authorized teachers of the order.

THE FORM OF THE LODGE.

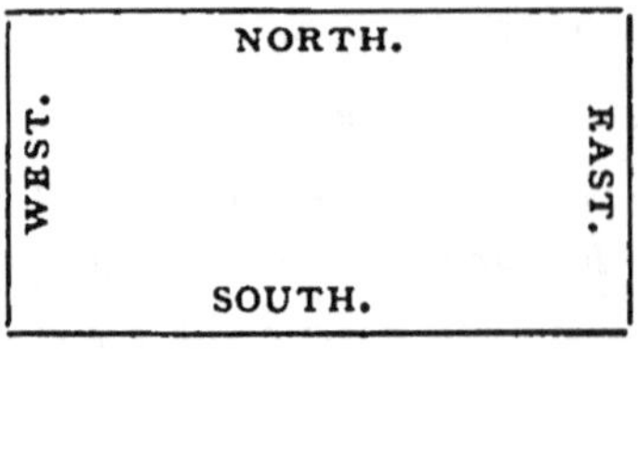

NORTH.
WEST.
EAST.
SOUTH.

From the Masonic ritual we learn that "the *form* of the lodge is that of an *oblong square*, extending from East to West, embracing every clime between the North and South." ("Hand Book," p. 92.) And Dr. Mackey, in referring to this universal form of Masonic lodges, explains in his "Manual of the Lodge," p. 44:—

"There is a peculiar fitness in this theory, which is really only making the Masonic lodge a symbol of the world." And in the "General Ahiman Rezon," p. 76, it is further asserted that "the double cube form is an expressive emblem of the united powers of *light* and *darkness* in the creation."

Also in the "Symbolism of Freemasonry," p. 102, we read:—

"The *form* of a Masonic lodge is said to be a parallelogram or oblong square, its greatest length being from east to west, its breadth from north to south." And again on p. 104 it is stated that "a Masonic lodge is therefore a symbol of the world."

The reason why this symbol is made use of in the Masonic philosophy, is given in a footnote on the same page, where it said that "to the vulgar and untaught eye the heaven or sky above the earth seems to be co-extensive with the earth, and to take the same form, enclosing a cubical space, of which the earth was the base, the heaven or sky the upper surface;" and Dr. Mackey further adds, that "it is to this notion of the universe the the Masonic symbol refers."

The lodge room then is brought before us as a symbol of the universe, governed by the sun-god, and its cubical form expressed in the language of the ritual is made to represent the united powers of light and darkness, and the constant conflict which is supposed to be always going on between them. Or, in other words, the lodge room is the real Masonic heaven, where the "god of nature,"—the "G. A. O. T. U."—always presides, where his symbol is always displayed, where his worship is always practiced, and when the "good Mason" dies he is simply transferred from this lower heaven or this "lodge below," to the Mount Olympus of the craft, called the "Grand Lodge above."

THE SUPPORTS OF THE LODGE.

In reference to this symbol, the Masonic ritual gives the following explanation:—

"The Masonic lodge, bounded only by the extreme points of the Compass, the highest heavens," (as in the last emblem,) "and the lowest depths of the central abyss, is said to be metaphorically supported by *three great* pillars, denominated *Wisdom*, *Strength* and *Beauty*."

The above figure represents these supports as given on the chart, and their positions are explained as follows by the Masonic text books:

"Manual of the Lodge," by Mackey, p. 46:—

"Of these, the Column of *Wisdom* is situated in the East part of the lodge, and is represented by the Worshipful Master. The Column of *Strength* is situated in the West part of the lodge, and is represented by the Senior Warden, and the Column of *Beauty* is situated in the South part of the lodge, and is represented by the Junior Warden."

And again, in the "Traditions of Freemasonry," by Pierson, p. 55:—

"The emblematical foundations, or support of a Masonic lodge, are three pillars denominated *Wisdom*, *Strength* and *Beauty*."

And now our next inquiry must be, where did the "Masonic fathers" of 1717 find these pillars? And why are they thus represented in Freemasonry? The answer comes from the "Grand East," and from its infallible ruling there is and there can be no appeal.

"Traditions of Freemasonry," by Pierson, p. 56:

"In the *Ancient Mysteries* these *three pillars* represented the great emblematical *Triad of Deity*, as with us they represent the three principal officers of the lodge. The three corresponding pillars of the Hindu Mysteries were also known by the names of *Wisdom*, *Strength* and *Beauty*, and placed *east*, *west* and *south*, crowned with three human heads."

We have it then, on the evidence of one of the best, if not actually *the* best informed Mason in America, that this emblem of the three pillars has not only been borrowed from the "Mysteries" of Hindostan, but that they actually retain the same names and positions in the Masonic institution that they formerly did, or do now, in the "secret initiations" of Brahma. And remembering the *Wisdom* of Solomon, the *Strength* of Hiram, King of Tyre, and the *Beauty* of the designs and work of Hiram, "the widow's son," we can easily understand the base cunning which prompted the adoption of these worthies as the first Grand Masters of the system, the better to hide its pagan origin, and to enable its infidel founders to carry out their base deception with greater facility.

But the three pillars, we are further informed, refer directly to the three principal officers of the lodge, and hence, to understand the true meaning of the symbol still more clearly, it must be also examined in that connection.

THE THREE PRINCIPAL OFFICERS.

The figures on the following page represent the three principal officers of the lodge, standing in their respective stations—the Worshipful Master in the East, the Senior Warden in the West, and the Junior Warden in the South. And now the question naturally arises, why are these officers thus situated? What do they really represent? And whence did the Masonic revivalists borrow the idea which at first led to this peculiar form of lodge government?

The Brahma, Vishnu and Siva of Freemasonry.

In the "Symbolism of Freemasonry," p. 106, we read:—

"The three principal officers of a lodge are, it is needless to say, situated in the east, the west and the south. Now bearing in mind that the lodge is a symbol of the world or the universe the reference of these three officers to the *sun* at its rising, its setting and its Meridian height must at once suggest itself."

And in the "Freemason's Guide," by Sickles, p. 66, this direct reference to the sun-god is further asserted. He says:—

"The Worshipful Master represents the sun at its rising, the Senior Warden represents the sun at its setting, and the Junior Warden represents the sun at Meridian."

In every symbol, ceremony and emblem of Freemasonry, we meet nothing but the *sun-god*—the "Ancient initiations"—the "Ancient Mysteries"—the old secret worship of Baal. But Past Grand Master Mackey, in referring to the Hindoo Mysteries, whence this particular Masonic emblem has been revived, and showing the coincidence between those "Mysteries" and the Masonic institution, gives the following copious explanation as the reason why the three principal lodge officers of Masonry are placed east west and south.

"Symbolism of Freemasonry," pp. 116, 117:—

"In the Brahminical initiations of Hindostan, which are among the earliest that have been transmitted to us, and may almost be considered as the cradle of all the others, of subsequent ages and various countries, the ceremonies were performed in vast caverns, the remains of some of which at Salsette and Elephanta and a few other places, will give the spectator but a very inadequate idea of the extent and splendor of these *ancient Indian lodges*."

"The interior of the cavern of initiation was lighted by innumerable lamps and there *sat in the east, the west and the south the princical Hierophants or explainers of the Mysteries*, as the representatives of Brahma, Vishnu and Siva."

"Now Brahma was the supreme deity of the Hindoos, borrowed or derived from the sun-god of their Sabean ancestors and Vishnu and Siva were but manifestations of his attributes."

And again on page 108:—

"We learn from the Indian Pantheon that when the sun rises in the east, he is Brahma, when he gains his meridian, he is Siva, and when he sets in the west, he is Vishnu."

Now if this is not an exact picture of Freemasonry and its symbolic teaching in reference to the sun or sun-god of its pagan worship, then there is no use in trying to understand the real meaning of words. In the Hindoo Mysteries the three principal officers who conducted the initiations, sat in the east, west and south and represented the sun-god Brahma in his three principal stations, at rising, at meridian and at setting. In the Masonic mysteries the three principal officers are situated in like manner, east, west and south and represent precisely the very same sun-god—"the

Worshipful Master," (as we are assured above) "representing the sun in the east, the Senior Warden the sun in the west, and the Junior Warden the sun in the south." And hence, it must unquestionably follow that the Worshipful Master of a Masonic lodge is but another name for the Brahma of the sun-worship of Hindostan, the Senior Warden but another name for Vishnu, and the Junior Warden but another name for Siva.

It could not be possible for Masonry to establish a clearer coincidence, nor could any stronger proof be adduced to identify the secret religious philosophy of the Masonic system with the ancient secret sun or Baal worship of pagan mythology.

But let us hear once more, what Past Grand Master Pierson has to say, in relation to this subject. Alluding to the three Masonic pillars, Wisdom, Strength and Beauty, in the Hindoo Mysteries, and their direct reference to Brahma or the sun-god of Hindostan, he goes on to explain.

"In the *east*, as the pillar of Wisdom, this deity—*i. e.* the sun-god—was called Brahma; in the *west*, as the pillar of Strength, Vishnu. And in the South, as the pillar of Beauty, Siva, and hence, in the Indian initiations the representative of Brahma was seated in the east, that of Vishnu in the west and that of Siva in the south. A very remarkable coincidence with the practice of Ancient Masonry."

And so then, the only difference between

the Brahmin lodges of Hindostan and the Masonic lodges of England and America is that instead of the names Brahma, Vishnu and Siva, found in the former, Freemasonry uses the terms Worshipful Master, Senior Warden and Junior Warden. The ceremonies are precisely the same, the positions of the Hierophants are the same, the duties the same, and the only difference is in the change of name, and, as we are informed elsewhere, this arises from change of country.

THE COVERING OF THE LODGE.

In regard to this symbol the Masonic *ritual* explains that:—

"The covering of the lodge is no less than that clouded canopy or starry decked heaven where all good Masons hope at last to arrive by the aid of that theological ladder which Jacob in his vision saw extending from earth to heaven." ("Hand Book," p. 93.)

This symbol is also derived from the "Ancient Mysteries," and has direct reference to the old sun-worship or sabaism of antiquity, as is abundantly proven by the following reference to both the *canopy* and *ladder* in the Masonic text-books.

In the "Manual of the Lodge," by Mackey, p. 40:—

The lodge continues throughout this degree to be presented to the initiated as a symbol of the world, and hence its covering is figuratively supposed to be the "clouded canopy," on which the host of stars is represented. * * * The mystical ladder which is here referred to is *a symbol that was widely diffused among the religions of antiquity*" *i e.* in the Ancient Mysteries—"where, as in Masonry, it was always supposed to consist of seven steps, because seven was a sacred number. In some of the *Ancient Mysteries* the seven steps represented the seven planets and then *the sun* was the topmost."

Again in the "Symbolism of Freemasonry," pp. 117, 118.

"The lodge, as a representative of the world, is of course supposed to have no other roof than the heavens."

"This mystic ladder which connects the ground floor of the lodge with its roof or covering, is another important and interesting *link* which *binds* with one common *chain* the symbolism and ceremonies of Freemasonry and the symbolism and rites of the ancient initiations."

And Pierson, referring to this same symbol of "Jacob's Ladder," in his "Traditions of Freemasonry, p. 50, uses the following language:—

"In the ladder we find another remarkable coincidence in the use of the same symbol in the Masonic institution, and the ancient mysteries to inculcate the same idea."

I have a strong desire to emphasize every word of these extracts, but in the absence of italics and with all the calmness possible under the circumstances, I will just remark, and do so, without any qualification whatever, that it would be impossible to conceive how the identity of Freemasonry with the old Baal or sun-worship of the "Mysteries" could be expressed in any stronger or plainer language than it is here affirmed in these quotations.

FURNITURE, LIGHTS, JEWELS.

It is only necessary to refer very briefly to these symbols and in this collective form, because they have been discussed somewhat extensively already, and it has been shown that with one single exception — the Holy Scriptures—they all refer to the Worshipful Master or the representation of the sun-god or "G. A. O. T. U." of Masonry. There are three articles of *furniture* in every Masonic lodge, as heretofore explained on page 123, the Holy Bible, Square and Compass, the Square being dedicated to the Master and the Compass to the craft. There are three lights—three burning tapers or three tallow candles — arranged in a triangular form, as in the above cut, and representing also the "sun, moon and Master of the lodge," and there are three immovable jewels, the square, level and plumb, again referring to the three principal officers, or to the sun-god in his three separate manifestations in the east, west and south, respectively. No matter, which way you turn in Masonry, or what emblem you investigete. you cannot get outside of the influence of sun-worship.

In reference to the symbol of the lights or the "three burning tapers," the lodge book explains as follows.

"Manual of the Lodge," by Mackey, p. 51:—

"The *three lights*, like the three principal officers and the three principal supports refer undoubtedly to the three principal stations of the sun —its rising in the east, its meridian in the south, and its setting in the west—and thus the symbol of the lodge, as typical of the world, continues to be preserved."

Now as the Worshipful Master in his own proper person represents the sun, and as it is stated here that the three principal officers and the three principal supports also represent the sun, therefore it follows as an undisputable fact that all these various symbolisms are absorbed in and are directly personated by the Master, who is therefore the Worshipful representative of the sun-god in the Masonic philosophy—the one chief object of veneration and reverence—the symbol of the god of Masonry.

THE ORNAMENTS.

In relation to this symbol the Masonic ritual declares that, "the ornaments of a lodge are the Mosaic Pavement, the Indented Tessel and the Blazing Star."—"Manual of the Lodge," p. 49.

Here then, we find three emblems included in one, and I presume it is needless to add that these, like all the preceeding ones have been derived from the old pagan temples, and refer in an especial manner to the Sabaism or star-worship of the ancient Egyptians where the "Mysteries" were first practiced.

In reference to "Mosaic Pavement," Masonry teaches as follows:—

Mosaic pavements, consisting of stones of various colors, so disposed as to represent different shapes or forms, were common in the temples of the ancients"—*i. e.* in the temple of Baal—"Fallows says that they represented the variagated face of the earth, in the places where the ancients formerly held their religious assemblies. "Manual of the Lodge," p. 49.

But how did the "Blazing Star" creep into

Freemasonry and what lesson, if any has it ever taught in the Masonic philosophy?

Dr. Mackey, having already quoted John Fallows as good authority on Freemasonry, it will surely be pardonable in us to follow his example and learn what he has to say concerning this symbol among the early Egyptians.

In his celebrated work "The Mysteries of Freemasonry," pp. 14, 15, he alludes to this Masonic emblem as follows:—

"I will here remark that the Anubis or Dog Star, so useful to the ancient Egyptians, is the Blazing Star of Masonry, and although the craft are ignorant of its origin as a Masonic symbol, yet they are actually taught the moral drawn from its original emblematical use. Webb in his "Monitor" says:—The *Mosaic Pavement* is emblematic of human life, checkered with good and evil, the *Beautiful Border* which surrounds it, is emblematic of those blessings and comforts which surround us and which we hope to obtain by a faithful reliance on Divine Providence, which is hieroglyphically represented by the *Blazing Star* in the center."

"This symbol is peculiarly if not exclusively applicable to the Egyptians who inhabited the Delta and who, by placing a reliance upon the warning, *providentially* given by this *star* and in consequence retiring to the higher ground with the produce of their agriculture might enjoy the "comforts" that surrounded them."

SITUATION OF THE LODGE.

The Masonic ritual prescribes that every lodge must be situated due east and west, and this custom like all the other customs, symbols and ceremonies of the institution has been derived from the situation of pagan temples of the ancient sun- or Baal-worship, as is evident from the following explanation. "Manual of the Lodge," p. 55.

"The orientation of lodges or their position east and west is derived from the universal custom of antiquity. The heathen temples," says Dudley, "were so constructed that their length was directed towards the east, and the entrance was by a portico at the western front, where the altar stood so that the votaries approaching for the performance of religious rites, directed their faces toward the east, the quarter of sunrise. The primitive reason for this custom undoubtedly is to be found in the early prevalence of *sun*-worship, and hence the spot where that luminary first made his appearance in the heavens was consecrated in the minds of his worshippers as a place entitled to peculiar reverence. Freemasonry retaining in its symbolism the typical reference of the lodge to the world and constantly alluding to the sun in his apparent diurnal revolution, imperatively requires, when it can be done that the lodge should be situated due east and west, so that every ceremony shall remind the Mason of the progress of that luminary."

How strangely anxious the teachers of Freemasonry must be, to establish the identity of Freemasonry with the "Ancient Mysteries," when it is "imperatively required" that even the very lodge rooms of the order must be situated due east and west, because of a similar custom which obtained in the situation of the pagan temples where the secret worship of Baal used to be formerly practised.

CHAPTER XIV.

THE POINT WITHIN A CIRCLE.—Lodge dedications. Refers to the Sun.—Borrowed from the Mysteries.—Represents the Phallus or Baal-peor of pagan worship.—Condemned by St. Paul.—Supported by Masonic ministers.—The Symbol of Masonic licentiousness.

Mr. Barton:—The last emblem on the "Master's Carpet" and the one which now demands our special attention, is that curious representation, commonly known among Masons as "The Point within a Circle."

The more we discuss the principles of Freemasonry, the closer we examine its hidden works of darkness and investigate the numerous symbols and ceremonies which it uses in the "dark chambers of its imagery," (Ezekiel viii. 12) in illustrating its religious philosophy, the more we are overwhelmed with astonishment at the immensity of its wickedness and at the wonderful ingenuity manifested in the construction of its entire system of idolatory. From the unanimous testimony of all its accredited teachers elicited thus far, while examining its different elements, it has been demonstrated as clearly as it is in the power of language to make it, that both in whole and in part, in its outward form and in its inward secret working the Masonic institution is an exact counterpart of the "Ancient Mysteries," and that all the ceremonies, symbols, emblems and rites which are now employed with so much pretended reverence and mock solemnity in conferring its heathenish degrees, are identical in every single feature with the initiatory rites and ceremonies that used to be formerly practised in the introduction of candidates into the secret worship of Baal or Osiris.

But in the explanation given in the Masonic text books of this emblem of "The Point within a Circle" we are furnished with such an accumulative mass of additional evidence as to its real character and philosophy, that in fact it would be more than sufficent of itself, and in the absence of any other proof, to brand Freemasonry as the must corrupt and demoralizing institution that the world ever saw.

Freemasonry and falsehood might without any impropriety be used as synonymous terms, but in all that pertains to the history and meaning of this symbol and from the duplicity and cunning so ingeniously displayed in concealing its real character from all but the "trooly loyal," it is scarcely possible to conceive how even the very father of lies himself could invent anything to beat it.

The first statement made in the Masonic text

book in relation to "The Point within a Circle" is as follows:—

"Manual of the Lodge," by Mackey, p. 55:—

"Modern Masons dedicate their lodges to St. John the Baptist and St. John the Evangelist, *who were two eminent patrons of Masonry;* and since their time there is represented in every regular and

well-governed lodge a certain point within a circle embordered by two parallel lines, representing St. John the Baptist and St. John the Evangelist. The point represents an individual member, the circle the boundary line of his duty."

The foregoing figure is an exact copy of this symbol as represented in every lodge room throughout the world, and by its accompanying quotation from the Manual we learn that Freemasonry sets forth the following as its pretended meaning: First, that the SS. John were eminent Christian patrons of Masonry; second, that since their time the "Point with a Circle" has been represented in every regular and well-governed lodge; third, that the two parallel lines represent St. John the Baptist and St. John the Evangelist; and fourth, that the *point* represents an individual member and the *circle* the boundary line of his duty.

Now there is not a single word of truth in any of these statements, but the whole averment is one continuous falsehood from beginning to end. "The Point within a Circle" is not only a pagan symbol, referring to the sun-god of Masonic worship from first to last, and borrowed directly from the "ancient initiations" of the old Baal mythology, but it is in fact as near a true representation of that lacivious idol—the Baal-peor of Moab—as common decency will permit the Grand High Priests of Masonry to represent it in books intended for general circulation. This and a great deal more concerning this vicious symbol will appear evident from the following Masonic testimony.

In regard to the "two parellel lines" we read

in the "Manual of the Lodge," by Mackey, p. 57:—

"The *two parallel lines* which in the modern lectures are said to represent St. John the Baptist, and St. John the Evangelist, *really allude* to particular periods in the SUN's annual course. At two particular points in this course the *sun* is found on the Zodiacal signs, Cancer and Capricorn, which are distinguished as the summer and winter solstices. When the sun is in these points, he has reached his greatest northern and southern limit. These points, if we suppose the circle to represent the sun's annual course, will be indicated by the points where the parallel lines touch the circle. But the days when the sun reaches these points are the 21st of June and the 22nd of December, and this will account for their subsequent application to the two Saints John, whose anniversaries the Church has placed near those days."

So then the "two perpendicular parallel lines," instead of referring to the "Forerunner of Christ," and the "Beloved Disciple," really allude to the tropic of Cancer to the north and the tropic of Capricorn to the south of the equator, while the *circle* itself alludes to the apparent course of the sun through the circle of the Zodiac. Even a common almanac will furnish sufficient proof that the "*Point within a Circle*" is a constant symbol of the *sun*. But again we read on the same page:—

"So the true interpretatoin of *the point within a circle* is the same as that of the Master and Wardens of a lodge. * * * The Master and Wardens are *symbols of the sun*—the lodge of the universe, or the world; the *point* also is the *symbol of the same sun*, and the surrounding *circle* of the *universe* while *the two parallel lines really* *point* NOT TO TWO saints, but to the two northern and southern limits of the sun's course."

The startling parallelsm so distinctly set forth in this last extract is worthy of attentive notice. The Worshipful Master is the symbol of the sun-god and the lodge of the universe; the *point* is also a symbol of the same sun-god and the circle of the universe, and therefore the *point* and the Master are one, while the circle and universe are also one. Now bearing this in mind, we shall perhaps be better enabled to realize the true "inwardness" of the Masonic philosophy, as expressed in the quotations that follow, on pp. 325, 326.

But in the "Traditions of Freemasonry," p. 84, Mr. Pierson also gives very elaborate explanations of this extraordinary symbol of the Masonic system, and everywhere refers it to the old sun-worship of the ancient pagan world. He says:—

"The *point within a circle* became a universal emblem"—*i. e.* among the pagans—"to denote the temple of the deity and was referred in the *planetary circle* in the *center* of which was fixed the *sun* as the universal god and father of nature."

"In the Druidical rites *the point within the circle* and the cube were emblems of Odin."

"The Hindoos believed that the Supreme Being was correctly represented by a perfect sphere, without beginning and without end."

And so then, in order to ascertain the true interpretation of "The Point within a Circle," we must seek for it, where alone we have found all the other symbols and ceremonies of the Masonic system, in the old Baal worship of paganism and among the Druids and Hindoos. But where did the "Masonic fathers" discover the two parallel lines? And who first introduced them into the system?

In the "Traditions of Freemasonry," p. 87, we find the answer:—

"The mysteries among the Chinese and Japanese came from India and had similar rites. In these *a ring* supported by *two serpents* was emblematical of the world protected by the power and wisdom of the Creator and *that is the origin of the two parallel lines* (into which time has changed the two serpents) *that support the circle in our lodges.* It is supposed that this addition of the two perpendicular parallel lines to the point within the circle was introduced by Dunckerley, as we find no allusion to them previous to his revision of the lectures."

And that no possible doubt may exist as to the real philosophic teaching of the Masonic system and the true import and design of this symbol, Mr. Pierson again asserts, in his Traditions, pp. 87, 88:—

"It is evident then that the *sun either as an object of worship* or of symbolization *has always formed an important part* of both the 'Mysteries' and the *system of Freemasonry.* * * * * The parallel lines will indicate the limits of the sun's extreme northern and southern declination when he arrives at the solstitial points of Cancer and Capricorn."

But not only does this symbol of "The Point within a Circle," in all its parts of parallel lines, point and circle, refer directly to the sun in its apparent annual course, and therefore to the fictitious sun-god of pagan worship, but it is also positively affirmed, that, like the emblem of the "three great pillars"—Wisdom, Strength and Beauty—it had a distinct existence in the "ancient initiations," bearing the same name that it does to-day in Masonry, and, consequently, that it was wholly transferred from that source into the Masonic system, without even the slightest change.

In relation to this fact we have the following, among many other proofs, from Dr. Oliver in his "History of Initiation," p. 88, where, in describing the mysteries of Greece, he says:—

"The following are some of the symbols of Pythagoras—the *equilateral triangle*, *the square*, the *perfect square*, the *cube* and *a point within a circle*, which was a symbol of the universe, because the most excellent body," (the sun) "ought to have the most excellent place, viz. the center."

All these pagan symbols are to be found to-day in every Masonic lodge and chapter in the world.

Again, on p. 181, when describing the Scandinavian mysteries:—

"The most prominent symbols in these celebrations were the cross and ring, already mentioned, the ash-tree, the POINT WITHIN A CIRCLE, the rainbow and a cube, the emblem of Odin."

But now the most important fact of all, in relation to this notorious Masonic symbol, remains to be stated, and the explanation here given of it by those who are most interested in imparting a knowledge of the wonderful mysteries of Freemasonry, and in proclaiming its extraordinary morality and virtue, when rightly understood, ought to be sufficient of itself to condemn this whole miserable system of duplicity and demon worship to lasting infamy. Hear what Past Grand Master Mackey teaches in his "Symbolism of Freemasonry," p. 353.

"The *point within a circle* is derived from the ancient sun-worship, and is in realty of *phallic* origin. It is a symbol of the universe, the *sun* being represented by the *point*, while the circumference is the universe."

And again on p. 352:—

"The lines touching the circle in the symbol of *the point within a circle* are said to reprent St. John the Baptist and St. John the Evangelist, but they really refer to the solstitial points Cancer and Capricorn in the Zodiac."

And lastly, in the "Manual of the Lodge," p. 56:—

"The *point within a circle* is an interesting and important symbol in Freemasonry, but it has been so debased in the interpretation of it in the modern lectures that the sooner that interpretation is forgotten by the Masonic student, the better will it be. *The symbol is really a beautiful* but somewhat abstruse *allusion to the old* SUN-WORSHIP, and introduces us for the first time to that modification of it, known among the ancients as the *worship* of the *Phallus.*"

And now our next inquiry must be, what was the *Phallus?* And what the nature of that ancient *phallic* worship, to which as we are here credibly informed, this Masonic symbol so distinctly refers? Hear the authoritative explanation of Masonry, as expressed in its text books and lodge monitors.

In the "Symbolism of Freemasonry," by A. G. Mackey, p. 112, we read:—

"Perfectly to understand this symbol, I must refer, as a preliminary matter, to the worship of the *Phallus*, a peculiar modification of sun-worship, which prevailed to a great extent among the nations of antiquity."

"The *Phallus* was a sculptured representation of the *membrum virile* or male organ of generation, and the worship of it is said to have originated in Egypt, where, after the murder of Osiris by Typhon, which is symbolically to be explained as the destruction or deprivation of the *sun's* light by *night*, Isis, his wife, as the symbol of nature, in the search for his mutilated body, is said to have found all the parts except the organ of generation, which myth is simply symbolic of the fact that the *sun* having set, its fecundating and invigorating power had ceased. The *Phallus* therefore as the symbol of the male generative principle was very universally venerated among the ancients, and that too as a religious rite."

"He is supposed by some commentators to be the god mentioned under the name of *Baal-peor* in the Book of Numbers, as having been worshiped by the idolatrous Moabites."

The language of this extract is so very plain, that any person of even average intelligence can readily understand its meaning, but our Masonic teachers, not willing, perhaps, that any mistake should be made in relation to this matter, express themselves in terms still more explicitly, in the lodge book.

Hear the "Manual of the Lodge," by Mackey, p. 56:—

"The *Phallus* was an imitation of the male generative organ. It was represented usually by a column which was surmounted by a circle at its base, in tended for the *cteis* or female generative organ. This union of the *Phallus* and the *cteis* which is well represented by the *point within the circle* was intended by the ancients as a type of the prolific powers of nature which they worshipped under the united form of the active or male principle and the passive or female principle."

And again, in the "Symbolism of Freemasonry," p. 352:—

"Phallus—representation of the virile member which was venerated as a religious symbol, very universally by the ancients. It was one of the modifications of sun-worship, and was a symbol of the fecundating power of that luminary. The *Masonic point* within a circle is undoubtedly of phallic origin."

And lastly, in the "Lexicon of Freemasonry," p. 353:—

"The *Phallus* was the wooden image of the *membrum virile*, which being affixed to a pole, formed a part of most of the pagan mysteries, and was worshiped as the emblem of the male generative principle. The phallic worship was first established in Egypt. From Egypt it was introduced into Greece, and its exhibition formed a part of the Dionysian mysteries. In the Indian Mysteries it was called the *lingam*, and was always found in the most holy place in the temple. It was adopted by the idolatrous Israelites, who took it from the Moabites when in the Wilderness of Sin, under the name of Baal-peor."

And now what information do we gather from all this voluminous Masonic testimony? And what instruction do we receive in relation to the "Point within a Circle" from the Most Worshipful Grand rulers of Masonry?

As we shall learn by and by, when discussing the Egyptian legend in the Master Mason's degree, Osiris, the chief deity or sun-god of Egypt, is said to have been treacherously slain by his brother Typhon, his body cut into fourteen different parts and buried or concealed in as many different places. Isis, or nature—the wife of Osiris—in her search for the mutilated body of her husband, is supposed to have found all the parts but one—the organ of generation. For this she made a "factitious representation," which the Masonic textbooks assure us, was in the shape of a "sculptured column, made of wood, and surrounded by a circle at its base, representing the *cteis* or female generative organ," and this she set up in the temple of Isis, that divine honor might be paid to it.

This monstrous abomination, as we are informed in the foregoing extracts, was the *Phallus* of the old pagan worship, and which we are positively assured is now represented in every Masonic lodge throughout the world, under the figure of "The

Point within a Circle." Being supposed to be a part of Baal or the sun-god, it was sometimes also called Baal-peor, and was always and everywhere worshiped with licentious worship. This was the chief deity of the Moabites, as we read in the twenty-fifth chapter of Numbers, and it was because the men of Israel joined themselves to this abominable idol and took part in its wicked worship indulging in the most flagrant licentiousness in honor of it, that twenty-four thousand of them were slain. And the Apostle Paul, alluding to this same *phallic* worship, speaks of it in terms of the highest reprobation, when he advises the Ephesian Christians to "have no fellowship with the unfruitful works of darkness, but rather reprove them. For," said he, "it is a shame to speak of the things that are done of them in secret." (Eph. v. 11, 12.) And yet notwithstanding all this, the ministers of our churches—those who claim to be commissioned by the Lord Jesus Christ, to preach the gospel of the grace of God, and to lead men from darkness to light, and the very representatives of that same Apostle Paul—these men I say go into those dark dens of infamy and sin, called Masonic lodges, join themselves to this very same Baal-peor, solemnly swear to maintain and support the wicked religious philosophy of which it forms an important part, use whatever in fluence they possess in inducing others to follow their example, and when questioned on the subject by even one of their own congregation, they either give a haughty, defiant reply, or else positively lie to hide their wickedness.

And now there is one other feature of this expressive symbol to which at least brief allusion ought to be made. We have learned that the *point* represents the male generative organ, that it represents an individual member and also that it represents the Worshipful Master, while at the same time the *circle* represents the lodge, the universe and the boundary line of Masonic duty. Now, putting all these facts together, and taking them in connection with the other meaning of the circle, and also with the further fact that the *phallic* worship was always licentious in character, it does not require a very great deal of penetration to understand that concubinage or free-love is one of the possible results of Masonic teaching, and that the individual Mason is only restricted so far as the wives, mothers, sisters and daughters of Master Masons are concerned, as prescribed in the obligation of the third degree. And yet to conceal all this abomination and wickedness, and to recommend Freemasonry to public favor, the figures of the Holy SS. John are placed on either side of this notorious symbol, while the Word of God is represented as being open on the vertex of the circle. Surely, if "righteousness exalteth a nation," and that "sin is a reproach to any people," it can scarcely be expected that the people of this land can long escape the sore judgments of the Almighty for the support and encouragement they are giving to this terrible form of idolatry and especially for the apathy and indifference with which they regard its very existence in the pulpit. May the Lord soon hasten the time when this fearful "covenant with hell shall be disannulled" and when this "agreement with death shall not stand," when the Lord Jesus Christ alone shall be the only object of worship and when "every tongue shall confess that He only is Lord to the glory of God the Father."

CHAPTER XV.

THE MASONIC LEGEND.—The Masonic revival. How effected and why.—Osiris and Hiram one and the same character.—Legend of Hiram Abiff.—Legend of Osiris.—Both identical.

Mr. Barton:—We are now done with the "Lesser Mysteries" or those initiatiory rites which constitute the first section of symbolic Masonry. We have examined all its ceremonies, have investigated all its symbols and the fearful truth has been made only too apparent, that every part of Freemasonry emphatically proclaims its pagan origin and that the god of its worship and religious philosopy is the old sun-god of the "Ancient Mysteries"—the Osiris of the Egyptians or the Baal of the idolatrous Israelites. We must now, my dear Henry, turn our attention to the sublime degree of Master Mason and to a discussion of that celebrated legend, which is regarded by all Masons the world over, as being decidedly the most impressive and instructive of all the Masonic rites, and which is called by way of eminence the "Temple legend," or the "Legend of the Builder." Some idea may be formed of the very high estimation in which this wonderful legend is held among the fraternity and of its pretended sublimity and great importance as an integral part of the Masonic institution from the following descriptive references copied from the monitors and text books of the lodge.

"Symbolism of Freemasonry," pp. 228, 229:—

"The most important and significant of the legendary symbols of Freemasonry is undoubtedly that which relates to the fate of Hiram Abiff, commonly called by way of excellence, the "Legend of the Third Degree."

"This legend has been considered of so much importance, that it has been preserved in the symbolism of every Masonic rite. No matter what modifications or alterations the general system may have undergone—no matter how much the ingenuity or the imagination of the founders of rites may have perverted or corrupted other symbols, abolishing the old and substituting new ones — the legend of the Temple Builder has ever been left untouched to present itself in all the integrity of its ancient mythical form.

And again in the "General Ahiman Rezon," by Sickles, p. 195, we read:—

"The ceremonial of the degree of Master Mason is unquestionably the most important, impressive and instructive portion of the Ritual of Ancient Freemasonry. That portion of the rite which is connected with the legend of the Tyrian Artist is well worthy the deep and earnest study of the thoughtful men. (Well, we are studying it thoughtfully and earnestly.) But it should be studied as a *myth* and not as a *fact*. Against the notion that it is the representation of a scene that actually occurred in the temple, it may well be urged that outside of Masonic tradition there is no proof that an event such as is related in connection with the Temple Builder ever transpired and besides the ceremony is older by more than a thousand years, than the age of Solomon. There are characters impressed upon it which cannot be mistaken. *It is thoroughly Egyptian.*"

And now the questions naturally suggest themselves, who is this "Hiram Abiff" or "Tyrian artist," who is referred to with so much apparent respect in the foregoing extracts, and whose "legend," as Dr. Mackey expresses it, "has become so intimately interwoven with Freemasonry as to make to all appearance a part of its very essence?" How did the "Masonic fathers" come to incorporate this man Hiram with the Masonic mysteries? And where, when and how did this celebrated "Temple Legend" first originate? To answer these inquiries in a satisfactory manner, and at the same time to get a further understanding of the true character of the Masonic philosophy, we must always remember that Freemasonry, as before stated, is the science of religious symbolism by means of which every Mason is professedly engaged in erecting a spiritual temple in his heart, pure and spotless, and to represent which the temple of Solomon has been adopted, as the most suitable type. The fact is, that the whole conception of the Masonic idea by the Apple-tree tavern philosophers was a wonderful scheme throughout—cunningly devised and carefully executed. Solomon, the principal character, connected with the construction of the Jerusalem temple, was a man, supposed to have been endowed with all *wisdom*; Hiram, King of Tyre, the next noted personage alluded to in the sacred narrative, supported or *strengthened*, as it were, King Solomon in carrying out that great undertaking, while "Hiram, the widow's son," by his surpassing skill as an artist, *beautified* and adorned the edifice. Now, in reviving the "Ancient Mysteries," with all their ceremonies and symbols, and in seeking for appropriate characters to represent the "three great pillars of Wisdom, Strength and Beauty," or the three manifestations of the sun-god in the east, west and south, as they existed in the "Ancient Initiations," who could be found to answer every purpose more suitably than Solomon and the two Hirams? And hence, as a matter of course, they were immediately dubbed the three first "Most Excellent Grand Masters" of this grand humbug, although we have abundant proof, from the very best and highest Masonic testimony on record, that one of them at least—King Solomon—knew no more of the mysteries of a Masonic lodge, as now constituted, than he did of the Marble cypher or the battle of Bunker Hill.

That important selection being once effected by the Masonic fathers, the rest of their revival work became quite simple. They merely changed the name of the hero-god in the Egyptian mysteries from Osiris to that of Hiram Abiff, composed a legend similar in all respects to that found in the "Ancient Initiatians" to record the manner of his pretended death, changed another name here and there to conceal the true character of the institution, and lest the mean pagan origin of the miserable swindle should be discovered, they "burned their manuscripts" in 1720, as we are credibly informed by James Hardie, in his "New Freemason's Monitor," p. 20. First they borrowed the secret worship of Baal, as a substitute for the religion of Christ, then they interspersed into its ritualistic jugglery the names of Solomon and Hiram to recommend it to the favorable acceptance both of Jew and gentile, and lastly they unblushingly appropriated the Holy Bible and the names of the SS. John to render it acceptable to the Christian public. All this, however was in the beginning of its wicked career, and before it had acquired a very solid foothold, but according as it grew older and gained new accessions to its ranks, deceiving into its midnight lodges even some of the best and purest men of both continents, its principal leaders, (when they found they could do so with impunity,) gradually threw off the flimsy cloak of hypocrisy in which its infidel and antichristian principles were only for a time enveloped, and proclaimed to the world its real philosophy. And strange as it may appear

Freemasonry is, to say the least of it, almost as popular to-day as Christianity itself, while its heathen mysteries are as much respected and upheld even by ministers of the gospel, as are the mysteries of the Christian faith. Its absolute identity with the "Ancient Initiations" has however been long since made manifest by all its principal teachers. Every one of its symbols, ceremonies and rites, as we have found, have been traced back with the most unerring accuracy to the secret initiations of Baal, and this celebrated legend of Hiram Abiff has in an especial manner been indisputably shown to have been the very self-same legend which formerly existed in every form of sun-worship throughout the pagan world, and is in realty to-day the religion of India and Japan.

This fact is so continually mentioned and is always affirmed with so much positive assurance by all the leading authors and most popular teachers of the Masonic institution, that if we reject their testimony concerning their own, best beloved system, then it would be hardly consistent in us to accept human testimony on any subject whatever. The identity of the Hiram of Masonry with the sun-god of the "Ancient Mysteries" has been already fully disposed of on pp. 235, 236 nevertheless, as I propose now to compare both legends—the Masonic and Egyptian—I shall refer once more to a few of the proofs heretofore given, and only very briefly.

"Traditions of Freemasonry," p. 159:—

"The *legend* and traditions of Hiram Abiff form the consummation of the connecting link between Freemasonry and the ancient mysteries.

And again on p. 240:—

"We readily recognize in Hiram Abiff the Osiris of the Egyptians, the Mythras of the Persians, the Bacchus of the Greeks," &c.

And again from the "Freemason's Guide," by Sickles, p. 236:—

"Osiris and the Tyrian Architect"—*i. e.* Hiram Abiff—"are one and the same."

It being undoubtedly true then, that the legend of Hiram has merely taken the place of the legend of Osiris and that as here expressed by the lodge book, "Osiris and Hiram are one and the same," the next point of interest perhaps, which ought to demand our attention, would be, to obtain a description of those ancient legends of the mysteries, and to ascertain exactly what facts or incidents they related, so as to be able to determine beyond any possibility of mistake, that the Masonic legend corresponds in every particular with the legend of Egypt. On this subject, as indeed on all other points tending in any way to establish the coincidence between Freemasonry and the ancient secret initiations of sun-worship, we have the fullest possible information and in the very clearest terms from all our Masonic teachers.

In the "Traditions of Freemasonry," by Pierson, p. 229, we read:—

"Everywhere, and in all their forms the mysteries were funereal in their character and celebrated the mythical death and restoration to life of some divine or heroic personage and the details of the legend and the mode of death varied in the different countries where the mysteries were practised.

And again on p. 232 he says:—

"Each legend represented the death by violence of some particular person; with some it was a god, with others a demi-god and with others a great warrior or person who had conferred signal benefits upon man in agricultural pursuits or in the arts and sciences. In consequence of such death *something was lost;* there was then a *search* made for that which was lost, a *finding of it* or of a part of it or of something that was adopted as a substitute for it—a beginning in sorrow and lamentation and an ending in joy and rejoicing. Such is a brief summary," he continues, "of the legend that accompanied the ceremonial of each of the systems of the mysteries of which we have any account, either historical or traditional that has ever been practised on this globe."

Having been thus made acquainted with the fact that the mysteries were all *funereal* in their character, and that they everywhere celebrated the death of some "cherished being" as the representative of the sun-god or the destruction of *light* by *night* and *darkness*, let us now compare the Legend of the "Tyrian Architect" with that of Osiris, and in that way ascertain to a certainty the coincidence that exists between them.

LEGEND OF HIRAM ABIFF.

The following is that wonderful legend of Hiram Abiff, which is rehearsed by the Worshipful Master to every candidate at the time he is made a Master Mason, or rather after he is "brought from a dead level to a living perpendicular."

"Fifteen Fellow Crafts seeing the temple about to be completed and being desirous of obtaining the secrets of a Master Mason or the Master's word whereby they might travel into foreign countries, work and receive Master's wages, entered into a horrid *conspiracy* to extort them from our Grand Master Hiram Abiff or take his life. But reflecting with horror upon the atrocity of the crime twelve of them recanted, the other three, however, persisted in their murderous design.

Our Grand Master Hiram Abiff was slain at the hour of ***high twelve.*** It was his usual custom at that hour, while the craft were called from labor to refreshment, to enter into the unfinished "sanctum sanctorum' or "Holy of Holies" of King Solomon's temple, there to offer his adorations to the Deity and draw his designs upon the trestle-board. The Fellow Crafts who persisted in their murderous design knowing this to be his usual custom placed themselves at the South, West and East gates of the inner court of the temple and there awaited his return.

Having finished his usual exercises he attempted to pass out by the South gate, where he was met by the *first ruffian*, Jubela, who thrice demanded of him the secrets of a Master Mason or Master's word and being thrice refused *he struck him with the twenty-four inch guage across the throat.*

He then attempted to retreat by the West gate, where he was met by the *second ruffian* Jubelo, who also demanded of him the secrets of a Master Mason, or the Master's word, and being again refused he *struck him with the square across the breast.*

He now attempted to make his escape by the East gate, where he was met by the *third ruffian*, Jubelum who in like manner thrice demanded of him the secrets of a Master Mason or the Master's word, and upon a like refusal, *he struck him a violent blow with the setting maul* on the forehead which felled him *dead* upon the spot.

They then buried him in the rubbish of the temple until low twelve or twelve at night, when they met by appointment, and conveyed him a westerly course from the temple to the brow of a hill west of Mount Moriah, where they buried him in a grave due east and west, six feet perpendicular, and planted an *acacia* at the head of the grave to conceal it, and that the place may be known should occasion thereafter ever require it.

They then attempted to make their escape out of the country.

Our Grand Master was not known to be missing until the following day, when King Solomon arriving at the temple and finding the craft in confusion he inquired the cause, and being informed that there was no work laid out and no designs upon the trestle-board, he inquired where was our Grand Master Hiram Abiff. He was informed that he had not been seen since high twelve yesterday, and fearing that he might have been indisposed he ordered strict search and due inquiry to be made in and about the several apartments of the temple to see if he could not be found. But strict search and due inquiry having already been made and our Grand Master Hiram Abiff being nowhere to be found, he feared that some fatal accident had befallen him and ordered the Grand Secretary to cause the several rolls of the workmen to be called, to see if any were missing and that returns be made as speedily as possible.

Upon roll-call three Fellow Crafts were found to be missing, namely, Jubela, Jubelo and Jubelum, who from the similarity of their names were supposed to be brethren and men of Tyre.

About this time the Fellow Crafts who recanted presented themselves before King Solomon, clad in white gloves and aprons, tokens of innocence, freely acknowledged their premeditated guilt and most humbly implored his pardon. King Solomon ordered them to divide themselves into parties and travel three East, three West, three North and three South, (with others, whom he should appoint) in *search* of the ruffians and return not without tidings.

The party who pursued a westerly course from the temple, on coming down near the port of Joppa, fell in with a wayfaring man of whom *they inquired* if he had seen any strangers pass that way. He informed them he had, three, and described them as workmen from the temple at Jerusalem, seeking a passage into Ethiopia, but not having King Solomon's pass, were unable to obtain a passage and returned back into the country. Deeming these to be tidings of importance they returned back to communicate them.

He then ordered them to disguise themselves and *travel* as before, with positive injunctions to find the ruffians and with as positive assurance that if they did not, the twelve Fellow Crafts would be deemed guilty of the murder and severally suffer for the crime committed.

They departed a second time and after *several days of fruitless search*, and when on their return one of their number, becoming more weary than the rest, sat down upon the brow of a hill, west of Mount Moriah to rest and refresh himself. On attempting to arise, he accidentally caught hold of an acacia, which easily giving way, excited his curiosity, whereupon he hailed his companions, and upon their return and examination found what had the appearance of a new-made grave. And whilst meditating upon this singular circumstance, they heard the following horrid exclamations from the clefts of an adjacent rock. The first was the voice of Jubela, who exclaimed, "O that my throat had been cut across, my tongue torn out by its roots and buried in the rough sands of the sea at low water mark, where the tide ebbs and flows twice in twenty-four hours, ere I had consented to the death of so great a man as our Grand Master

Hiram Abiff." The second was the voice of Jubelo, who exclaimed, "O that my left breast had been torn open, my heart plucked out and given as a prey to the wild beasts of the field and the fowls of the air, ere I had been accessory to the death of so good a man as our Grand Master Hiram Abiff." The third was the voice of Jubelum who exclaimed in tones of greater horror than the others, "O that my body had been severed in twain, my bowels taken from thence and burned to ashes and the ashes scattered to the four winds of heaven, so that no more trace or remembrance might be had of so vile and perjured a wretch as I, ere I had caused the death of so great and so good a man as our Grand Master Hiram Abiff. Ah, Jubela and Jubelo, it is I who am more guilty than you both; it was I who struck the fatal blow, it was I who killed him!" Whereupon they rushed in, seized and bound them and brought them before King Solomon, who upon a due conviction and confession of their guilt ordered them to be taken without the gates of the city and be there executed according to their several imprecations whilst hidden in the clefts of the rock.

King Solomon then ordered the Fellow Crafts to go in *search* of the body and when found to observe whether the Master's word or a key to it or anything pertaining to the Master's degree be on or about the body. The body of our Grand Master Hiram Abiff was found in a grave dug due east and west, six feet perpendicular, a westerly course from the temple, where a weary brother sat down to rest and refresh himself, but there was nothing found on or about the body, by which it could be designated, except the jewel of his office which they bore up to King Solomon.

He then ordered the Fellow Crafts to form a solemn procession to go and assist him in raising the body and as the Master's word was then *lost*, he proposed that the first sign made upon arriving at the grave, and the first word spoken after the body should be raised, should be *adopted* as the sign and word for the regulation of all Master's lodges until future generations should find out the right."

Such is the celebrated legend of "Hiram the Builder," the name of the sun-god of the Masonic mysteries, and now let us refer to its great antitype—the equally famous legend of Osiris the King, or the name of the sun-god of the "Ancient Mysteries."

LEGEND OF OSIRIS.

In the "Traditions of Freemasonry," p. 229, we read:—

"Osiris, King of Egypt, willing to confer an indescribable benefit on all the nations around him, by communicating to them the arts of civilization, left the government of his kingdom to the care of his wife Isis and made an expedition of three years to effect his benevolent purpose.

On his return he fell a sacrifice to the intrigues of his *brother* Typhon who had formed a *conspiracy* in his absence to destroy him and usurp his throne. At a grand entertainment, to which

Osiris was invited, when none but the conspirators were present, Typhon produced a valuable chest adorned with work of gold. He had secured without suspicion a measurement of the person of Osiris and had caused the chest to be made of such proportions as would exactly fit his body During the entertainment, and while the guests were extolling the beauty of the chest, Typhon promised to give it to any person present, whose body it should most conveniently hold. Osiris was tempted to try the experiment, but was no sooner laid in the chest, when the lid of it was nailed down and thrown into the river.

The body of Osiris thus committed to the mercy of the winds and waves, was cast up at Byblos in Phœnicia, and *left at the foot of a tamarind tree.*

As soon as Isis was informed of the death of the unfortunate Osiris, and that his body had been shut up in a coffin, in the extremity of sorrow and despair at the loss of her husband, she set out in company with Thoth *in search* of the body.

Uncertain as to the route she ought to pursue, uneasy and agitated, her heart lacerated with grief, in mourning garb, making the air re-echo with her lamentations, she interogates every one whom she meets.

After encountering the most extraordinary adventures she is informed by some young children that the coffin which contains the body of her husband had been carried by the waters out to sea and thence to Byblos, where it was stopped and was now reposing *upon a plant* (erica) which had put forth a superb stalk. Isis, actuated by a divine impulse, arrived in Byblos and discovered the coffin and engaged herself as nurse for the King's Children. As a reward for her services she demanded that the precious column should be given to her. Disengaging the coffin from the branches by which it was covered she took out the body and sent the branches to the King who deposited them in the temple of Isis.

She then returned to Egypt where her son Horus reigned and deposited the body in a secret place, intending to give it a splendid interment. By the treachery of Typhon she was again deprived of the body which was severed into *fourteen* parts and deposited in as many different places.

Isis, with unparalleled zeal and perserverance undertook a *second* journey to *search* for these scattered remnants."

And Dr. Mackey finishes this interesting narrative in his "Masonic Lexicon," p. 130:—

"One piece of the body," he says, "however she could not find, the *membrum virile.* For this she *substituted* a factitious representation which she consecrated and which under the name of *Phallus* is to be found as the emblem of fecundity in all the ancient mysteries."

"This legend," he further states "was purely astronomical. Osiris was the sun, Isis the moon."

Such is the celebrated legend of the sun-god Osiris of Egypt, as furnished us by the most authentic Masonic documents in the world and in relation to which Past Grand Master Pierson further observes in his "Traditions of Freemasonry," p 231:—

"The Masonic reader will be struck with the remarkable coincidences which the above legend presents *with one with which he is acquainted.*"

Concerning this legend and all the others of the sun-god of the "Mysteries," by whatsoever name that myth had been worshipped, whether as Osiris in Thebes, or as Baal in Samaria and Jezreel, we have the following general description in addition to that already given, from the "Traditions of Freemasonry," p. 232:—

"The legend of every one of the different phases of the mysteries irrespective of country or language, had the same general character, in fact *were all indentical* except in the name of individuals. We have presented that of the Egyptian mysteries, because it has been generally regarded as the parent of all others."

This being the case then and having both the Masonic and Egyptian legends fairly before us and also remembering that our Masonic teachers furnish all these historical facts for the sole purpose of proving that the legend of the third degree is identical with all the legends of antiquity let us now examine carefully and enumerate one by one the various incidents connected with the supposed death of the hero-god, as formerly rehearsed in the secret worship of the sun in the old temple of Baal, and as they are now rehearsed in the very same secret worship in the different temples of Masonry.

In the Egyptian legend of Osiris we notice the following principal details:—

1st:—There is the possession of some valuable thing.—Osiris possessed a Kingdom.

2nd:—There is a conspiracy. — Typhon and his fellows conspire against Osiris.

3d:—There is a conflict.—Typhon and his fellows had a conflict with Osiris.

4th:—There is a death. — Osiris is slain and enclosed in a chest.

5th:—The death is by the hand of a brother.—Osiris is slain by his brother Typhon.

6th:—The body is buried at the foot of a tamarind tree.

7th:—There is a first search.—Isis searches for her husband's body.

8th:—She interogates every one whom she meets.

9th:—The search is accidentally successful. — Isis finds the body and disposes of it.

10th:—There is a second search.—Isis searches for the scattered remnants of the body of Osiris a second time.

11th:—There is a finding.—Isis finds all the parts of the body but one.

12th:—There is a loss.—One part of the body is missing.

13th:—There is a substitution.—Isis substitutes the Phallus for the missing part.

Now compare all these various incidents with those related in the Masonic legend and note the identity between the two. In the Masonic legend

1st:—There is the valuable possession.—Hiram possessed the Master's word.

2nd:—There is a conspiracy.— Fifteen Fellow Crafts conspire against Hiram.

3d:—There is a conflict.— Three ruffians attack Hiram Abiff at high twelve.

4th:—There is a death.— Hiram is slain by Jubelum.

5th:—This death is by the hand of a brother.— Hiram is slain by his brother Jubelum.

6th:—The body is buried at the foot of a tamarind or acacia tree.

7th:—There is a first search.— Twelve Fellow Crafts search for the ruffians.

8th:—They interogate every one whom they meet

9th:—This search is accidentally successful.—The ruffians are found in the clefts of a rock and disposed of.

10th:—There is a second search.— Three Fellow Crafts go in search of the body.

11th:—There is a finding. — The body is found in a grave dug due east and west.

12th:—There is a loss.—The Master's word is lost.

13th:—There is a substitution. — The first word spoken after the body is raised is subtituted.

Thus we discover at length as the result of our investigation that even in the very minutest particulars the Masonic legend of Hiram Abiff and the old Egyptian legend of Osiris or Baal are one and the same. All the incidents connected with the death of the hero-god — the search for the body — the finding—the loss of one part and the substitution for that which was lost, are identically the same, the only difference being that the name Osiris was dropped by the "Masonic fathers" and the name of Hiram Abiff was substituted in its place.

This is unquestionably the strongest proof which Masonry has hitherto furnished of the pagan origin of its religious philosophy and of the undoubted fact that in every conceivable feature it is the identical religion of the "Ancient Mysteries."

CHAPTER XVI.

THE MASONIC TRAGEDY.—Murder of Hiram **historically** false.—A substitute for Osiris.—Candidate kneeling to pray.—Personates the sun-god in his conflict with *night*.—Is slain by Jubelum.—Body concealed.—Buried at foot of a tamarind tree.—Search for the ruffians.—Accidental discovery.—Search for the body.—Loss of Master's word.—Substitution of Mahhah-bone.—Procession.—Prayer at the grave.—Raising of the body.

Mr. Barton:—The celebrated drama or scenic representation of the pretended death of Hiram Abiff, based upon the foregoing legend is unquestionably the most interesting if not the most important portion of the whole Masonic system, and is that which gives to the Master Mason's degree the character of "Sublime." But nevertheless, like every other part of the Masonic philosophy, it is a "sublime" falsehood, and in the end becomes to the candidate a "sublime" farce. No such event ever transpired at the building of the temple, but on the very contrary, it is distinctly stated in the Scriptures that Hiram, the widow's son of Tyre not only was not slain "before the temple was completed," but that he actually *finished* all the work he had to make for King Solomon for the house of the Lord.

In I. Kings vii, 40, we read:—

"And Hiram made the lavers and the shovels, and the basins. So Hiram *made an end of doing all the work* that he made King Solomon for the house of the Lord."

And again in II. Chron. iv, 2:—

"And Hiram made the pots, and the shovels, and the basins. And Hiram *finished all the work* that he was to make for King Solomon for the house of the Lord."

But Hiram, in the manner previously explained, having been adopted as the hero-god of Masonry to substitute Osiris or the sun-god of the "Mysteries," the scenic representation of his pretended death is performed with all the mock solemnity imaginable, and the candidate is made to represent him in every single element of the Masonic legend because that was the mode of initiation into the "Greater Mysteries" and true or false, Freemasonry must establish beyond any question its perfect identity with that secret system of sun-worship. In proof of this we read in the "Lexicon of Freemasonry," p 130, as follows:—

"The *Mysteries of Osiris* formed the third degree or summit of the Egyptian initiations. In these the Murder of Osiris by his brother Typhon was represented and the god was personated by the candidate."

In perfect harmony with this explanation we

have its literal counterpart in the Masonic philosophy, so that it might be correctly read—"the mysteries of Hiram form the third degree or summit of Ancient Craft Masonry. In these the death of Hiram by his brother Typhon is represented and the god *is* personated by the candidate." Both legends and both scenic representations are exactly the same, and all there is to be done, is to change one name for another and use the present tense in describing the ceremonies of the lodge. Again:—

"Typhon was the symbol of winter which destroys the fecundating and fertilizing powers of the sun, thus as it were, depriving him of life. This was the catastrophe celebrated in the mysteries, and the aspirant was made to pass fictitiously through the suffering and death of Osiris."

Again in the "Traditions of Freemasonry," p. 233:—

"The candidate in these initiations was made to pass through a mimic representation or repetition of the conflict and destruction of Osiris and the eventual recovery of his body, and the explanation made to him after he had received the full share of light to which the painful and solemn ceremonies through which he had passed, had entitled him constituted the secret doctrine, the object of all the mysteries."

This is precisely what takes place in the Master Mason's degree. The candidate is made to represent the death of the sun-god or the "fecundating and fertilizing power of the sun," under the fictitious name of Hiram Abiff, and this dramatic representation is the last great link which connects this idolatrous system of demon mythology to the old Baal or sun-worship of the "Mysteries." We shall now examine this drama in detail and follow the candidate in all the various incidents of his conflict, death and the subsequent disposal of his body, as related in the legend of Osiris.

Having passed through the first section of the degree, and having resumed his clothing in the preparation room, and being invested with his apron and with a small plumb, suspended from his neck, he is ushered into the lodge and all necessary preparations for the sublime (?) drama which is to follow having been already made by the Senior Deacon as detailed in the "Hand Book," pp. 194, 195, the candidate is called to the East and addressed as follows, by the Worshipful Master.

Worshipful Master:—"Bro. Hunt, you now no doubt consider yourself a Master Mason, and as such entitled to all the rights and privileges of a Master Mason, do you not?"

The candidate either nods his head in affirmation, or else answers "I do."

Worshipful Master:—"I presumed you did from the jewel you wear, it being the jewel of one of the principal officers of this lodge [alluding to the small plumb hanging from his neck]. But, my brother, it becomes my duty to inform you that you are not yet a Master Mason; neither do I know that you ever shall be. You have yet a rough and rugged road to travel, one beset with ruffians, and it may be with murderers, and should you lose your life in the conflict, yours will not be the first. But remember in whom you placed your trust and 'he that endureth unto the end the same shall be saved.' On a former occasion you had some one to pray for you, but now you have none; you must pray for yourself. You will therefore suffer yourself to be again *hoodwinked*, kneel where you now stand, and pray, either mentally or orally as you see fit, but when done signify the same by saying 'Amen,' aloud."

The Senior Deacon now steps forward and again fastens a hoodwink securely over the candidate's eyes and causes him to kneel on both knees, as it were, to pray. The Worshipful Master stands up, removes his hat and gives three raps, calling all the brethren to their feet, and thus standing, they await for some minutes, till the candidate is supposed to have done praying and says "Amen" aloud.

The figure on next page accurately represents the minister or saloon-keeper as he is again blindfolded and kneels once more to make a mockery of prayer in a Masonic lodge, with the brethren standing round and hugely enjoying his miserable appearance. Having said "Amen" he is ordered to "arise and make his progress," the lodge being again seated. The various incidents detailed in the previous legend of Hiram now begin to be enacted. The candidate is assisted to his feet by the Senior Deacon and conducted in the usual manner once round the lodge. When they approach the Junior Warden's station in the South, he is accosted by a pretended ruffian (or perhaps a real one), named

Jubela, who thrice demands of him the secrets of a Master Mason or the Master's word, and being, in his behalf, thrice refused by the Senior Deacon, he strikes him lightly with the twenty-four inch gauge across the throat.

He is then rushed towards the Senior Warden's station in the West, where he is met by a second ruffian named Jubelo, who also demands of him the secrets of a Master Mason or the Master's word, and being again refused he strikes him with the square across the left breast.

Faint and bleeding as it were, he is now hurried along to the "East gate," but in the north-east corner he is attacked by the third ruffian, Jubelum, who in like manner demands of him the secrets of a Master Mason or the Master's word and upon a like refusal he strikes him a blow with a leather mallet called a "setting maul," and pitches him backward into a canvas, held for the purpose by six of the brethren. He is now supposed to be dead, and in this manner the first five incidents in the legend of Osiris are performed. Hiram, or the candidate, is claimed to have had a *valuable possession.* There is a *conspiracy* to obtain that valuable possession at any hazard. Then follows the *conflict*—that conflict ends in *death*, and that death is by the hand of a *brother.*

The figures on the following page represent the sun-god personated by the candidate, passing through these scenes of fierce and terrible conflict with the conspirators, representing Typhon or the powers of darkness, at the South, West, and Northeast.

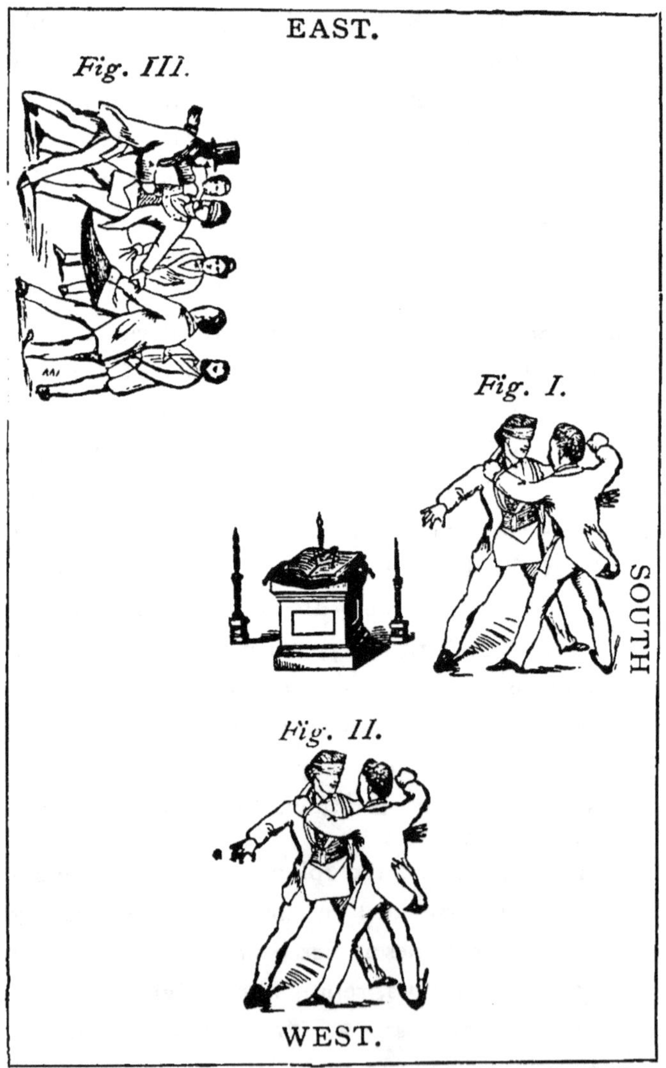

The Candidate representing the Sun god in his *Conflict* with *Night* or *Darkness.*

Now to understand all this, let us remember that the candidate represents Osiris, or Baal, or Hiram which are all one and the same principle, and that that principle is "the fertilizing and fecundating powers of the sun"—"the sun-god." Let us also bear in mind that there is supposed to be a constant, unceasing conflict going on between this sun-god and *night* or *darkness.*

Now the sun, appearing in the east in the morning, rises higher and higher in the heavens until at Meridian he attains his highest point of elevation in the SOUTH. The moment he arrives at the "south gate" however, that moment he begins to descend and there receives, as it were, the first blow from Typhon or *night.* Continuing to decend, and constantly hurrying towards the "*west* gate" he at length sets behind the western horizon and there the sun-god is supposed, symbolically, to receive the second blow. After the setting of the sun there is but a feeble light (represented by the feeble condition of the candidate), as is natural enough after having received two terrific blows, and so in a weak and wasted condition twilight lingers on, still engaged in deadly conflict with his relentless enemy, until at last he is entirely overcome—*night* swoops down upon the earth and *darkness* everywhere prevails—the sun-god having received. as it were, the final blow which deprives him of life. On page 358 Fig. 1 represents the mortal strife between *light* and *darkness* at the Meridian; Fig. 2 represents the conflict in the West which causes the sun-god to disappear, and Fig. 3 represents his death, when light becomes entirely extinct and night is triumphant. The lights in the lodge room are also turned down, and everything is shrouded in gloom, in mournful sympathy with the loss of the beloved Osiris, personated by the candidate. This whole scene is termed the "*Aphanism*," and is explained in the "Symbolism of Freemasonry," p. 317, as follows.

"In each of the initiations of the ancient mysteries there was a scenic representation of the *death* or disappearance of some god or hero whose adventures constituted the legend of the mystery. That part of the initiation which related to and represented the death or disappearance was called the *Aphanism*. *Freemasonry which has in its ceremonial form been founded after the model of these ancient mysteries*, has also its aphanism in the third degree."

The candidate having been struck by the *setting maul* of Jubelum and thrown back into the canvass as already stated, is then laid upon his back on the floor and covered up. All the brethren except the three pretended ruffians—Jubela, Jubelo and Jubelum—retire to their seats, and these, standing near their victim and realizing in some measure the enormity of their crime, determine to conceal the body "in the rubbish of the temple until low twelve or twelve at night, when they agree to meet again and give it a more decent burial."

They then lay hold of the canvass and slowly convey the dead body of Hiram or the sun-god to the south-east corner, where they cover it with anything that comes next to hand, representing its *concealment* in the rubbish, while Jubelum sits near "to watch," and the other two repair toward the west end of the lodge, as the ritual expresses it, "to dig a grave."

In the meantime the Master or Secretary strikes "low twelve" on a gong or bell always kept for that purpose, indicating *midnight* and hence the complete annihilation of *light*. Jubela and Jubelo again stealthily approach the spot where the body is concealed and after mutual recognition and inquiry between the supposed ruffians, it is agreed that they convey it a westerly course to a spot where a pretended grave has been prepared and there bury it. Accordingly the dead candidate, or the murdered sun-god, is again lifted up and borne in slow and solemn procession on the shoulders of the brethren to the Senior Warden's station, where he is finally interred, or laid on the floor in a due east and west position, and the Senior Warden's column is placed standing near his head to represent the *acacia* or "tamarind tree," at the foot of which the body of Osiris was buried, as related in the legend. The three "ruffians" then propose at once to make their escape, Typhon, or *night* and *darkness*, to all appearance has now completely triumphed. Osiris or Baal—the "fertilizing and fecundating power of the sun"—is now apparently buried out of sight, the lodge becomes a house of mourning, and Isis or nature weeps for the *loss* of her husband. Referring to this melancholy scene and at the same time conclusively proving what has been already stated, that the so-called "higher degrees" are but so many developments of the "Sublime degree of Master Mason," we read as follows in the "Book of the Ancient and Accepted Scottish Rite," pp. 355, 356:—

M.·.P.·.—"My brethren, the power of darkness has prevailed over the prince of light. The earth mourns and is wrinkled with frost. All nature laments, and we share the common sorrow. Excellent Senior Warden, let prayers be offered up in the tabernacle for the return of *light* and the re-ascension of the Sun.

Senior Warden:—Most Puissant, our ancient taskmasters on the banks of the Nile mourn for Osiris. The Chaldeans lament for Bel (or Baal) and the Phœnicians for Tammuz. The Phrygian women clash their cymbals and weep for Atys; while far in India the Brahmins pray for the return of Cama."

M.·.P.·.—We, like our ancient Masters weep for Osiris—the type to us of the sun, of light, of life. Weep, my brethren, for Osiris! Weep for light lost, and life departed, and the good and the beautiful oppressed by evil."

This from such "high" authority proves beyond any power of denial that the dead candidate in the Masonic lodge and the Osiris or Baal of the "Mysteries" are one and the same characters, while it also explains as clearly as it can possibly be done, the true meaning of Ezekiel viii. 14, 15, 16, where a similar scene is described as being impiously practised in the secret worship of the idolatrous Jews.

"Then he brought me to the door of the gate of the Lord's house which was toward the north; and behold, there sat women weeping for Tammuz. Then said he unto me, hast thou seen this, O son of man? turn thee yet again and I will show thee greater ABOMINATIONS than these. And he brought me into the inner court of the Lord's house, and, behold at the door of the temple of the Lord, between the porch and the altar, were about five and twenty men, with their backs toward the temple of the Lord, and their faces toward the *east*; and they *worshipped the* SUN *toward the east.*"

Precisely what is done in a Masonic lodge and as an act of worship.

The figures on the following page represent the candidate in the three positions before described. Fig. 1 represents him where he is supposed to have been slain. In Fig. 2 he lies in the southeast corner of the lodge, concealed under the rubbish, and in Fig. 3 he is buried in a grave dug due east and west, at the foot of a "tamarind tree." Now to understand the reason for these different

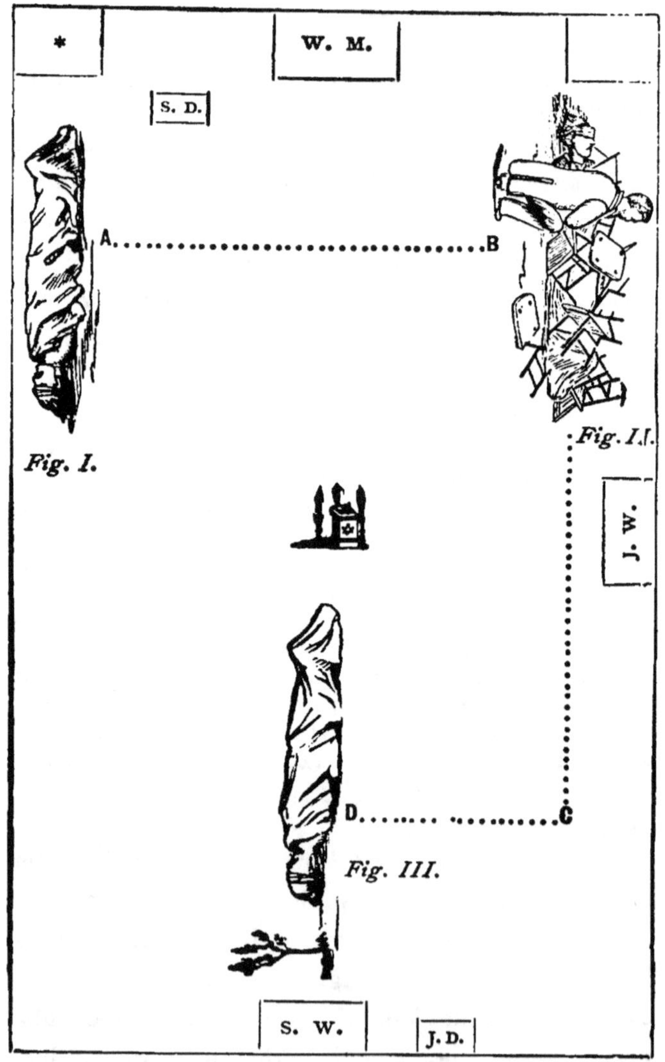

The Candidate representing Osiris—slain by Typhon at A, borne by the river Nile to B, and buried at D.

movements of the candidate's body, we must refer once more to the Egyptian legend. When Osiris was slain by Typhon and his body enclosed in a chest, it will be remembered that he was thrown in the river Nile and borne out to the Mediterranean Sea. This is represented by conveying the candidate's body from A to B.

The winds and waves of the Mediterranean, it is further asserted, bore Osiris' body a westerly course, "to a place called Byblos in Phœnicia, where it finally reposed at the foot of a tamarind tree," in like manner represented by bearing the candidate's body from B to D and burying it as before described at the foot of a "tamarind" or "acacia" tree, thus reproducing scene the sixth in the Osirian legend.

As soon as the supposed ruffians have effected their escape, as alluded to on p. 362, there is quite a commotion in the lodge room. Every one seems to be trying how crazily he can act, but after a few minutes the Worshipful Master raps with his gavel, and all again is prefectly still. Grand Master Hiram is reported missing—no work is laid out and no designs are upon the trestle-board. About this time an alarm is heard at the door, and the announcement is made that twelve Fellow Crafts who of course are Master Masons under the name of Fellow Crafts, "are without, clad in white gloves and aprons who say they have important tidings to communicate, and desire an audience with his majesty, *i. e.*, with the Worshipful Master, who throughout the whole of this ceremony represents King Solomon. The Fellow Crafts are admitted, and proceeding at once to the Master's station in the east. They relate at length all the supposed facts connected with the *Conspiracy* against Hiram, their own share in the wicked plot at first, their subsequent recantation,and now, freely acknowledging their premeditated guilt, they on their bended knees "most humbly implore his pardon."

In relation to the meaning and use of the number 12 in the Masonic system the lodge book explains as follows, "Mackey's Manual" p. 100:—

"The number 12 was celebrated as a mystical number in the ancient system of sun-worship *of which it has already been said that Masonry is*, *a philosophical* development. The number there referred to the 12 signs of the Zodiac, and in those Masonic rites in which the Builder" [*i. e.*,[Hiram "is made the symbol of the sun, the twelve F.·.C.·. refer to the twelve signs in which alone the sun is to be found."

THE FIRST SEARCH.

The seventh act in the Masonic drama is now performed. King Solomon orders that these "Fellow Crafts divide themselves into parties and travel, three east, three west, three north and three south, in *search* of the ruffians and return not without tidings." All the brethren of course take their seats except three who are always supposed to be well posted and thoroughly drilled in doing what is technically called the "floor-works" and these now proceed with their search to represent Isis, in the Egyptian legend, searching for the body of Osiris. They pass out by the "preparation-room" door and enter the lodge again after a few minutes by the ante-room door, where they meet the Junior Deacon, carelessly lounging and representing a "wayfaring man," when the following dialogue takes place, performing the eighth act as related in the legend.

INTERROGATITG WHOEVER THEY MEET.

Fellow Craft:—(in search of the ruffians) "Hallo, friend! Have you seen any strangers pass this way?"

Junior Deacon:—"I have; three."

Fellow Craft:—"What sort of appearing men were they?"

Junior Deacon:—"They appeared to be workmen from the temple at Jerusalem seeking a passage to Ethiopia, but not having King. Solomon's pass, were unable to obtain a passage and returned back into the country."

Fellow Craft:—(addressing his companions) "Why, these are the very men of whom we are in search. [turning to Junior Deacon] You say they returned back into the country?"

Junior Deacon:—"They did."

Fellow Craft:—(to his compinions) "Why, these are important tidings; let us go up and report this to King Solomon."

The following engraving represents the Fello Crafts *interrogating* every one whom they meet in the prosecution of their *search*, just as Isis interrogated every one whom she met when searching for the body of Osiris.

Having reported their conversation with the "wayfaring man," and having received strict injunction from King Solomon (the Worshipful Master) to be sure and find "the ruffians," they once more continue their "search," which, like that of Isis, is also pretended to be long and wearisome. They pass out the "preparation room" door as before and returning after a short absence by way of the ante-room door, they approach the spot where the candidate is lying. One of them, pretending to be very tired, and all feeling more or less dejected because of the fruitlessness of their efforts to find "the ruffians," he sits down near the head of the supposed grave, as he says, "to rest and refresh himself." Having made up their minds to continue the *search* in another direction, this weary brother is called upon to "arise" and go along, and on attempting to do so, *accidentally* as it were, catches hold of the acacia or little column standing near the candidate's head, and pretending to have pulled it up by the roots, calls upon his companions to return. They do so, and while wondering at "this singular circumstance," they hear three horrid exclamations proceeding from the preparation-room, and recognizing the voices of the escaped "ruffians," they finally rush in, seize and bind them and bring them in mock captivity before King Solomon (the Worshipful Master). And thus the ninth item of the legend is represented—they *accidentally* find the object of their *search*, just as Isis discovered her husband's body the first time.

THE SECOND SEARCH.

The "ruffians" being disposed of according to "ancient usage," and as prescribed in the several penalties of Symbolic Masonry, the three Fellow Crafts are now commanded to "go in *search* of the *body* and when found to observe whether the Master's word or a key to it or anything appertaining to the Master's degree be on or about the body." This second journey in search of Hiram's body is to represent the second journey undertaken by Isis in search of the body of Osiris and as the latter was found in a *mutilated* condition, so in like manner the Fellow Crafts discover the body of Hiram in a similar condition. And thus the eleventh and twelfth incidents of the Osirian legend are represented. Having found the body, they now search for the Master's word or a key to it, according to the orders of King Solomon.

The above engraving represents the Fellow Crafts—two saloon keepers and a Jew peddler—as they scratch and fumble over the body of the dead candidate—Doctor of Divinity or gambler—pretending to *search* for the "Master's word" and which of course they know well he never possessed. After a while, however, they lay hold of the little *plumb*, previously mentioned as being suspended from his neck, and pretending even to be ignorant of what that is, or to what especial use it might be put, they conclude to report the whole matter to King Solomon, and "if he said nothing about the

Master's word or a key to it, they would not."

They accordingly do this, and it being then ascertained beyond a doubt, that although the body was *found*, yet the Master's word was unfortunately *lost*, the last great incident of this unearthly mystery in its coincidence with the legend of Osiris is then represented.

THE SUBSTITUTION.

The Worshipful Master rising to his feet, and very reverently receiving the plumb from the brother who presents it, pronounces it "indeed the Jewel of our Grand Master Hiram Abiff," and then continues as follows:—

> "There can be no longer a doubt of his untimely end. You twelve Fellow Crafts will now form a solemn procession and go and assist me in raising the body; and, my worthy companion of Tyre, (addressing the Senior Warden as Hiram, King of Tyre) since the Master's word is now lost, I propose that the first sign made upon arriving at the grave and the first word spoken after the body shall be raised, shall be *adopted* as the sign and word for the regulation of all Masters' lodges until future generations shall find out the right." "Hand Book," p. 119.

In the mysteries of Osiris, the substitute was called *Phallus*, in the mysteries of Hiram, it is called *Mah-hah-bone.* And as "the Point within a Circle" represents the Phallus and as it also, as we have previously learned, represents tbe Worshipful Master, and lastly as the Worshipful Master represents the sun-god rising in the east, therefore it undoubtedly follows that *Mah-hah-bone* is the real name of the god of Masonry, the "G. A. O. T. U." of its worship, which Freemasons are always to pronounce "with awe and reverence," and which, in fact, they are solemnly (?) sworn never to speak above their breath, and even then only "upon the five points of fellowship." And this being unquestionably the case, the religion of Masonry ought in all consistency to be called the "Mysteries of Mah-hah-bone," as the religion of Egypt was anciently called the "Mysteries of Osiris."

But to continue. The Master and brethren, as above indicated, approach the spot where the candidate has been lying during all this time, and his hoodwink being now slipped off, they march in solemn procession three times around the pretended grave, singing a "doleful ditty" ("Hand Book," p. 218).

The following cut illustrates this procession with the Doctor of Divinity still lying on the floor shamming death. It is Saturday night and drawing close to twelve o'clock. This man thus lying there is expected to occupy some Christian pulpit on the approaching Sabbath. How does this picture suit you? You ask can a man be a Mason and a Christian? My dear sir, answer your own question, can this man—this minister—lying here on the lodge room floor be a Christian? He is undoubtedly a sworn worshipper of Baal, for in fact he is just now representing the Baal or Tammuz of the "Ancient Mysteries." Tell me then, through all his initiatory ceremonies thus far, and more especially in his present position, can you say that he is a follower of the Lord Jesus Christ?

And now whence did this ceremony come, and why is it performed in the Masonic lodge—room? The answer is given, as in the case of all the other ceremonies of Masonry, that it was directly borrowed from the pagan religion of the "Mysteries."

In Sharp's "Egyptian Mythology," p. 10, we read that:—

"The death of Osiris was piously *lamented* by Isis and her sister Nephtys; and once a year the Egyptians joined their priests in a *melancholy procession* through the streets, *singing a doleful ditty*, called the Maneros or Song of Love which was to console the goddess for the loss of her husband."

And because the Egyptian sun-worshippers "joined" their priests in a melancholy procession, "singing a doleful ditty" in commemoration of the death of Osiris, so the Masonic fraternity or the modern Baal worshippers, in imitation of their ancient brethren, join their priests in a similar procession and for precisely the same purpose.

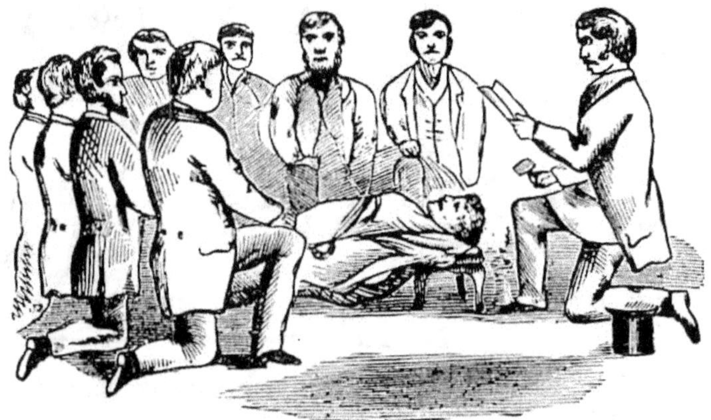

The procession being ended, they again surround the body and by request of "King Solomon" two attempts are made to raise it, but both fail in consequence of its supposed putrefaction, in the first instance, "the skin slipping from the flesh," and in the other "the flesh cleaving from the bone." The Master and brethren then kneel and another mock prayer is mumbled in solemn blasphemy over the prostrate minister as represented by the above engraving. At the close of this so-called prayer the Master takes hold of the candidate's right hand

by the strong grip of a Master Mason, or "lion's paw," as in the annexed figure, and with the assistance of the Senior Warden raises him to his feet on the "five points of fellowship" and whispers *Mah-hah-bone* into his ear. All the lights are again turned on, there is a very general feeling of pleasurable relief, and thus, as it was in the "Mysteries," so it is also in Masonry, the ceremonies "that were begun in sorrow and lamentation," as Pierson expresses it ("Traditions," p. 232), "are now ended in joy and rejoicing."

The annexed figure correctly represents the Master and candidate on the "five points of fellowship," while this "Grand Masonic word"—Mah-hah-bone, the unspeakable name of the god of Masonry, is being communicated.

And thus, my dear Henry, every incident recorded in the "Legend of Osiris," as being connected with his supposed tragical death, the subsequent search of Isis, and the finding of his body, is literally reproduced in the Masonic *drama* i , relation to the supposed death burial, and pretended *raising* of Hiram Abiff.

Osiris has a valuable possession —a kingdom.	Hiram has a valuable possession —the Master's word.
Typhon and his fellows conspire against Osiris.	Fifteen Fellow Crafts conspire against Hiram.
The conspirators have a conflict with Osiris.	The three ruffians have a conflict with Hiram.
Osiris is slain by his brother Typhon.	Hiram is slain by his brother Jubulum.
Osiris' body is buried at the foot of a tamarind tree.	Hiram's body is buried at the foot of an acacia tree.
There is a first search by Isis.	There is a first search by the Fellow Crafts.
Isis accidently discovers the body.	The Fellow Crafts accidently discover the three ruffians.
There is a second search by Isis for the mutilated body of Osiris.	There is a second search by the Fellow Crafts for the mutilated body of Hiram.
Isis discovers, the body, but one part is lost.	The Fellow Crafts discover Hiram's body, but the Master's word is lost.
Isis substitutes the Phallus for the lost part.	King Solomon, alias the Worshipful Master, substitutes Mahhah-bone for the lost part.

Every single point in the mysteries of Osiris has its literal counterpart in the mysteries of Masonry, so that no doubt can possibly remain as to the absolute identity of both systems. Even the *manner* of raising Hiram in the Masonic lodge, the *position* of the Worshipful Master over the prostrate candidate (as seen on p. 375), and the *means* adopted for his supposed restoration to life—"the lion's paw"—were actually represented among the hieroglyphics of ancient Egypt and have all been borrowed from that source alone. The accompanying complex figure was copied by the Abbe Pluche from the collection of Montfaucon, and which he says is painted on a mummy at the Austin-Friars of La Place des Victoires, representing the death and resurrection of Osiris.

The sign of *Leo*, or the *lion*, is transformed into a couch, upon which Osiris is laid out as dead, under which are three canopi of various capacities, denoting the state of the Nile at different periods. The first is terminated by the head of the dog-star, which gives warning of the approach of the overflow of the river; the second, by the head of the hawk, the symbol of the Etesian wind, which tends to swell the waters, and the third, by that of the Virgin, which indicates that when the sun had passed that sign the inundation would have nearly subsided. To this is superadded a large Anubis—the dog-star—who, with an emphatic gesture, turning towards Isis, who has an empty throne on her head, intimates that *the sun, by the aid of the lion*, had cleared the difficult pass of the tropic of Cancer, and was now in the sign of the latter, and although in a state of exhaustion, would soon be in a condition to proceed on his way to the South. It is through the instrumentality of *Leo* that Osiris, the sun-god, is relieved from his perilous condition. The strong *paw* of the *lion* wrests him from the clutches of Typhon, or the spirit of night and darkness, and places him in his wonted course. Anubis, the dog-star, is the herald of this event(see page 224). Here we see the archetype of the *raising* or restoration of our Grand Master Hiram by the "strong grip or lion's paw," and it will be seen that the position of the Worshipful Master, when in the act of raising the candidate(as on p. 375) is a fac-simile of that of Anubis over the body of Osiris (Fellow's Mysteries, p. 22).

"We may distinguish two points in the heavens,"says Dupuis,when explaining the philosophy of the Osirian Mysteries, "which limit the duration of the creative action of the sun, and these two points are those where the night and the day are of equal length. Scarcely has the sun in his annual route attained one of these points than an active and prolific force appears to emanate from his rays and to communicate movement and life to all sublunary bodies which he brings to light by a new organization. It is then that the resurrection of the god takes place, and with his, that of all nature. Having arrived at the opposite point that power seems to abandon him and *nature*" (or Isis) "becomes sensible of his weakness. It is Atys whose mutilation Cybele deplored! It is Adonis wounded in the virile parts of which Venus regretted the loss; it is Osiris precipitated in the tomb of Typhon, and whose organs of generation the disconsolate Isis never found."

And I shall add,as the modern counterpart of either, it is Hiram Abiff, "buried in a grave dug due east and west, six feet perpendicular," with the supposed loss of the Master's word. This, and this only, is the true interpretation of the Masonic drama. Through the fecundating power of the sun's rays, nature, as it were, becomes pregnant in Spring and Summer, and brings forth in Autumn, and hence in the Pagan mythology of Egypt, the *earth*, or more properly *nature*, was represented as a *female* and a goddess, and designated by the name of Isis, while "the fecundating and fertilizing power of the sun" was represented as a *male*, and the chief deity, or the ruler and governor of nature, and was called Osiris or Baal. But when the sun reaches the Autumnal equinox his prolific powers seem to decay, and as he passes farther south his rays become weaker and weaker, until at last, during the winter months, nature becomes entirely barren. Typhon, or the genius of evil and darkness, has finally prevailed over the sun-god, and Osiris is slain. He is restored again, however, by the sign, *Leo* or the "lion's paw," after the vernal equinox, when the earth once more rejoices into bloom and Typhon, or Winter is overcome. The supposed conflict between *day and night*, or light and darkness, which recurs through the diurnal motion of the earth, was another phenomenon which gave rise to this philosophical myth, as already illustrated and explained on pp. 358 and 359. This is the same death and resurrection so graphically represented in the Master Mason's degree by the pretended death and burial of the candidate, and his subsequent *raising* by the "paw of the lion," and the god recognized in this Pagan philosophy—the god of nature, or the fecundating power of the sun—is the god to whom prayers are offered in Masonic worship. The names given to this fictitious deity, as has been already explained, were different in different countries, so that the Baal of Samaria was the Osiris of Egypt, and is unquestionably the Hiram of Masonry. In the eighth chapter of Ezekiel this idol is designated by the name of Tammuz, and, as we shall see hereafter, is the self-same deity whom every Mason, minister, as well as rum-seller, must personate in the sublime mysteries of the third degree.

CHAPTER XVII.

TAMMUZ.—Identical wlth Hiram.—His secret worship revealed to Ezekiel.—The acacia or evergreen.—The beautiful virgin.—The all-seeing eye.—Forty-seventh problem of Euclid.—Corn, wine, and oil.—Romanism and Masonry compared.—The beast and his image.—Case submitted.—Henry's resolve.

"Then he brought me to the door of the gate of the Lord's house, which was toward the north, and behold there sat women weeping for Tammuz." (Ezekiel viii. 14).

Now, who was this Tammuz? What did he represent, if anything? And what is meant by "women weeping" for him? You will remember, my dear Henry, that it has been demonstrated over and over again as clearly as possible, that the Osiris of the old Egyptian Mysteries and the Hiram of modern Freemasonry are one and the same; also, that Osiris and Adonis were but different names applied by people of different countries to the same principle—the sun-god, or "the fecundating and fertilizing powers of nature." Now, let us examine what Freemasonry has to say concerning *Tammuz* and his identity with the hero-god or the Baal of the old Pagan Mysteries.

In the "Lexicon of Freemasonry," by Mackey, p. 19, I read:

ADONIS, MYSTERIES OF:—"The Mysteries, which in Egypt, the cradle of all the Pagan rites, had been consecrated to Osiris in passing over into Phœnicia were dedicated to Adonis. *Adonis*, in the Phœnician language, like Adon, in the Cognate Hebrew, signifies Lord or Master. THE IDOL TAMMUZ, mentioned in the eighth chapter of Ezekiel, was considered by Jerome, and after him by Parkhurst, as identical with Adonis."

Again, in the "Symbolism of Freemasonry,"p. 3-4:

"In the mythology of the philosophers Adonis was a symbol of the sun, but his death by violence, and his subsequent restoration to life, *made him the analogue of Hiram Abiff in the Masonic system* and identify the spirit of the initiation in his Mysteries, which was to teach the second life with that of the third degree of Freemasonry."

From all this testimony, then, which could be easily multiplied, you will at once perceive that Tammuz and Adonis are identical, and inasmuch as Hiram, Osiris and Adonis are also identical, therefore, it unquestionably follows that the Hiram of the Master Mason's degree is precisely the same character as that formerly worshiped by the wicked and rebellious Jews under the name of Tammuz.

But we have yet a fuller explanation concerning the worship of this idol, the lamentation made for him by the women of Judah, and his absolute identity with the Baal of Ahab's time in "Godwyn's, Moses and Aaron," as follows:

"The sun was also worshiped by the house of Judah under the name of *Tammuz*, for Tammuz, saith Hierom, was *Adonis*, and Adonis is generally interpreted the sun, from the Hebrew word *Adan*, signifying *dominus*, the same as Baal, or Moloch, formerly did the *lord or prince of the planets.* The month which we call June, was by the Hebrews called Tammuz; and the entrance of the sun into the sign cancer was in Jews' astronomy termed *Tekupha Tammuz*, the revolution of Tammuz. About the time of our Saviour, the Jews held it unlawful to pronounce that essential name of God, Jehovah; and instead thereof, read Adonai, to prevent the heathen blaspheming that holy name by the adoption of the name Jove, etc., to the idols. Concerning Adonis, whom some ancient writers call Osiris, there are two things remarkable. The death, or loss of Adonis, and the finding of him again; as there was great lamentation at his loss, so was there great joy at his finding. By the death or loss of Adonis, we are to understand the departure of the sun; by his finding again, the return of that luminary. Now he seemeth to depart twice in the year; first, when he is in the tropic of cancer, in the farthest degree northward; and, secondly, when he is in the tropic of capricorn, in the farthest degree southward. Hence, we may note, that the Egyptians celebrated their Adonai in the month of November, when the sun began to be farthest southward, and the house of Judah theirs in the month of June, when the sun was farthest northward; yet both were for the same reasons. Some authors say that this lamentation was performed over an *image* in the night season; and when they had sufficiently lamented, a candle was brought into the room, which ceremony might mystically denote the return of the sun, then the priest, with a soft voice, muttered these words, '*Trust ye in God, for out of pains salvation is come to us.*' "

We learn from this corroborative testimony, then, that the idolatrous Jews in Jerusalem worshiped the sun-god under the name of Tammuz, that they made an image of a man, which they laid out(on a bed of let tuce)as dead, that lamentation was made "in the night season" over this supposed dead body, and that the being so represented as dead was in other countries recognized as Osiris, Baal or Adonis. In the Master Mason's degree there is precisely the same scenic representation, as we have already seen. A man is slain by violence and is laid out as dead. This tragic performance is invariably at night; the lodge room is shrouded in gloom and darkness, grief and lamentation for the loss of the hero-god is everywhere apparent, and at last, when a sufficient time has elapsed, the sun-god, or Hiram, is again restored to life, light is introduced, and in the language of Hutchinson, as in the above extract, the candidate is raised "from the grave of iniquity to the faith of salvation." Thus, then, there can be no question whatever as to the identity of Tammuz with the Hiram of Masonry, and neither can there be any doubt as to the absolute idolatry of Masonic worship and its positive and emphatic condemnation by the Word of God. And inasmuch as God himself not only revealed to Ezekiel the *secret* mysteries of the Tammuz worship, but also pronounces, in verse eighteen, a most terrible judgment on the wicked and back-slidden worshipers,so we are undoubtedly to learn from the same Scriptures that it is his divine will that the *secret* mysteries of Hiram should be also revealed, and that the false and idolatrous worship of that ancient idol (though under a modern name) be forever banished from his church and from any fellowship whatever with the Gospel of Christ.

But there is yet another important link which connects the Osirian and Hiramic mysteries, and which demonstrates still further that the idolatrous worship which used to be practiced in Jerusalem, in honor of *Tammuz*, is literally reproduced to-day in Freemasonry, an dis engaged in by those ministers, class-leaders, Sunday-school superintendents and other professing Christians, who, in the madness of their blind folly, voluntarily swear eternal allegiance to the despotic laws and edicts of that stupendous system. In witnessing Masonic funerals you have doubtless observed that every member of the fraternity carries a *sprig of evergreen*, which he finally deposits in the grave of the deceased, with the exclamation, "Alas, my brother!" This *evergreen* is the *acacia* so often mentioned in the ritual of the Master Mason's degree, and which is supposed to have been planted at the head of the grave where Hiram's body is said to have been buried, and which also led to the *accidental* discovery of his remains. (See Handbook, p. 210.) Concerning the origin of this Masonic emblem, and the reason why it occupies so prominent a position, both in the lodge and and ritual we have the following explanation from our Masonic teachers. In the "Traditions of Freemasonry," by Pierson, p. 207, we read as follows:

"In all the ancient *systems* of *religion* and *mysteries* of *initiation* there was always some one plant consecrated in the minds of the worshipers and participants by a peculiar symbolism, and therefore held in extraordinary veneration as a sacred emblem. Thus, the *ivy* was used in the mysteries of Dionysius, the *myrtle* in those of Ceres, the *erica* or *heath*, in the Osirian, the *lettuce* in the Adonisian, the *misletoe* in the Celtic, and the *lotus*, or water-lily, in those of India and Egypt. The coincident symbol of Freemasons is the cassia, or *acacia*."

And again on page 212.

"One fact is admitted, that the Masonic sprig (of acacia) is a substitute for the lotus, the erica, the ivy, the myrtle, the misletoe, etc., the sacred plant of the Ancient Mysteries."

This is precisely the very same evergreen shrub, or *branch*, which is also referred to in Ezekiel viii. 17, and the religious services and secret mysteries with which that emblem was associated in Jerusalem, by the idolatrous Jews, are precisely the same religious ceremonies, and the same secret mysteries, with which it is connected in our own day in the Masonic lodge.

"Is it a light thing for the house of Judah," says Jehovah, speaking to the prophet, "that they commit the abominations which they commit here? For they have filled the land with violence, and have returned to provoke me to anger, and lo, *they put the branch to their nose*." (Ezekiel viii. 17.)

This *branch* is the *acacia* of Freemasonry, and it is also the *palm* or *evergreen* of the false worship of Rome.

But, to conclude our investigation of the sublime(?) mysteries of Hiram Abiff, I shall offer a few more proofs, though in a collective form, from the emblems of the Master Mason's degree (and these shall be the last) to show that not even the most minute particular is wanting, to demonstrate the absolute identity of our modern system of Freemasonry with the old Baal, or Tammuz, or Osirian worship of the "mysteries."

THE HIEROGLYPHIC FIGURE.

The accompanying figure occupies a conspicuous and prominent place on the "MASTER'S CARPET" in every Masonic lodge room and in every Masonic Man-

ual of any note throughout the world. It consists, as we are informed in the ritual (see "Hand-book," p. 235), of a "beautiful virgin weeping over a broken column. Before her a book open; in her right hand an acacia, in her left an urn; behind her Time, standing, unfolding her ringlets and counting her hair." Now, what is the real origin of this figure? Who first introduced it into Masonry? And whence was the idea of this emblem borrowed?

Its true history is found in Pierson's "Traditions of Freemasonry," p. 220, as follows:

"Within the last fifty years there has been added to the American emblems of Freemasonry that which is sometimes termed a 'hieroglyphical figure'—a female weeping over abrokencolumn,a book open before her; in her right hand a sprig, in her left an urn; Time standing behind her with his fingers enfolded in the ringlets of her hair. *This figure was designed* by the Rev. Jonathan Nye, for the *Hieroglyphic Monitor*, published by Jeremy L. Cross, in 1819. *The idea doubtless was aerived from the legend of Isis* weeping at Byblos, over the column torn from the palace of the king, which contained the body of Osiris, while *Horos*, the god of Time, pours ambrosia on her hair." (See p. 346.)

THE ALL-SEEING EYE.

The Abbe Pluche, in referring to Osiris, the cheif deity of the Egyptians, in his "*History of the Heavens*" (*Historie du Ciel*), goes on to relate that

"That luminary (the sun), as it was the grandest object in nature, had also its peculiar character, or mark, in the symbolical writing. It was called Osiris. This word, according to the most judicious and most learned among the ancients, signified the inspector, the coachman, or the leader, *the king*, the guide, the moderator of the stars, *the soul of the world*, *the governor of nature*." (The god of Masonic worship is termed the "Great Architect of the Universe"—the "Supreme Ruler of the Universe.") "From the energy of the terms of which it was composed it signified, in general, the governor of the earth, which amounts to the same sense. And it is because they gave that name and function to the sun that it was expressed in their writing sometimes by the figure of a man bearing a sceptre, sometimes by that of a coachman carrying a whip, or plainly, by AN EYE." (See, also, Pierson's "Traditions," p. 231, where the same account is literally given.)

This, then, is the origin of the Masonic emblem called the "All-Seeing Eye," which, as we have seen, is nothing more than a symbol of the sun, made use of by the ancient Egyptians, and from them descended to the Masons. To make it represent the true God would be in direct violation of the Divine command. (See Ex. xx. 4, 5; Isa. xl. 18, 25.)

THE FORTY-SEVENTH PROBLEM OF EUCLID.

And now, as to the true origin of the Forty-seventh Problem of Euclid as a Masonic emblem, and the last to which I deem it necessary to refer.

In the "Traditions of Freemasonry," by Pierson, p. 83, I read as follows:

"The mysteries among the Chinese and Japanese came from India, and had similar rites. The *equilateral triangle* was one of their symbols"(as it is in Masonry),"and so was the mystical Y, both alluding to the Triune God, and the latter being the ineffable name of Deity, and for which symbol the modern Masons have substituted the Forty-seventh Problem of Euclid, from its similarity in shape, having lost the explanation of the original symbol."

Even the symbol of *corn*, *wine* and *oil*, used in all Masonic consecrations, and which is also mentioned in the ritual of the second degree, as referring to the wages of a Fellow Craft, or to Masonic truth, is borrowed from the old Baal worship of the mysteries, and is alluded to by Hosea, when reproving the Israelitish Church for her wicked idolatries:

"For she did not know that I gave her *corn* and *wine* and *oil*, and multiplied her silver and gold, which she prepared for Baal." (Hosea ii. 8.)

There is but one *key* which can unlock the real secret of Freemasonry, and but one *source* from which to obtain the true meaning of all Masonic symbolism, and that *key* and that *source* are plainly furnished us in the following extract, from one of the standard and most popular *manuals* of the order.

In the "General Ahiman Rezon, or Freemason's Guide," by D Sickles, 33° p. 56, we read as follows:

"It is our duty, then, to make Freemasonry the object of a profound study. We must consult the Past. We must stand by the sarcophagus of the murdered, but restored, Osiris, in Egypt; enter the caverns of Phrygia and hold communion with the Cabiri; penetrate the Collegia Fabrorum of ancient Rome, and work in the mystic circles of Sidon. In a word, we must pursue our researches until we find the THOUGHT that lay in the minds of those who created the institution and founded our mysteries. *Then we shall* know precisely what they mean."

This is exactly what we have done, and the result is before you. We have carefully examined every part of the Masonic system and philosophy from the *cable tow* and *hoodwink* of the "*preparation room*," and the "Lesser Mysteries" to the grave of Osiris, as we saw it dug on the brow of a hill and his body buried at the foot of a *tamarind tree.* We have traced back every ceremony, accounted for every symbol, and pointed out the true source and significance of all its emblems. We have stood by the supposed couch of Tammuz, or Adonis, in Jerusalem, and heard the lamentations made over him by the women of Judah. We have been to the Wilderness of Sin, and to the plains of India and Persia, and have witnessed, with loathing and disgust, the lascivious worship of *Baal Peor* and the *Lignam.* We have even knelt before the blazing altars of Popery, sat as attentive listeners in the Councils of Lateran and Trent,and have ransacked the musty old documents of the Vatican. We have done precisely what Masonry itself commands us to do, and as the result of our examination and study what have we found? We have demonstrated beyond the possibility of a doubt or contradiction, that Freemasonry both in whole and in part, is literally and truly the secret worship of Baal, or the sun-god, as that worship used to be practiced among the old Pagan nations, and that Romanism is its exact counterpart. In a word, we have discovered, beyond a question, that Freemasonry is the vile, miserable, idolatrous old Pagan *Beast*, and that Popery is the very express *Image* of that *Beast.*

The Pontifex Maximus of Pagan Rome we have in the Pope; the Collegium in the sacred College of Cardinals: the Pagan priests of various classes with their shorn crowns we have in the shorn-headed priests of Romanism and in the varying classes of monks and nuns; the multiplication of demi-gods we have in the canonization of the saints; the ancient ceremonies of the Pantheon we have in Rome at this very hour almost unchanged; the wafer called the "Mola" we have in the *unbloody sacrifice of the Mass;* the intermediate state between hell and Elysium, as sung by Virgil, we have in purgatory; and the cruelty of Domitian and his tools and their persecution of the Christians we have vividly represented in the infamous, detestable conduct of the Pope and his cardinals for generations past. Romanism is unquestionably the *image* of what Pagan Rome formerly was, while Freemasonry is the veritable Pagan beast of the "mysteries," without a single material change. (Rev. xiii. 15.) I am aware, however, that the commonly accepted interpretation of this passage, especially among anti-masons, is, that Romanism is the *Beast* and that Masonry is the *Image*, but upon a closer examination of the whole chapter I think it will be found that if either view of the case is the correct one, the interpretation I have here ventured to suggest will be found to accord more with the real meaning of the prophecy.

Let us compare, for instance, the mysteries of Hiram Abiff in the Master Mason's degree with the mock solemn mysteries of the Romish Mass. Take away the "sacrifice of the Mass" from Romanism and you destroy it; strike out the sacrifice of Hiram from Freemasonry and there is nothing left. Both are, undoubtedly, Pagan ceremonies, performed by Pagan priests in Pagan temples, with altars that are Pagan, lighted candles that are Pagan, lustration that are Pagan, and with the chief priests of both systems decked out in the gaudy vestments of Paganism.

Both sacrifices are also but *theatrical representations* the *little round wafer* manipulated by the priest in the "unbloody sacrifice of the Mass," being the "Mola" first instituted by Numa, and commanded to be offered as an "unbloody sacrifice" in the old Roman-Pagan worship, while the *candidate*, manipulated by the *chief hierophant*, or priest, of Masonry *literally* represents Osiris, or Baal, or Tammuz, and is made to pass through all the mythical scenes related in the common legend of the "Mysteries."

In the annexed figure we behold the representation of a Romish priest in the act of *performing his Latin Mass.* Before him is the *altar* with its lighted candles, beside him are his assistants, while in his hand he holds the little round *wafer*, or "Mola," called *the host*, which has just been transubstantiated into a god, and which is now about to undergo a destructive change—the real body of Christ being seen under the form of bread, and the real blood of Christ under the form of wine, and now the priest eats the one and drinks the other. Can we imagine this to approximate, even in the remotest degree, to Christian worship, or is it possible for us to conceive that Paul, or Peter, or John ever engaged in such a stupid, meaningless and idolatrous ceremony? Now, let us turn to page 358, and there we behold, in like manner, the Masonic priest engaged in performing the tragedy of Hiram Abiff. Here we have the *altar* and the *lighted* candles, as in the *Mass*, here the assistants, and here, too, is, not alone a little wafer, but a veritable *man*, which, for the time being is converted into a hero-god,and which, as in the other instance, is now about to undergo a destructive change, by being slain at the hands of Jubelum, precisely as it used to be done in the old Pagan worship of the "Mysteries."

In the Romish Mass, also, as you may observe, the priest is the chief actor, the altar is the stage, the congregation the spectators, and the church the theatre, while in the Master Mason's degree the Worshipful Master is the star actor, the East is the stage, the members the spectators, and the lodge the theatre.

But, while the *Mass* is a theatrical representation of the various incidents connected with the *passion* and *death* of the Redeemer, though it holds precisely the same relation to the history of Christ that Richard III., Henry VIII., John II., or any other of the historical plays of Shakspeare do to the characters and times which they represent, the tragedy of Hiram Abiff is a *theatrieal representation* of a veritable Pagan *myth*, with no allusion whatever to Christ, but on the contrary, his name absolutely expunged even from any Scripture passage in which it may occur. And hence, in comparing the two as Pagan institutions, Freemasonry must unquestionably be the *substance* (as being the most Pagan) and Romanism the *shadow*, or Image. But I shall not pursue the subject any further. This is how the question presents itself to me after the most careful and thorough investigation of the two systems, and with my knowledge of both I am unable to comprehend how their relative positions could be otherwise changed.

And now, my dear Henry, I confidently submit my case. I have fully explained to you the *real secrets* of a Master Mason's lodge(of which nineteen-twentieths of the Craft are themselves ignorant). I have traced every single part of the Masonic system back to its original source. I think I have clearly established its thoroughly anti-Christian and Pagan character, and now, that I hope you are tolerably familiar with its false philosophy and worship, you can exercise your own judgment intelligibly,and seek affiliation with the midnight idolatrous lodges of Freemasonry, or not, as duty, honor and conscience may dictate.

Henry:--I am very thankful,indeed, my dear father, for the very clear and complete exposition you have given me of the whole Masonic philosophy and its undoubted heathen origin, and you may rest assured, that instead of having any desire to become a Mason, I am firmly resolved, with God's assistance, to oppose it all I can, being fully persuaded that man is wicked and corrupt enough by nature, without voluntarily returing to Pagan practices, and swearing to support and maintain a Pagan religious institution.

APPENDIX.

(Note A, p. 27.)

The following is the manner of admitting a new member into a tribe of Gypsies, together with the oath and articles, as administered by the principal Mannder or roguish Strowler. (See Fellows' Mysteries, p. 224.)

"The name of the person is first demanded, and a nick-name is then given him in its stead, by which he is ever after called, and in time his other name is quite forgotten. Then standing up in the middle of the fraternity, and directing his face to the Dimber-Damber, or prince of the gang, he swears in this manner, as is dictated to him by one of the most experienced:

"'I, Crank-Cuffin, do swear to be a true brother, and will in all things obey the commands of the great Tawney Prince, and keep his counsel, and not divulge the secrets of my brethren.

"'I will never leave nor forsake this company, but observe and keep all the times of appointments, either by day or by night, in any place whatsoever.

"'I will not teach any one to cant; nor will I disclose aught of our *mysteries* to them, although they flog me to death.

"'I will take my prince's part against all that shall oppose him, or any of us according to the utmost of my ability; nor will I suffer him, or any belonging to us, to be abused by any strange Abrams, Rufflers, Hookers, etc., but will defend him or them as much as I can against all other outlyers whatever.

"'I will not conceal aught I win out of Libkins, or from the Ruffmans; but will preserve it for the use of the company.'"

The canters have, it seems, a tradition, that from the three first articles of the oath, the first founders of a certain boastful, worshipful fraternity, who pretend to derive their origin from the earliest times, borrowed of them both the hint and form of their establishment; and that their pretended derivation from the first Adam is a forgery, it being only from the first Adam-Tiler.

The same author has given the meaning of the cant terms here used as follows:—Abrams, shabby beggars; Rufflers, notorious rogues; Hookers, petty thieves; Libkin, a house to lie in; Ruffmans, the woods or bushes; Adam-Tiler, the comrade of a pickpocket, who receives stolen goods or money and scours off with them.

(NOTE B, p. 38.)

As an apt illustration of the practical working of Masonic Charity, even to a dead brother, the following is copied in full from the "Voice of Masonry," for June, 1879, pp. 478–480.

SAD DISREGARD OF MASONIC DUTY! E.·.SIR WILLIAM ROUNSEVILLE'S REQUEST FOR MASONIC BURIAL DISREGARDED!

One of the saddest events within our knowledge of Masonry and of Knight Templarism is that which we now have to record. It pains us exceedingly to speak of it, but duty to the dead and to the living cannot now be waived. There are times when "silence is golden," and we devoutly wish that this were such a time, but it is not; the command of duty is imperative and we must obey it. There are other times when mere expediency may prevail and govern, now it can not, for an irreparable injury has been done to Masonry and, especially, to Knight Templarism. The right of Masonic burial has been willfully disregarded and not to rebuke the uncharitable, un-valiant and unmagnanimous act, would greatly imperil the present and future prosperity of the entire Fraternity, therefore, while the VOICE would gladly spread over this un-Masonic deed the broad mantle of charity, and forever shut it from mortal view, it can not—dare not. Now, let us state the facts, as we see and understand them. For years past Eminent Sir WILLIAM ROUNSEVILLE was a constant sufferer from partial paralysis, caused by overwork in behalf of his family, his church, and the Masonic Fraternity. Never receiving compensation for his services that enabled him to make provision for a time of distress, about three years since he found himself almost destitute, and would have died of want rather than have called on the Fraternity for the assistance to which *he was entitled*, so great was his horror of being in any way dependent on what might be esteemed charity. A visit of his son-in-law, Mr. G. S. Knapp, to him in Peoria, then revealed his need of aid. Mr. Knapp immediately made arrangements to remove Bro. ROUNSEVILLE, and his wife and daughter to Chicago, and there to provide for them as best he could in his own then straitened circumstances. In this he was aided by Bro. ROUNSEVILLE's son, William, now a young man past twenty-one years of age. Bro. ROUNSEVILLE was unable to perform any manual labor, and his only way of earning anything was by his writing for the VOICE, for which he was paid an average of ten dollars, monthly. Knowing his need of help from the Fraternity, we called attention to the fact, in the VOICE, and applied, by letter, to the brethren in Peoria for aid to him, and they responded. We thought then, and still think, he should have received aid from the Grand Lodge Charity Fund, and we so wrote the then Grand Master, and received the response that when the Masonic Bodies to which Bro. ROUNSEVILLE belonged had exhausted their ability to contribute to his relief, then the Grand

Lodge could and would aid him, which was all right as a rule, but exceptions had been made, promptly and and without hesitation, in cases no more meritorious, and thus the precedent for aid to him had been established, and it should have been granted. The trait in his character already alluded to, and his desire that we should say no more of his need in the VOICE, and let him suffer rather than burden the Craft in Peoria, deterred us from further public efforts to procure him Masonic assistance. During all this time Mr. Knapp, and the son, William were doing all in their power, and their earnings came by their daily labor, not from business, or landed estates, or government bonds, to render Bro. ROUNSEVILLE'S condition as comfortable and pleasant as possible. They did their whole duty, while the Masonic Fraternity did not do theirs. For the latter there is the excuse that many were not aware of Bro. ROUNSEVILLE'S residence in Chicago, nor of his pecuniary and physical distress, and this partly accounts for the inattention shown him, both before and after his death.

In the latter part of April last, Bro. ROUNSEVILLE had an attack of erysipelas, from which it was believed he would recover, but early in May, his paralytic trouble complicated his case so that it became apparent he could not long survive. Monday morning, May 5, it was evident his death was near at hand. The dearest wish he had concerning his body had been expressed to his friend, Sir John B. Gavin, and hethen proceeded to do his part toward fulfilling it. He, and William Rounseville, Jr., came to our office, and, not finding us in, left word, which, not being given to us as received, entirely misled us, and the consequence was we went on with our work, entirely in ignorance of Bro. ROUNSEVILLE'S dangerons illness *and of his death*, which occurred the following day.

Bro. Gavin proceeded from our office to the office of Eminent Sir Gil. W. Barnard, Grand Recorder of the Grand Commandery of Illinois, who, on hearing a statement of the facts, immediately wrote and mailed the following letter:

CHICAGO, Ill., May 5, 1879.

C. F. HITCHCOCK, Esq.—*Dear Sir and Frater*—Bro. WILLIAM ROUNSEVILLE is not likely to live over to-night. The Masons here desire to grant his request to be buried with Masonic honors but, no one seems to know his standing in lodge, etc. Will you kindly telegraph John B. Gavin, 87 West Lake street, Chicago, what his standing is, and, if good if the Masons of Peoria desire to take any part, in the affair?

With fraternal regards, I am courteously yours,

GIL. W. BARNARD, Gr. Sec.

To this was added the postscript:

"I am just leaving the city for a week or I would have answer sentt o me."

At the same time, Sir John B. Gavin wrote and posted the following letter:

CHICAGO, Ill., May 5, 1879.

MICHAEL E. ERLER, *Recorder Peoria Commandery No. 3.*—*Dear Sir*—WILLIAM ROUNSEVILLE, Past Eminent Commander of Peoria Commandery, No. 3, is now dying, and, as a friend of his and his family, and being also a K. T., he requested me to see that the Fraternity took charge of him. When I saw him last night he was hardly able to talk, and could scarcely recognize any one, unless an old friend. The doctor thinks he may drop off any moment, or may linger a few days. Unless the lodge or commandery of Peoria, of which he is a member, express their wish to have the Fraternity here take charge of the matter and so write us, I don't know how we will be able to do so. He has been sick and absent from the meetings of the different bodies so long, not through his fault, but by his misfortune, that few know him as a Mason, except by his writings in the VOICE OF

MASONRY. The March number contains a sketch of his life, which is full of interest. Now, what I wish, and it is also the wish of all the Masons I have spoken to, is to have Peoria Commandery request Chicago Commandery to take charge of him, and do honor to the man who has been an honor to the Fraternity.

Please let us hear from you immediately, for, in case he should die, something will have to be done quite soon.

Yours respectfully, JOHN B. GAVIN.

That (Monday) evening a regular conclave of Chicago Commandery was held, when Eminent Sir Knight ROUNSEVILLE's condition and request were formally made known by Sir John B. Gavin, who is a member thereof, and, after due consideration, the first three officers were appointed a committee, with full power to act in the matter. The following morning the letters above named and copies were received in Peoria, by the Sir Knights, to whom they were addressed, and they immediately gave attention thereto. Eminent Sir C. F. Hitchcock promptly sent the following telegram:

PEORIA, Ill., May 6, 1879.

To JOHN B. GAVIN, 87 West Lake Street, Chicago —Brother ROUNSEVILLE is in good standing in all the bodies. Desire Chicago Commandery to take charge and bury him. C. F. HITCHCOCK.

This was soon delivered to the Eminent Commander of Chicago Commandery, Sir Alexander White, who put it in his pocket, and subsequently called at Mr. Knapp's residence, spending, we are informed, not over two and a half minutes in making inquiries, giving the family no information, and manifesting no desire to see the deceased.

But Eminent Sir C. F. Hitchcock did not stop at sending the above telegram; he also wrote and posted the following letter:

PEORIA, Ill., May 6, 1879.

JOHN B. GAVIN, Esq., Chicago, Ill.—*Dear Sir and Frater*,—I am in receipt of Sir Knight Gil. W. Barnard's letter stating condition of Sir Knight WILLIAM ROUNSEVILLE, and wired you, this morning, request to Chicago Commandery to take charge and bury him. Sir Knight ROUNSEVILLE is Past Eminent Commander of Peoria Commandery, and in good standing in the several bodies. He is, and ever has been, held in high esteem among the Fraternity of Peoria; of late years unfortunate in business adventures, but always ready and willing to do to the extent of his ability. It is not probable that any of the Masons here would desire to take part in the services. I do not know as it would be convenient for any to be present. In behalf of Peoria Commandery, and the Masons of Peoria, would respectfully request Chicago Commandery to take charge of his remains and bury him with Knightly honors.

We do not know anything respecting the circumstances of his friends. We understand he has been living with a son or daughter, and suppose they are able to meet the expense of his funeral, but whatever expenses it may be necessary for Chicago Commandery to incur, can send the bill to me for settlement.

Courteously yours, C. F. HITCHCOCK.
E.·. C.·. Peoria Commandery, No. 3.

This letter was received by Sir Knight Gavin Wednesday morning, May 7. Sir Knight ROUNSEVILLE's death had then occurred. The Eminent Commander of Chicago Commandery, Sir Alexander White had also sent the following telegram:

CHICAGO, May 6, 1879.

TO CHARLES F. HITCHCOCK, *Eminent Commander of Peoria Commandery Knights Templars*—Sir Knight ROUNSEVILLE died this P. M. He requested to be buried by the Fraternity. *Chicago Commandery* DECLINES TO ACT *unless Peoria Commandery* GUARANTEES PAYMENT OF EXPENSES INCURRED. If you desire Chicago Commandery to act, send full instructions by wire immediately. *The expenses will be* AT LEAST TWO HUNDRED DOLLARS.

ALEXANDER WHITE, E.·.C.·.
900 West Madison Street.

This telegram was delivered to Eminent Sir C. F. Hitchcock at about 11·30 o'clock P. M. Feeling that he could not take the responsibility of answering immediately, he waited until morning. Then he sought advice from members of the respective bodies. The general expression was: "*This is unusual.* The amount seems extravagant. Reasonable expenses we will pay. We don't see how we can pay or raise that amount, and, as *two hundred dollars* is the *least* amount named, it may be three or four hundred dollars." The question was asked by every one: "Why can't the remains be brought to Peoria?" and agreed in saying: "We will pay the expenses of bringing him and the family here, and their return, and give him the largest Masonic funeral here for years." Accordingly Eminent Sir C. F. Hitchcock sent the following telegram:

PEORIA, May 7, 1879.

To ALEXANDER WHITE, E.·. C.·. 900 West Madison Street, Chicago, Ill.—We withdraw our request to Chicago Commandery; we can't bear the expense. *Can't the remains be sent to Peoria?*

C. F. HITCHCOCK, E.·.C.·.

This telegram reached Sir Knight White prior to Sir Knight Gavin's call on him with the above letter. Then he said the telegram superseded the letter. Sir Knight Gavin was accompany by Sir H. H. Pond, Generalissimo of Chicago Commandery, and one of the committee appointed with full power to act, and they jointly urged and begged Sir Knight White to comply with the request of Peoria Commandery.

No. 3. He replied that not a dollar should be granted for expenses, that not a man should turn out, and that ended it. Then, mortified beyond the power of words to express, the Sir Knights named left him. To the question: "Can't the remains be sent to Peoria?" he deigned no reply, and imparted no information of it to any of the friends or family.

The enormity of his offense will more clearly appear when it is stated that there had been no call on his commandery by Sir Knight ROUNSEVILLE or his relatives to bear any part of the burial expenses, but only to turn out, and perform the burial service. But further, had there been such a call the utmost necessary expenses could not have exceeded one hundred and twenty dollars. This would have included a good burial case, ten carriages, hearse, and flowers. It would not have paid for a band and a display of plumes, but of that there was no need.

It was about 2 o'clock P. M., of Wednesday, and every effort made by Sir Knight Gavin to secure Masonic burial for Sir Knight ROUNSEVILLE's remains had failed. In despair, he and Sir H. H. Pond wended their way to Mr. Knapp's residence. Sir Knight Pond said: "I never can face the family with such news; you will have to impart it." Oh, direful task! but it was performed. How? Sir Knight Gavin rung the door-bell. It was answered by Mrs. Knapp, daughter of Eminent Sir Knight ROUNSEVILLE. With blood stilled, and cheeks paler than those of the corpse within, he entered the house, and then, overcome by his emotion, fell back against the door. Mrs. Knapp, burdened with grief, exclaimed: "What is the matter?" and he found voice to answer: "They utterly refuse to do anything."

Up to that moment, all the family had entertained an exalted opinion of Masonry, and therefore, the shock to them was terrible; they could not understand why their request could not be granted; and they concluded that all Masonic profession was the grossest sham and hypocrisy. But they could not be idle, and again Mr. Knapp, and the son, William, performed the service that was due from the Masonic Fraternity. To them the highest praise is due, and there can be no wonder at their feeling that Eminent Sir Alexander White has inflicted upon Eminent Sir Knight ROUNSEVILLE, upon them, upon all his relatives and friends, and upon Freemasonry, an irreparable wrong, for which he should be expelled from all Masonic rights and privileges. This can be better understood when it is stated that they knew the service Sir Knight ROUNSEVILLE had rendered the Order; that they were familiar with his articles on Masonic funerals; thatthey had seen the look of serenity which had spread over his countenance when Sir Knight Gavin assured him, just before he died, that his request for Masonic burial would be fully complied with, and that their faith in Freemasonry, up to that time, was unshaken. They sent for us to visit them and explain the wrong, if we could. What could we say, but that it was a blunder caused by inexcusable ignorance, or an abuse of Freemasonry unparalleled within our experience or knowledge. They insisted that we should expose this wrong, that others might be saved from a similar experience hereafter. To the best of our ability we have performed the duty, keeping in view throughout the welfare of all concerned, and penning no word herein with any other feeling than that of the deepest sadness, that Eminent Sir Knight ROUNSEVILLE's request for Masonic burial was not complied with.